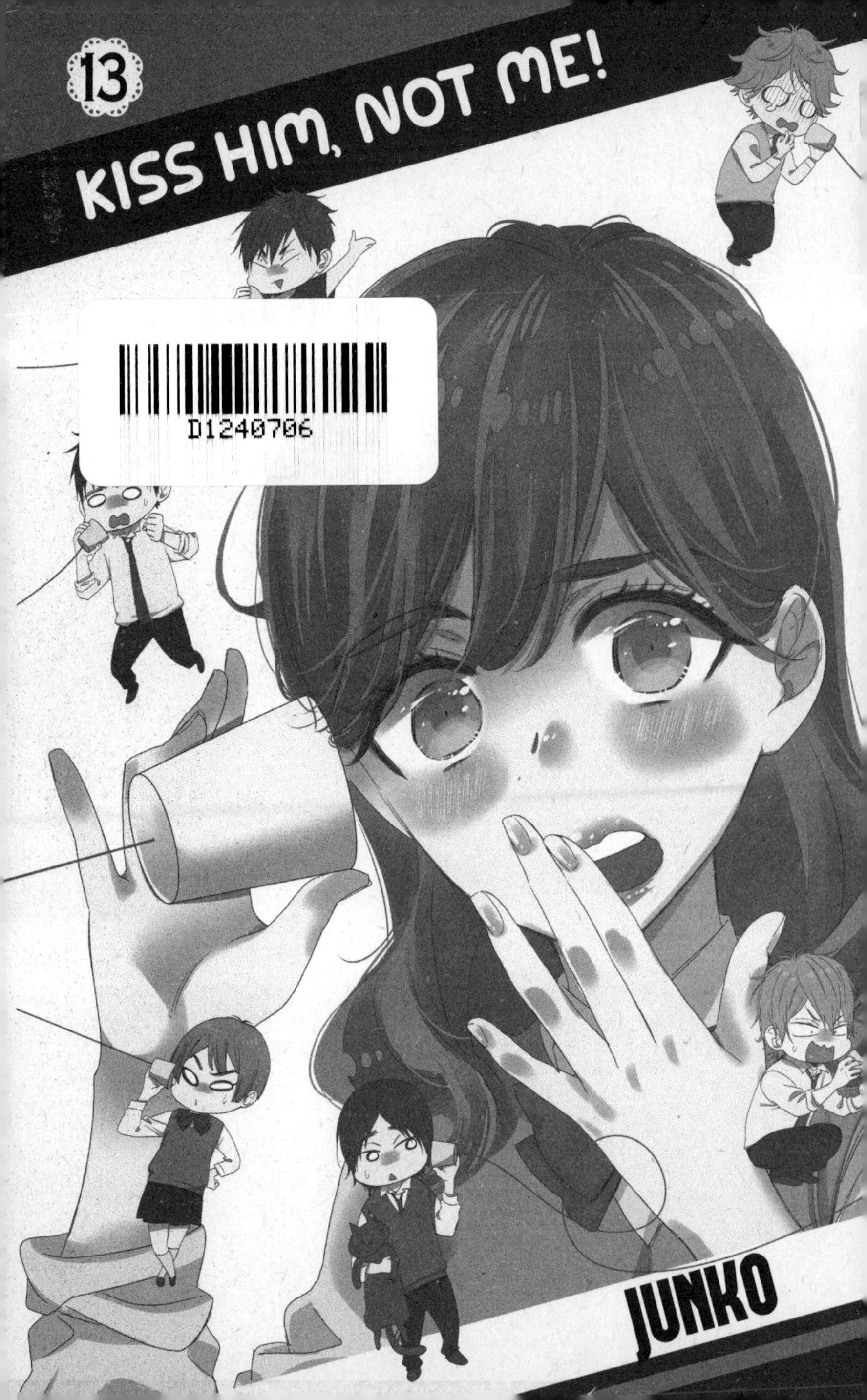
13
KISS HIM, NOT ME!
JUNKO

CONTENTS

STORY

MUTSUMI AND **KAE** FINALLY BEGIN THEIR **RELATIONSHIP!** ♥ DURING THESE ROMANTIC DAYS, **KAE** HEARS THE GOOD NEWS THAT HER BELOVED ANIME "MIRAGE SAGA" IS GETTING A SEQUEL AND A PROMOTIONAL EVENT. HOWEVER, THE EVENT IS ON THE SAME DAY AS HER DATE WITH **MUTSUMI**. **KAE** PROMISES MUTSUMI TO ONLY GO TO THE FIRST PART OF THE EVENT, BUT HER RESOLVE WAVERS WHEN SHE'S ENTICED BY **YASHIRO'S** FRONT-ROW TICKETS TO THE SECOND PART... **HAVING BROKEN HER PROMISE TO MUTSUMI,** SHE APOLOGIZES TO HIM THE NEXT DAY, BUT...?!

I ♥ BL

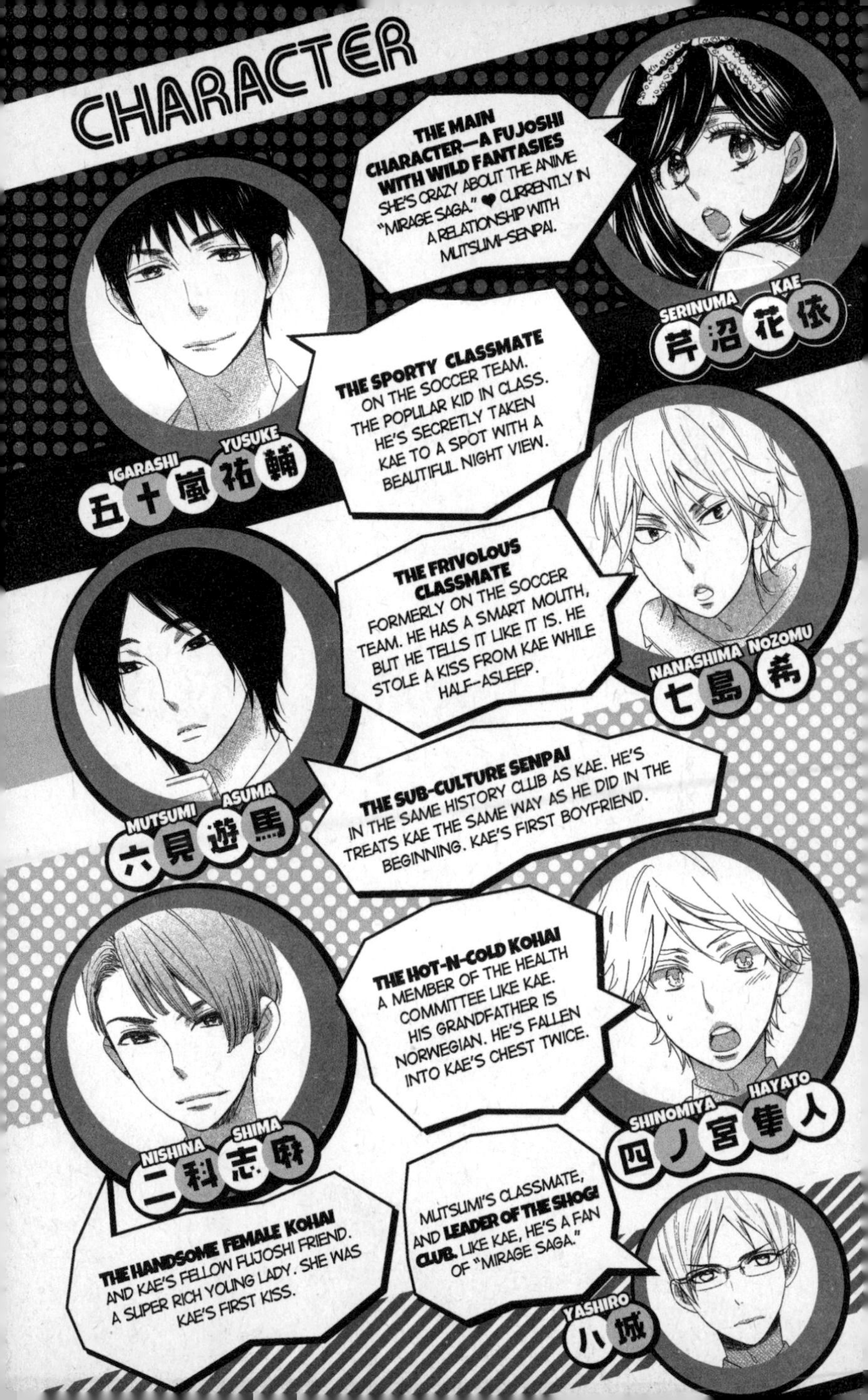
CHARACTER
SERINUMA KAE
芹沼花依
THE MAIN CHARACTER—A FUJOSHI WITH WILD FANTASIES
SHE'S CRAZY ABOUT THE ANIME "MIRAGE SAGA." ❤ CURRENTLY IN A RELATIONSHIP WITH MUTSUMI-SENPAI.
IGARASHI YUSUKE
五十嵐祐輔
THE SPORTY CLASSMATE
ON THE SOCCER TEAM. THE POPULAR KID IN CLASS. HE'S SECRETLY TAKEN KAE TO A SPOT WITH A BEAUTIFUL NIGHT VIEW.
NANASHIMA NOZOMU
七島希
THE FRIVOLOUS CLASSMATE
FORMERLY ON THE SOCCER TEAM. HE HAS A SMART MOUTH, BUT HE TELLS IT LIKE IT IS. HE STOLE A KISS FROM KAE WHILE HALF-ASLEEP.
MUTSUMI ASUMA
六見遊馬
THE SUB-CULTURE SENPAI
IN THE SAME HISTORY CLUB AS KAE. HE'S TREATS KAE THE SAME WAY AS HE DID IN THE BEGINNING. KAE'S FIRST BOYFRIEND.
SHINOMIYA HAYATO
四ノ宮隼人
THE HOT-N-COLD KOHAI
A MEMBER OF THE HEALTH COMMITTEE LIKE KAE. HIS GRANDFATHER IS NORWEGIAN. HE'S FALLEN INTO KAE'S CHEST TWICE.
NISHINA SHIMA
二科志麻
THE HANDSOME FEMALE KOHAI
AND KAE'S FELLOW FUJOSHI FRIEND. A SUPER RICH YOUNG LADY. SHE WAS KAE'S FIRST KISS.
YASHIRO
八城
MUTSUMI'S CLASSMATE, AND LEADER OF THE SHOGI CLUB. LIKE KAE, HE'S A FAN OF "MIRAGE SAGA."

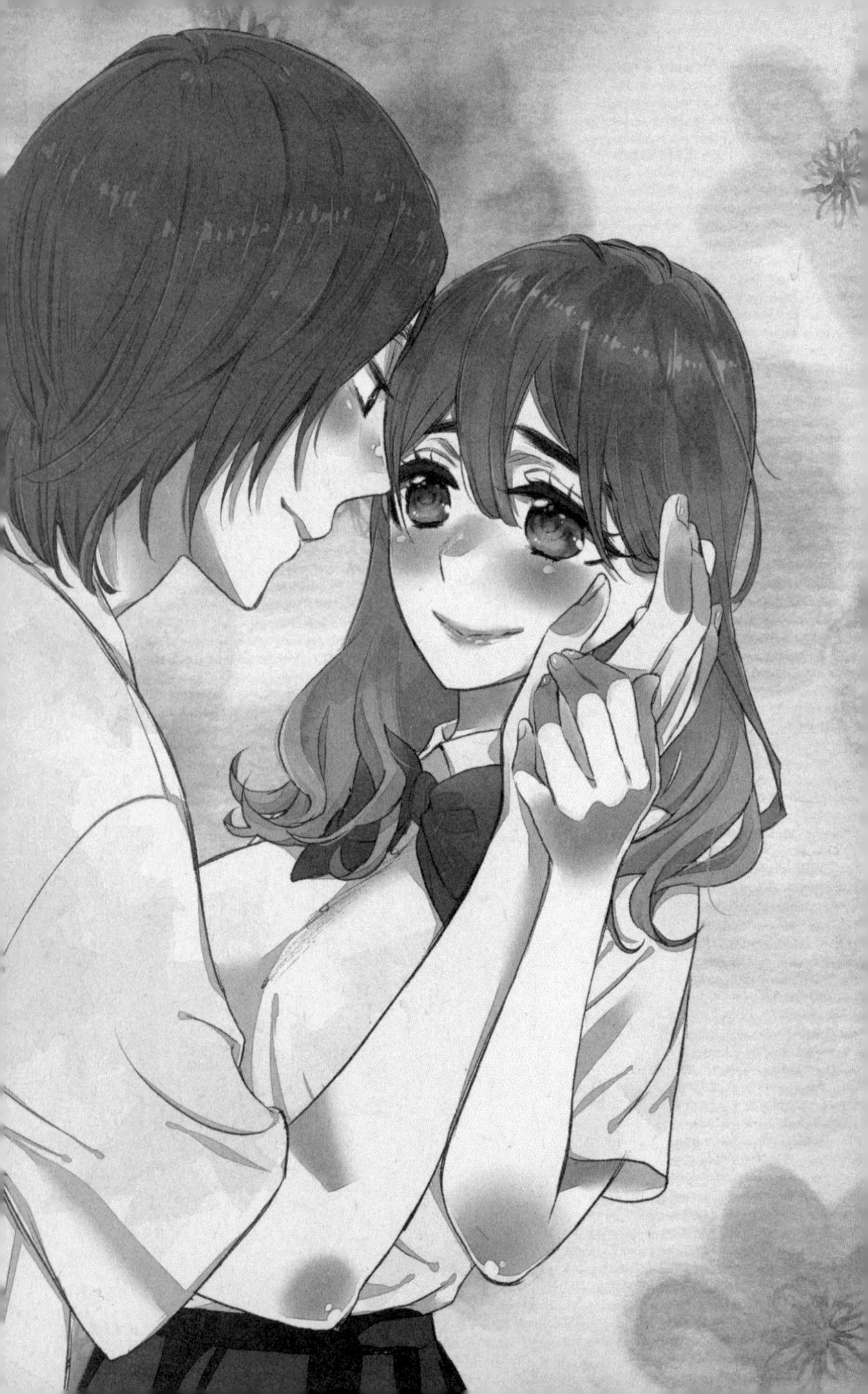

#48 CAN SHE OVERCOME HER DESIRES?

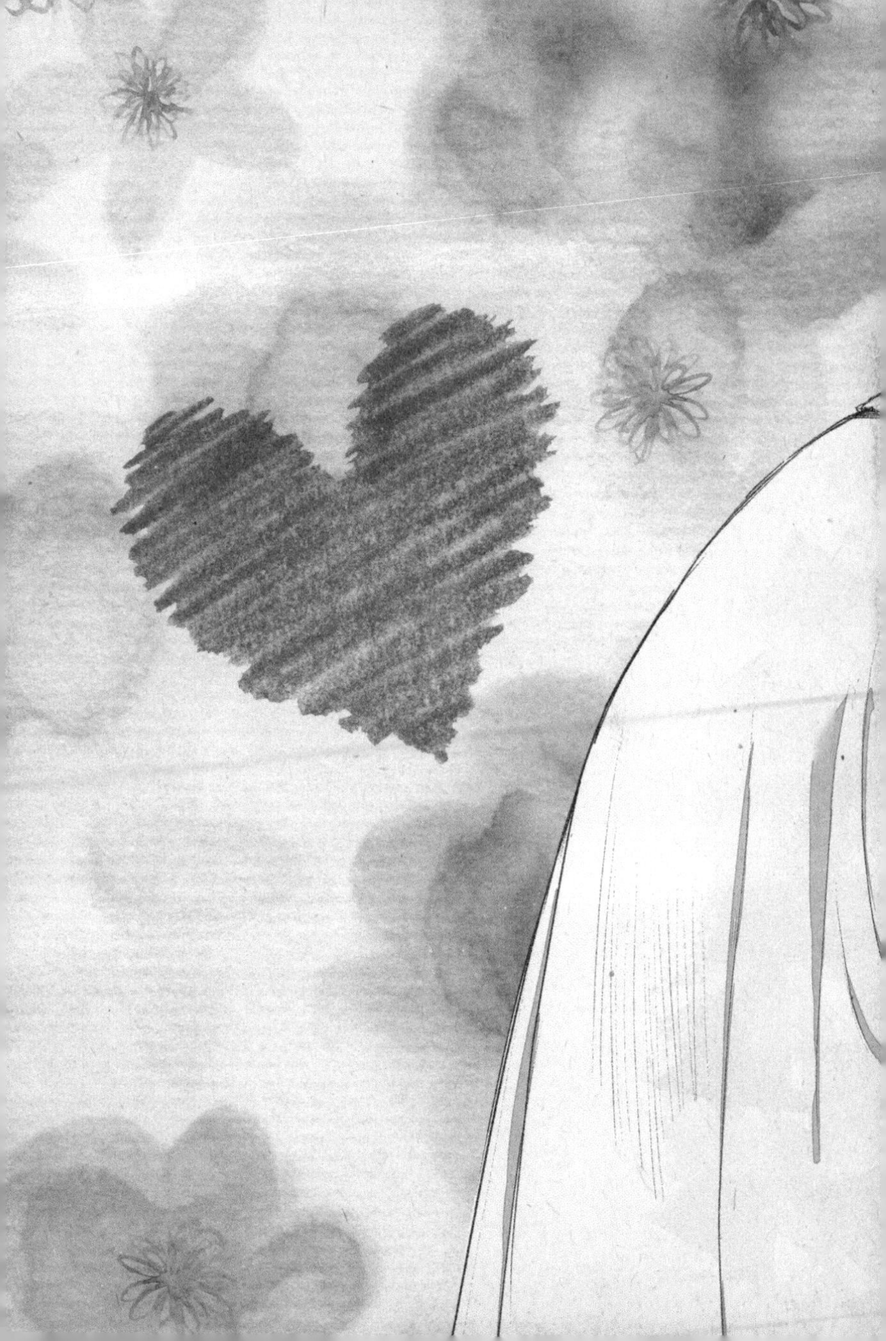

KiSS HiM, NOT ME!

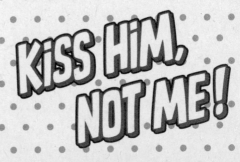

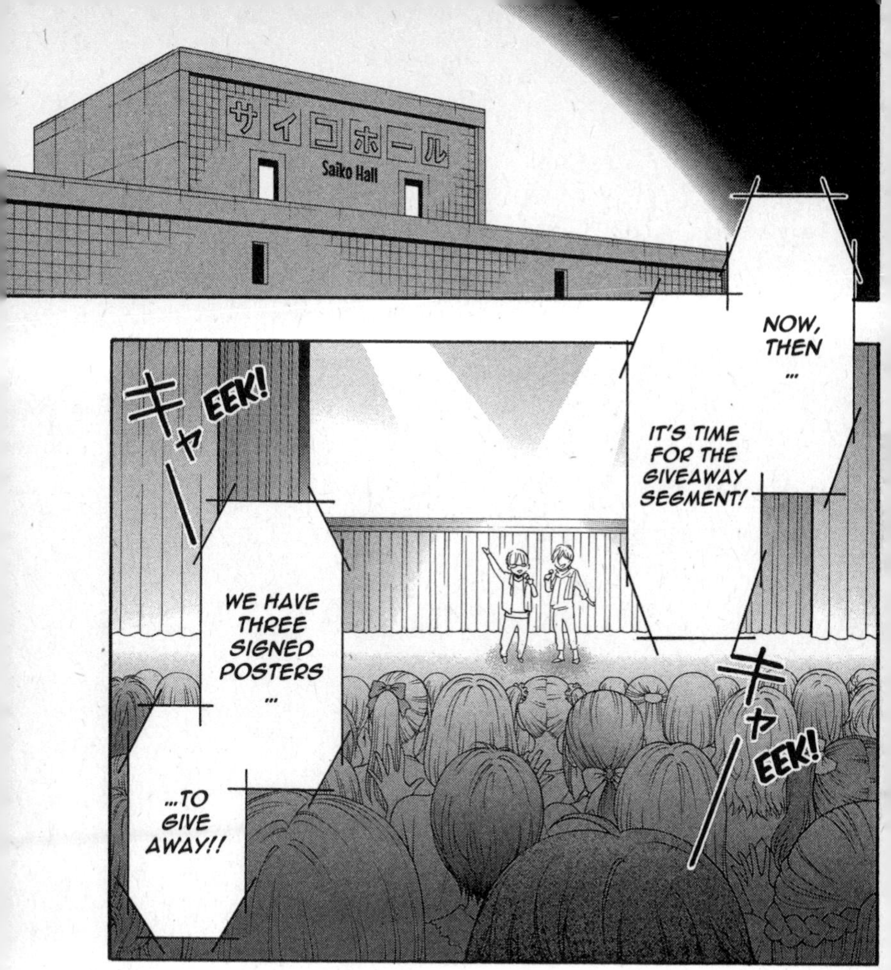
サイコホール
Saiko Hall
NOW, THEN ...
IT'S TIME FOR THE GIVEAWAY SEGMENT!
キャー
EEK!
WE HAVE THREE SIGNED POSTERS ...
...TO GIVE AWAY!!
キャー
EEK!

KiSS HiM, NOT ME!

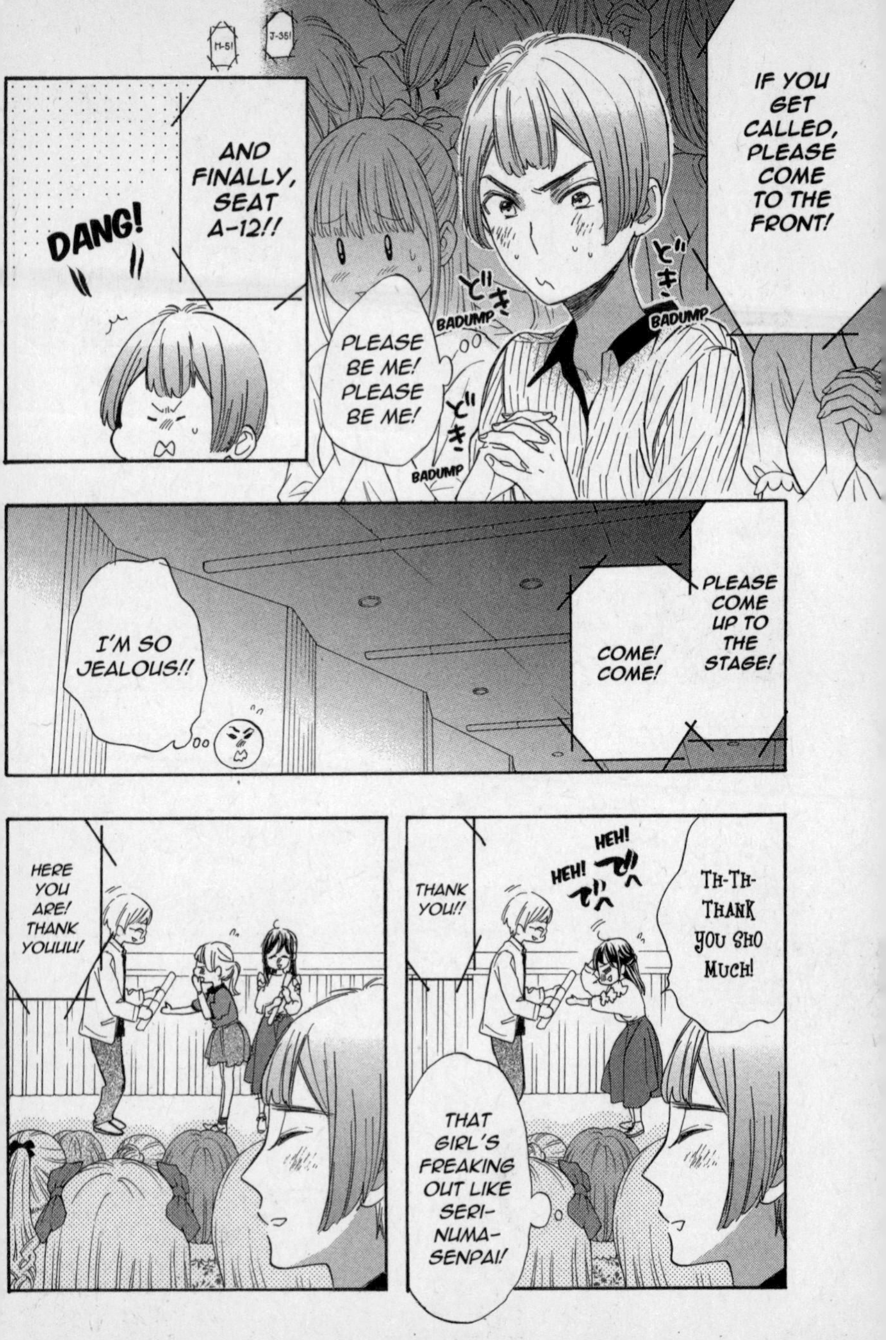
J-35!
H-5!
IF YOU GET CALLED, PLEASE COME TO THE FRONT!
どき
BADUMP
どき
BADUMP
PLEASE BE ME! PLEASE BE ME!
どき
BADUMP
AND FINALLY, SEAT A-12!!
DANG!
PLEASE COME UP TO THE STAGE!
COME! COME!
I'M SO JEALOUS!!
TH-TH-THANK YOU SHO MUCH!
HEH!
でへ
HEH!
でへ
THANK YOU!!
THAT GIRL'S FREAKING OUT LIKE SERI-NUMA-SENPAI!
HERE YOU ARE! THANK YOUUU!

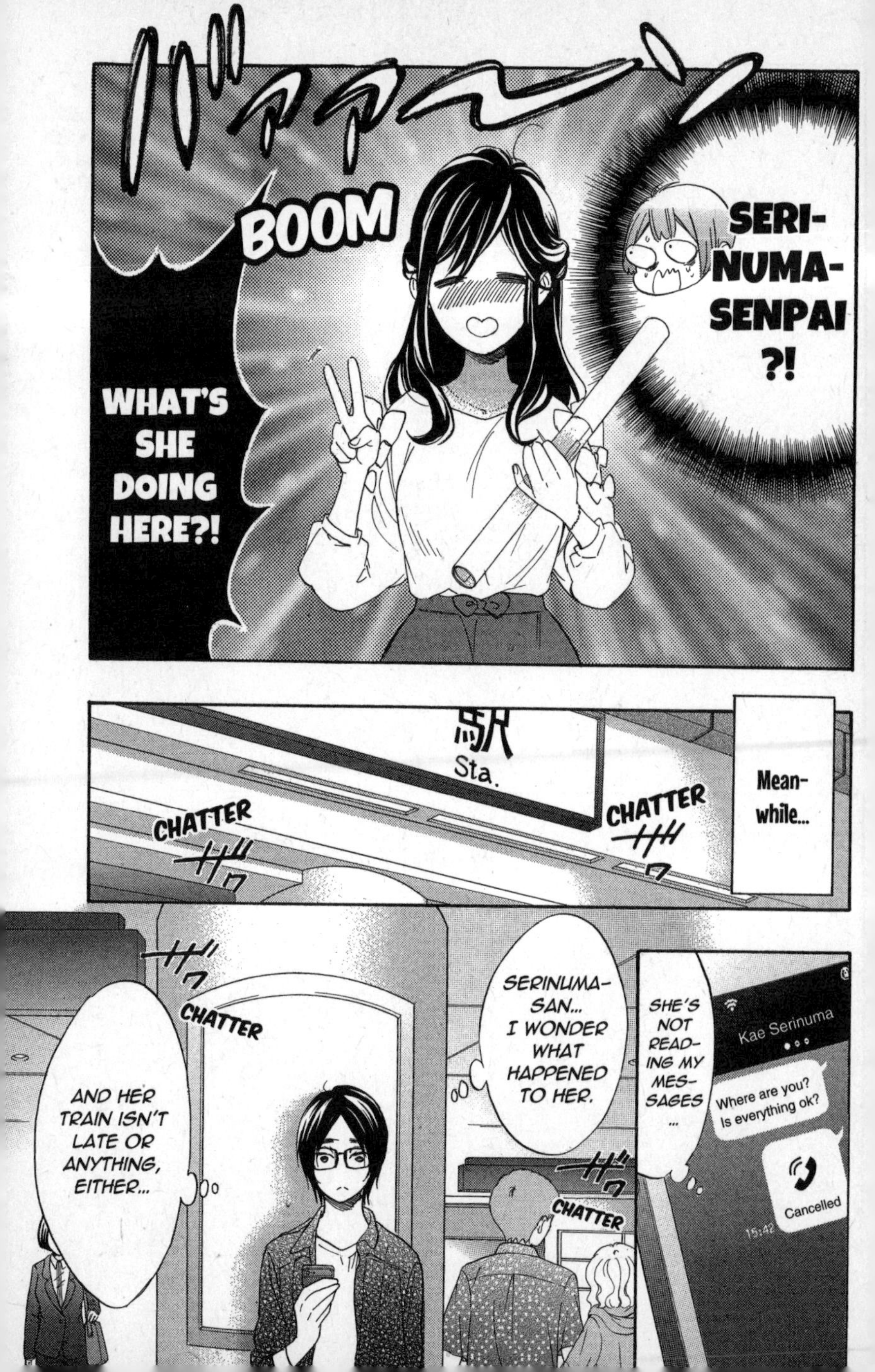
BOOM
SERI-NUMA-SENPAI?!
WHAT'S SHE DOING HERE?!
Mean-while...
駅
Sta.
CHATTER
CHATTER
Kae Serinuma
Where are you? Is everything ok?
Cancelled
15:42
SHE'S NOT READ-ING MY MES-SAGES...
SERINUMA-SAN... I WONDER WHAT HAPPENED TO HER.
CHATTER
AND HER TRAIN ISN'T LATE OR ANYTHING, EITHER...
CHATTER

I HOPE SHE DIDN'T GET INTO AN ACCIDENT...!

V-VM!

GASP

Shin Yashiro
New Message

?

UH, YA-SHIRO-KUN...

!

I'm at a "Mirage Saga" event right now, and I bumped into your girlfriend.

PING

your girlfriend.

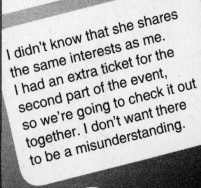

I didn't know that she shares the same interests as me. I had an extra ticket for the second part of the event, so we're going to check it out together. I don't want there to be a misunderstanding.

Later.

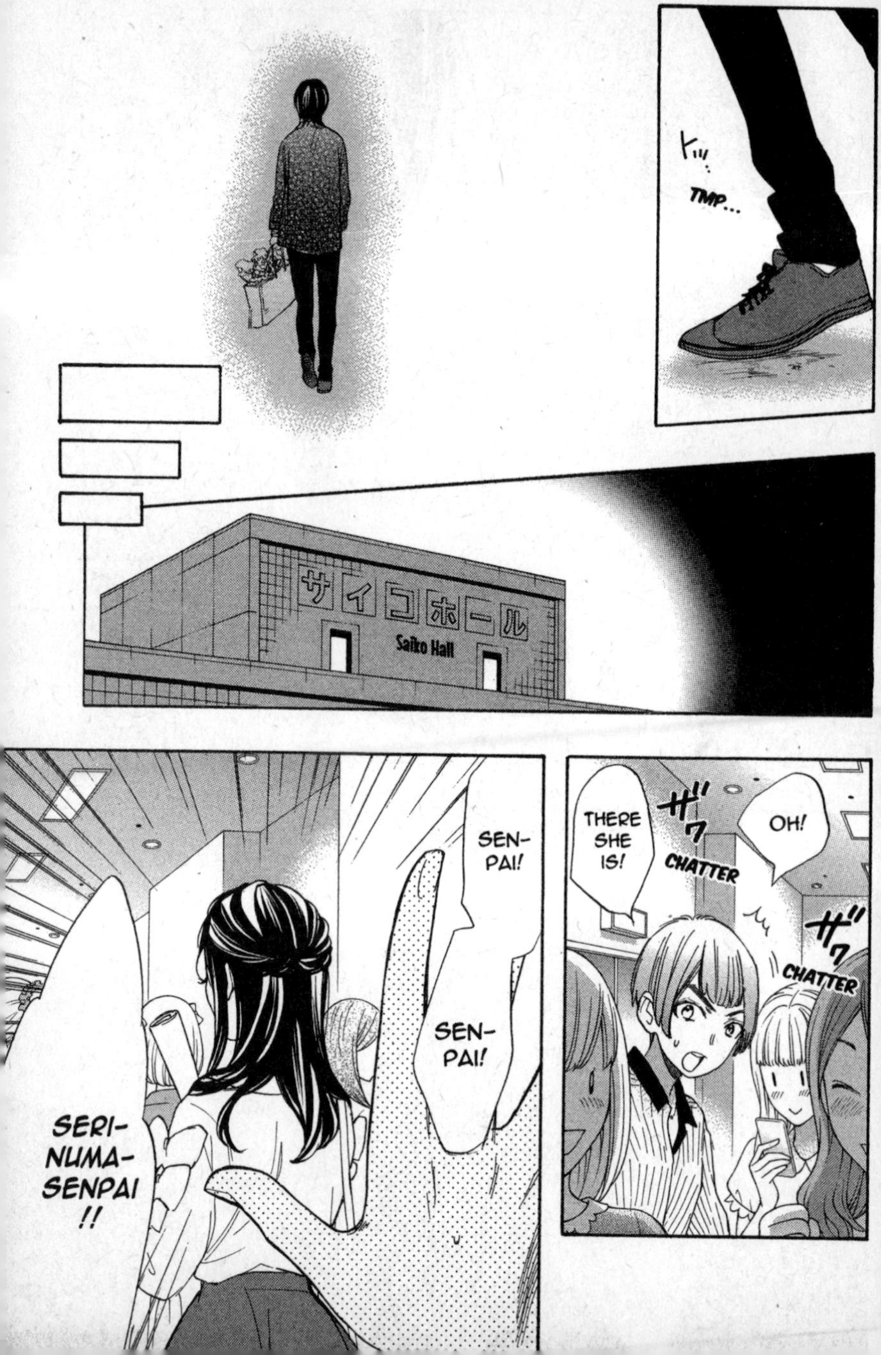
ドッ
TMP...
サイコホール
Saiko Hall
CHATTER
OH!
THERE SHE IS!
CHATTER
SEN-PAI!
SEN-PAI!
SERI-NUMA-SENPAI!!

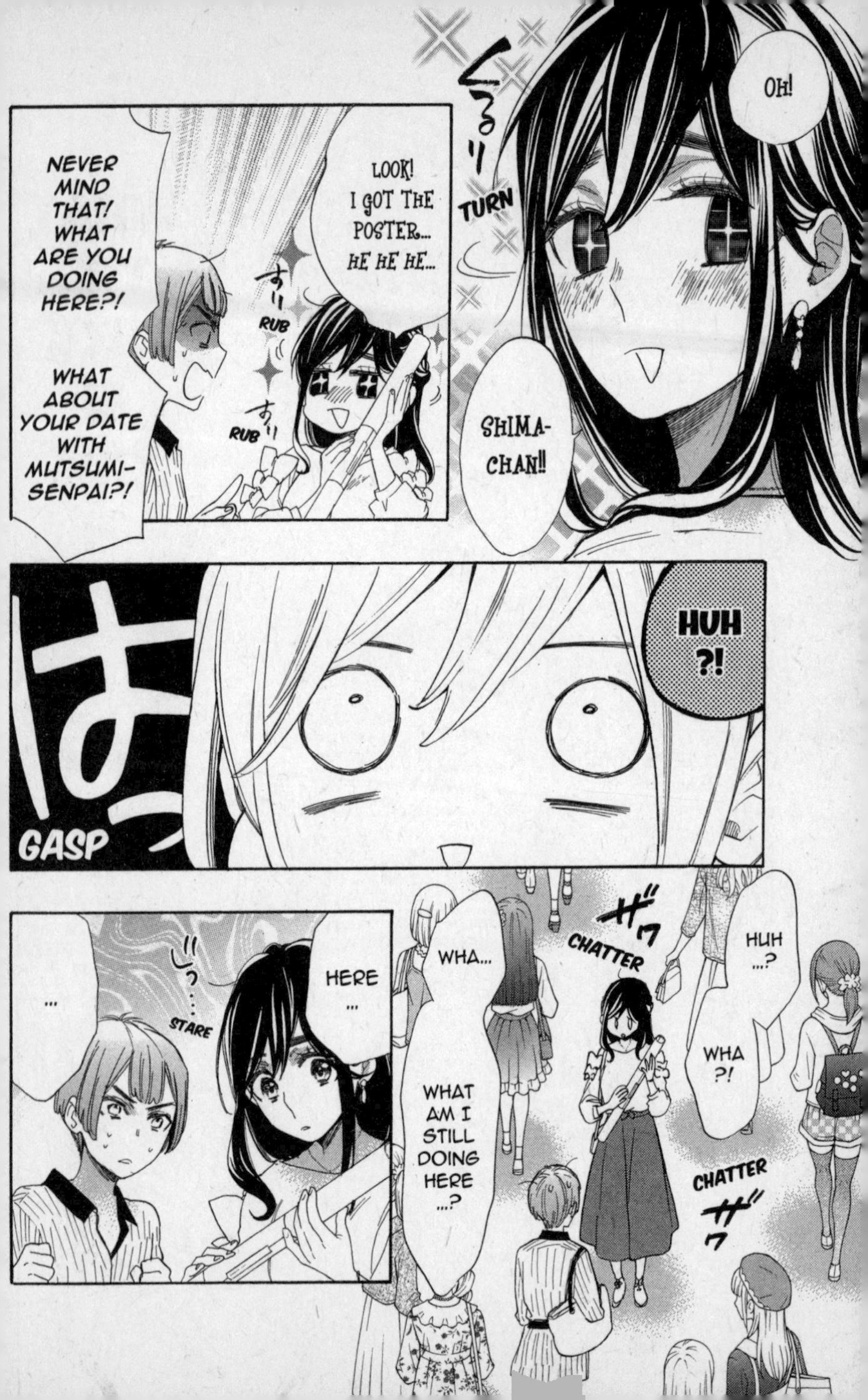
OH!
TURN
SHIMA-CHAN!!
LOOK! I GOT THE POSTER... HE HE HE...
RUB
RUB
NEVER MIND THAT! WHAT ARE YOU DOING HERE?!
WHAT ABOUT YOUR DATE WITH MUTSUMI-SENPAI?!
HUH ?!
GASP
HUH ...?
CHATTER
WHA ?!
WHA...
WHAT AM I STILL DOING HERE ...?
CHATTER
HERE ...
STARE
...

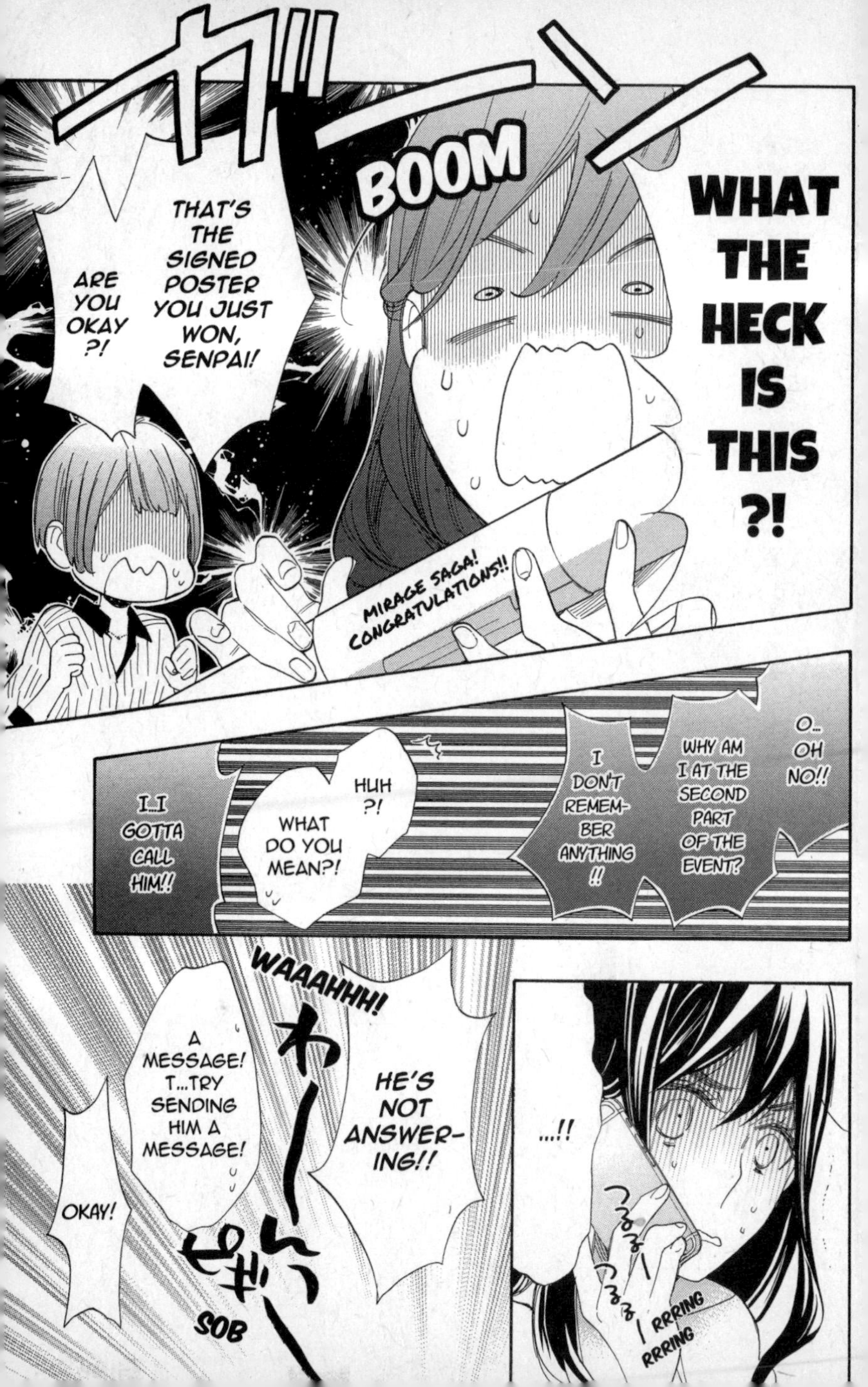
BOOM
WHAT THE HECK IS THIS ?!
THAT'S THE SIGNED POSTER YOU JUST WON, SENPAI!
ARE YOU OKAY ?!
MIRAGE SAGA! CONGRATULATIONS!!
O... OH NO!!
WHY AM I AT THE SECOND PART OF THE EVENT?
I DON'T REMEMBER ANYTHING !!
HUH ?!
WHAT DO YOU MEAN?!
I...I GOTTA CALL HIM!!
...!!
RRRING RRRING
HE'S NOT ANSWERING!!
WAAAHHH!
A MESSAGE! T...TRY SENDING HIM A MESSAGE!
OKAY!
SOB

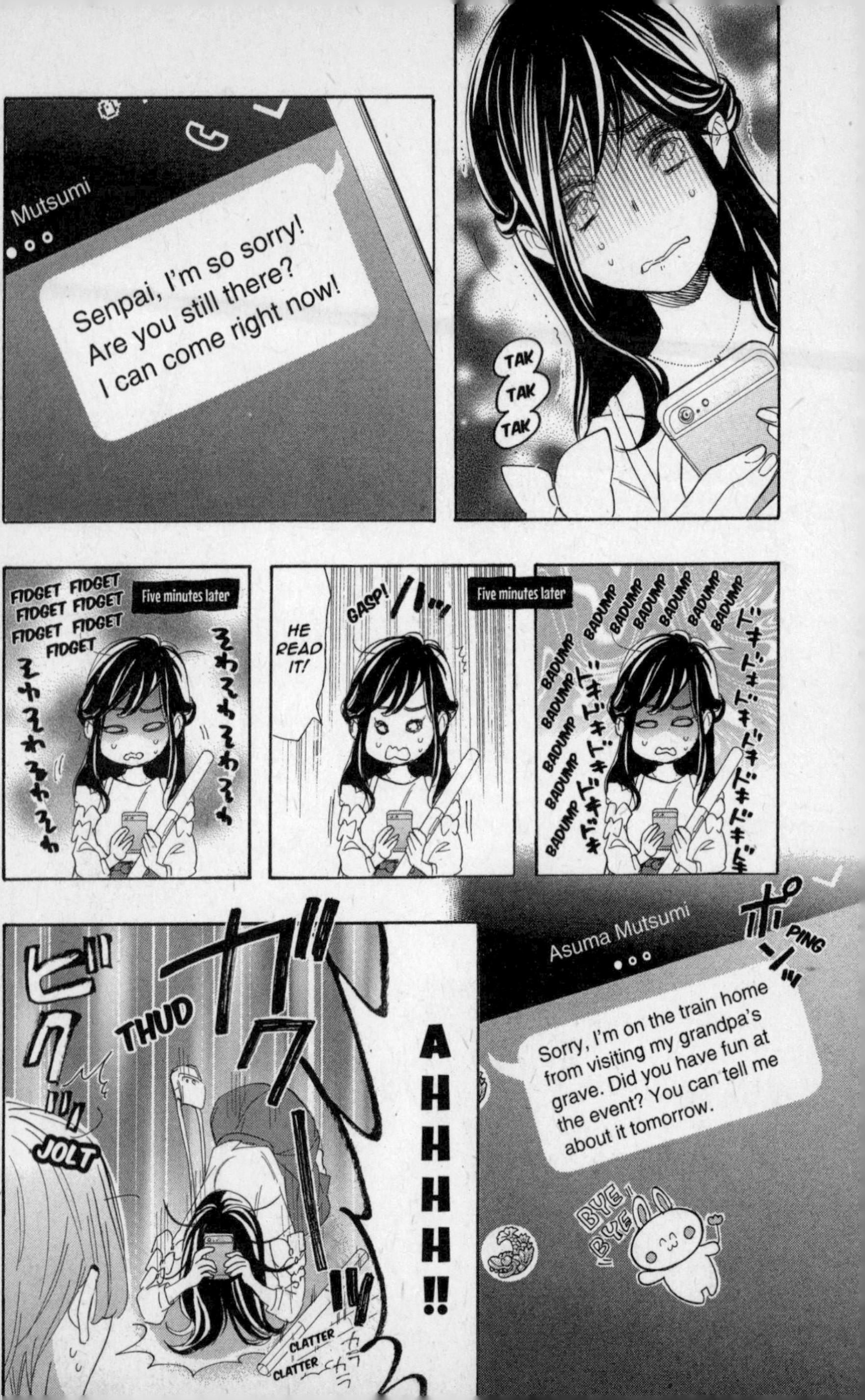

TAK
TAK
TAK
Mutsumi
Senpai, I'm so sorry! Are you still there? I can come right now!
BADUMP BADUMP BADUMP BADUMP BADUMP BADUMP
BADUMP BADUMP BADUMP BADUMP BADUMP BADUMP
Five minutes later
GASP!
HE READ IT!
Five minutes later
FIDGET FIDGET FIDGET FIDGET FIDGET FIDGET FIDGET
Asuma Mutsumi
PING
Sorry, I'm on the train home from visiting my grandpa's grave. Did you have fun at the event? You can tell me about it tomorrow.
BYE BYE
AHHHH!!
THUD
JOLT
CLATTER
CLATTER

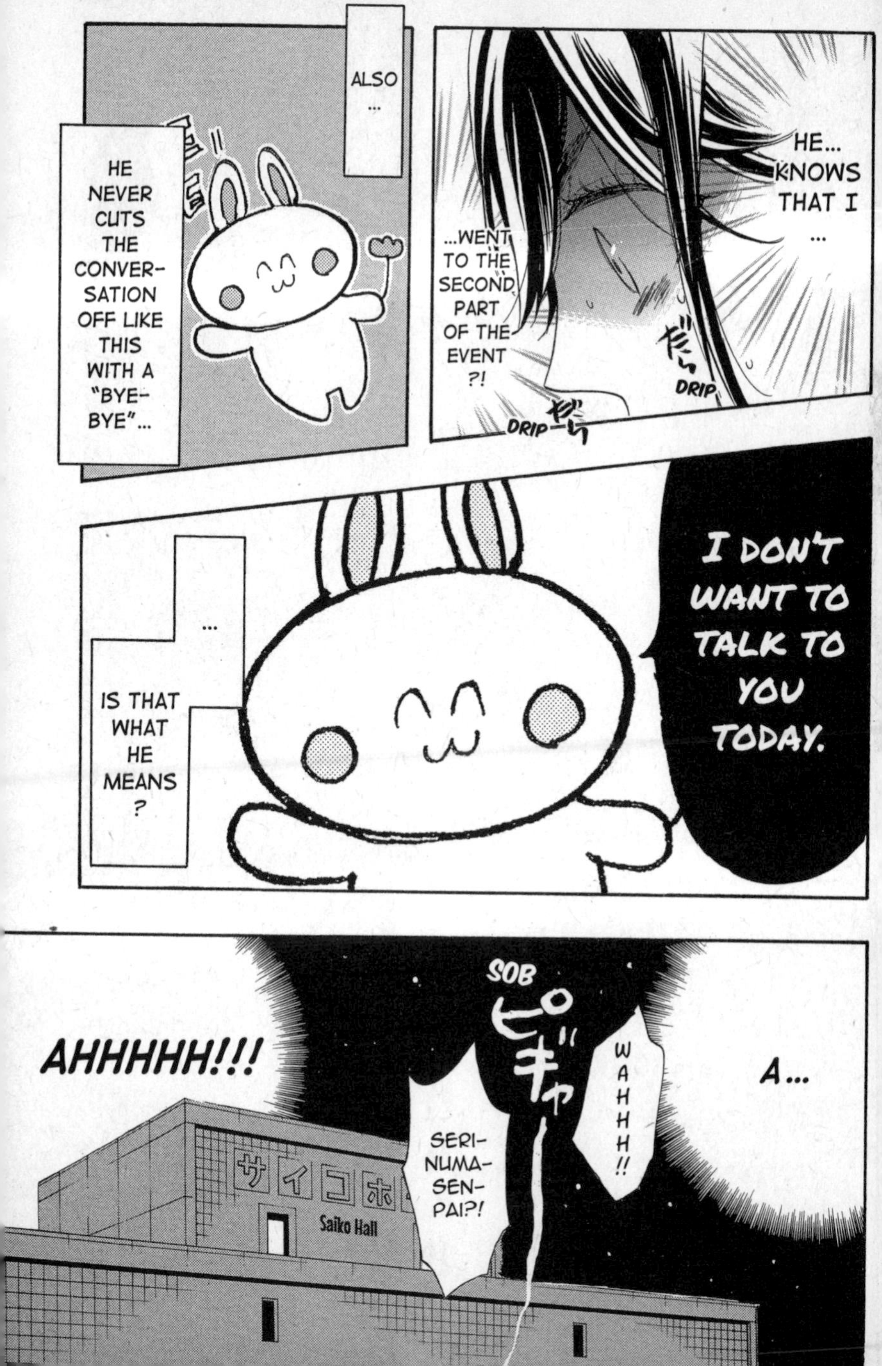
HE... KNOWS THAT I ...
...WENT TO THE SECOND PART OF THE EVENT ?!
DRIP
DRIP
ALSO ...
HE NEVER CUTS THE CONVER-SATION OFF LIKE THIS WITH A "BYE-BYE"...
I DON'T WANT TO TALK TO YOU TODAY.
...
IS THAT WHAT HE MEANS ?
A...
SOB
WAHHHH!!
SERI-NUMA-SEN-PAI?!
AHHHHH!!!
Saiko Hall

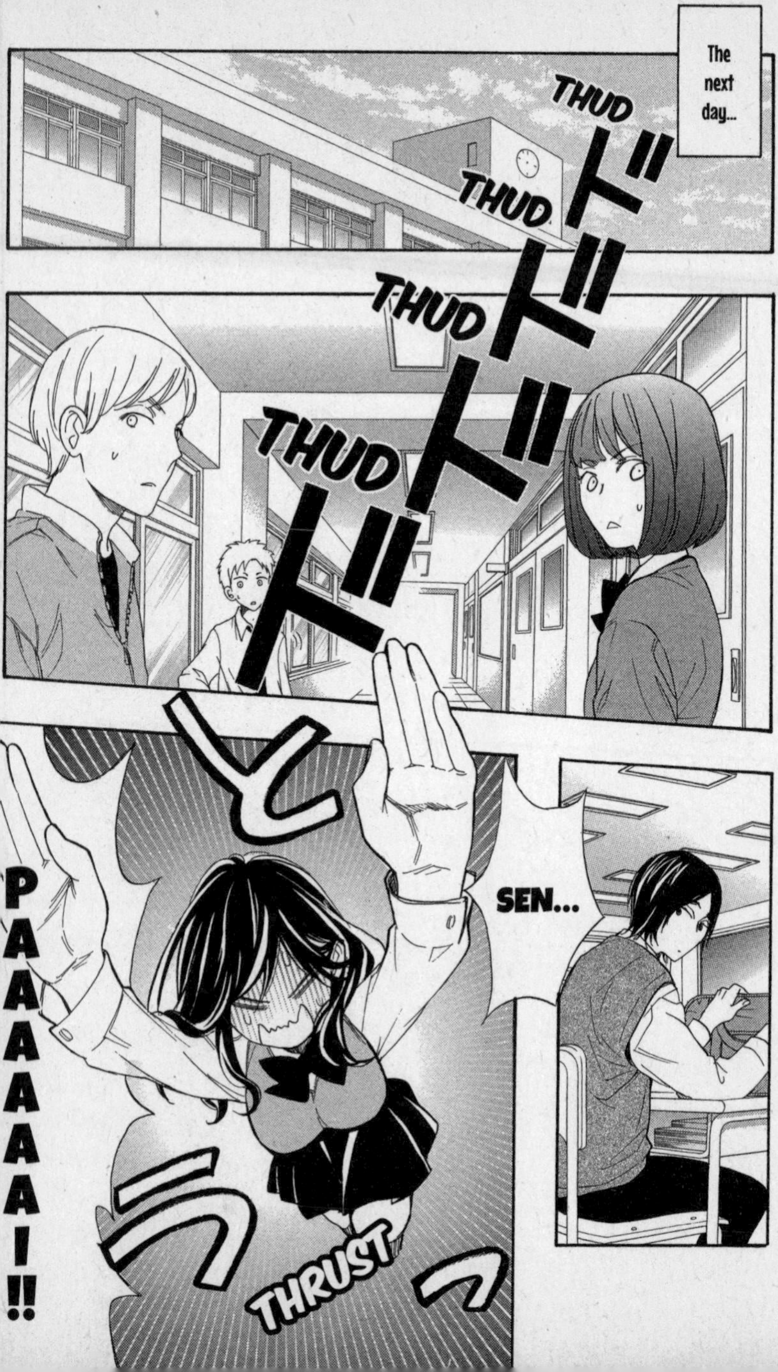
The next day...
THUD
ドド
THUD
ド
THUD
ド
THUD
ド
SEN...
PAAAAAAAAI!!
と
う
THRUST
っ

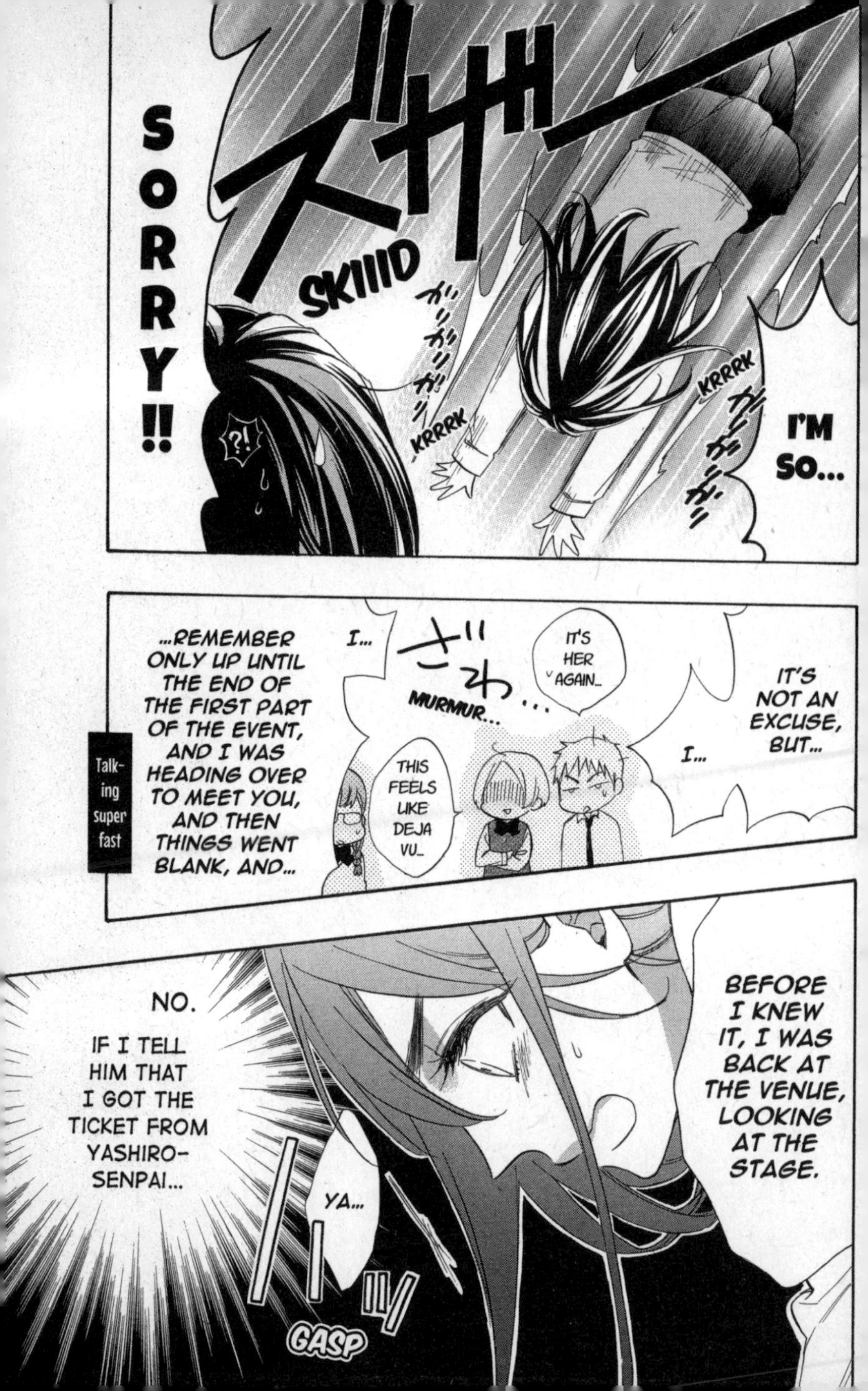
I'M SO...
SKIIID
KRRRK
KRRRK
?!
SORRY!!
IT'S NOT AN EXCUSE, BUT...
I...
IT'S HER AGAIN...
ざわ...
MURMUR...
THIS FEELS LIKE DEJA VU...
I...
...REMEMBER ONLY UP UNTIL THE END OF THE FIRST PART OF THE EVENT, AND I WAS HEADING OVER TO MEET YOU, AND THEN THINGS WENT BLANK, AND...
Talking super fast
BEFORE I KNEW IT, I WAS BACK AT THE VENUE, LOOKING AT THE STAGE.
NO.
IF I TELL HIM THAT I GOT THE TICKET FROM YASHIRO-SENPAI...
YA...
GASP

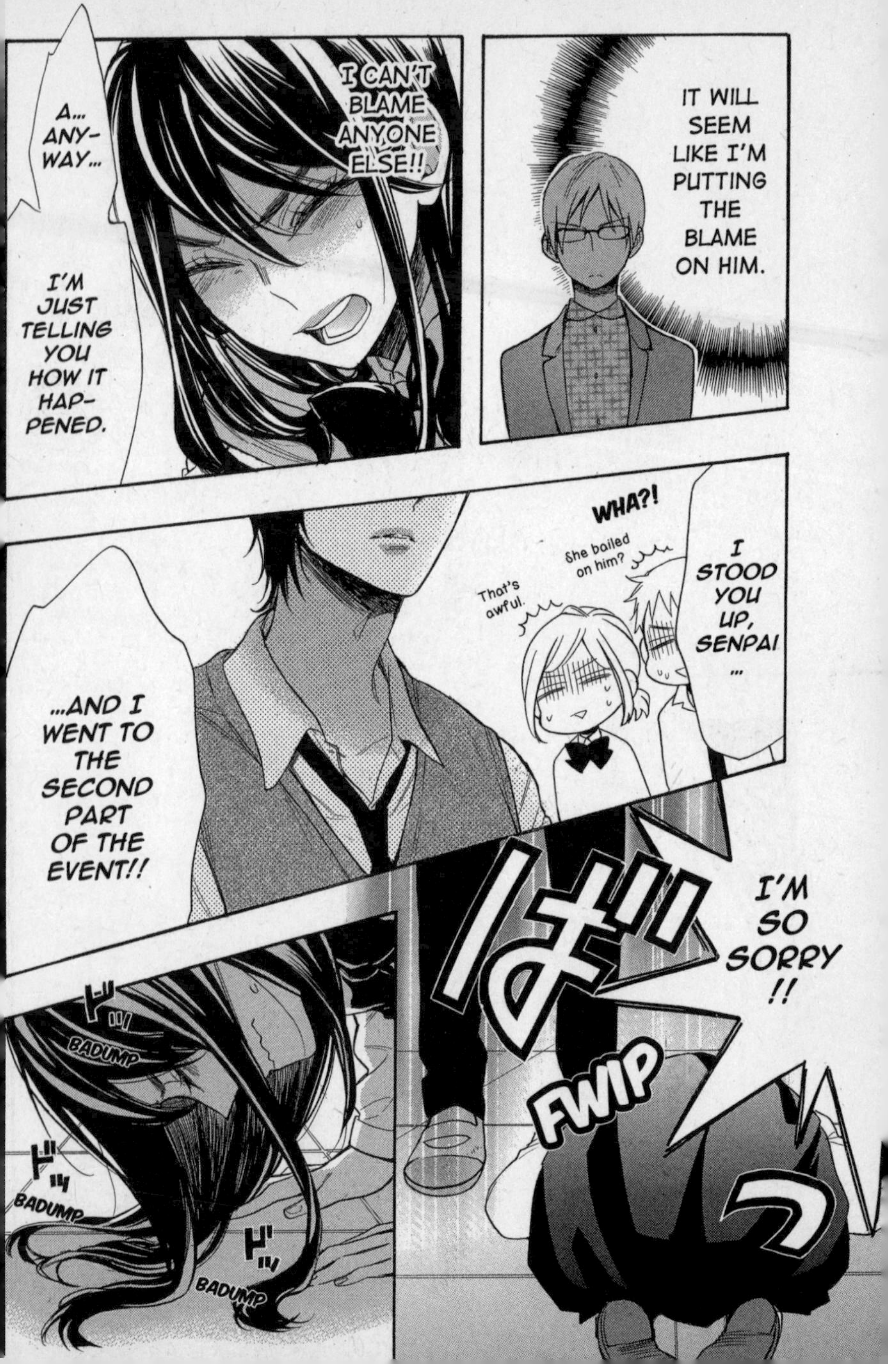
IT WILL SEEM LIKE I'M PUTTING THE BLAME ON HIM.
I CAN'T BLAME ANYONE ELSE!!
A... ANY-WAY...
I'M JUST TELLING YOU HOW IT HAP-PENED.
I STOOD YOU UP, SENPAI...
WHA?!
She bailed on him?
That's awful.
...AND I WENT TO THE SECOND PART OF THE EVENT!!
I'M SO SORRY!!
FWIP
BADUMP
BADUMP
BADUMP

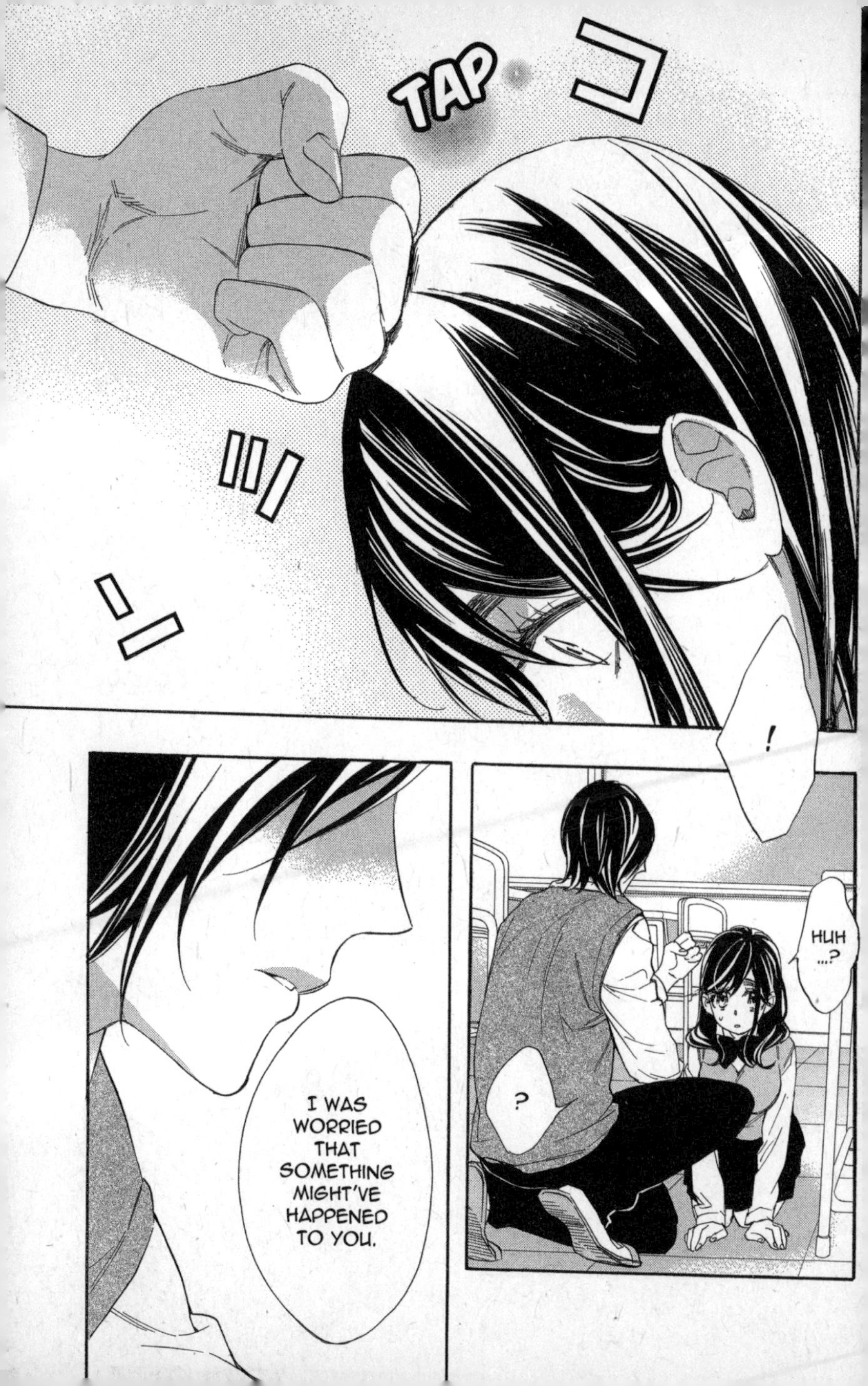
TAP
!
HUH ...?
?
I WAS WORRIED THAT SOMETHING MIGHT'VE HAPPENED TO YOU.

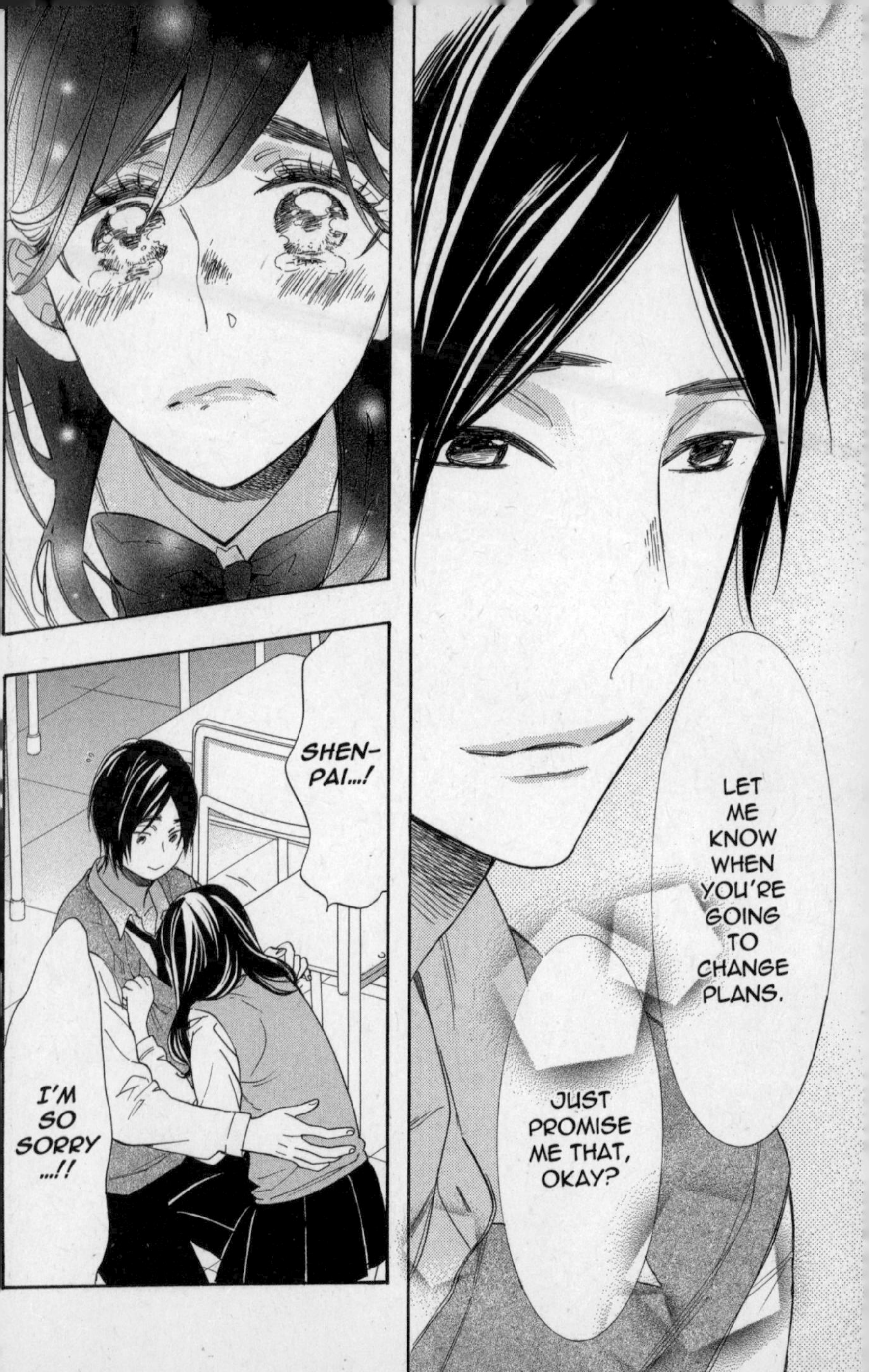
LET ME KNOW WHEN YOU'RE GOING TO CHANGE PLANS.
JUST PROMISE ME THAT, OKAY?
SHEN-PAI...!
I'M SO SORRY ...!!

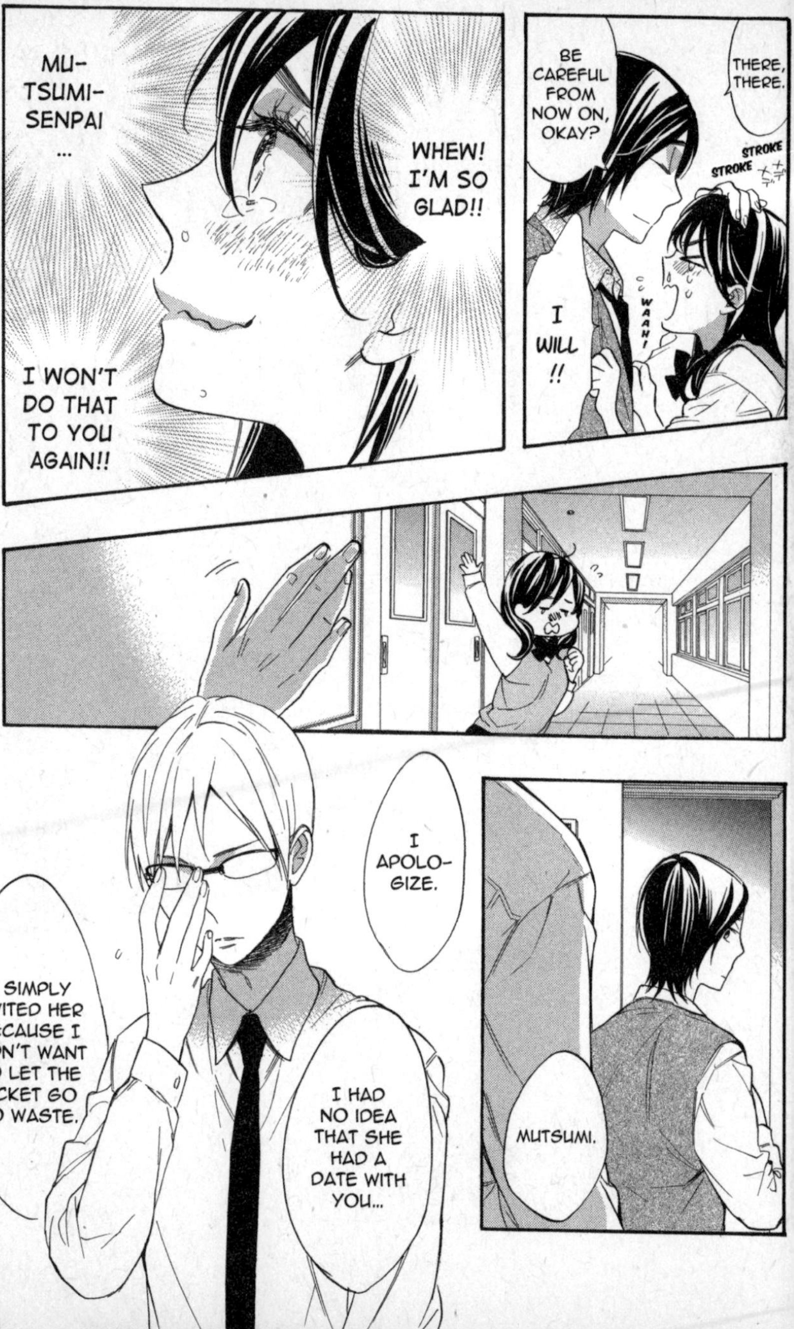
THERE, THERE.
BE CAREFUL FROM NOW ON, OKAY?
STROKE STROKE
WAAH!
I WILL!!
WHEW! I'M SO GLAD!!
MU-TSUMI-SENPAI...
I WON'T DO THAT TO YOU AGAIN!!
MUTSUMI.
I APOLO-GIZE.
I HAD NO IDEA THAT SHE HAD A DATE WITH YOU...
I SIMPLY INVITED HER BECAUSE I DIDN'T WANT TO LET THE TICKET GO TO WASTE.

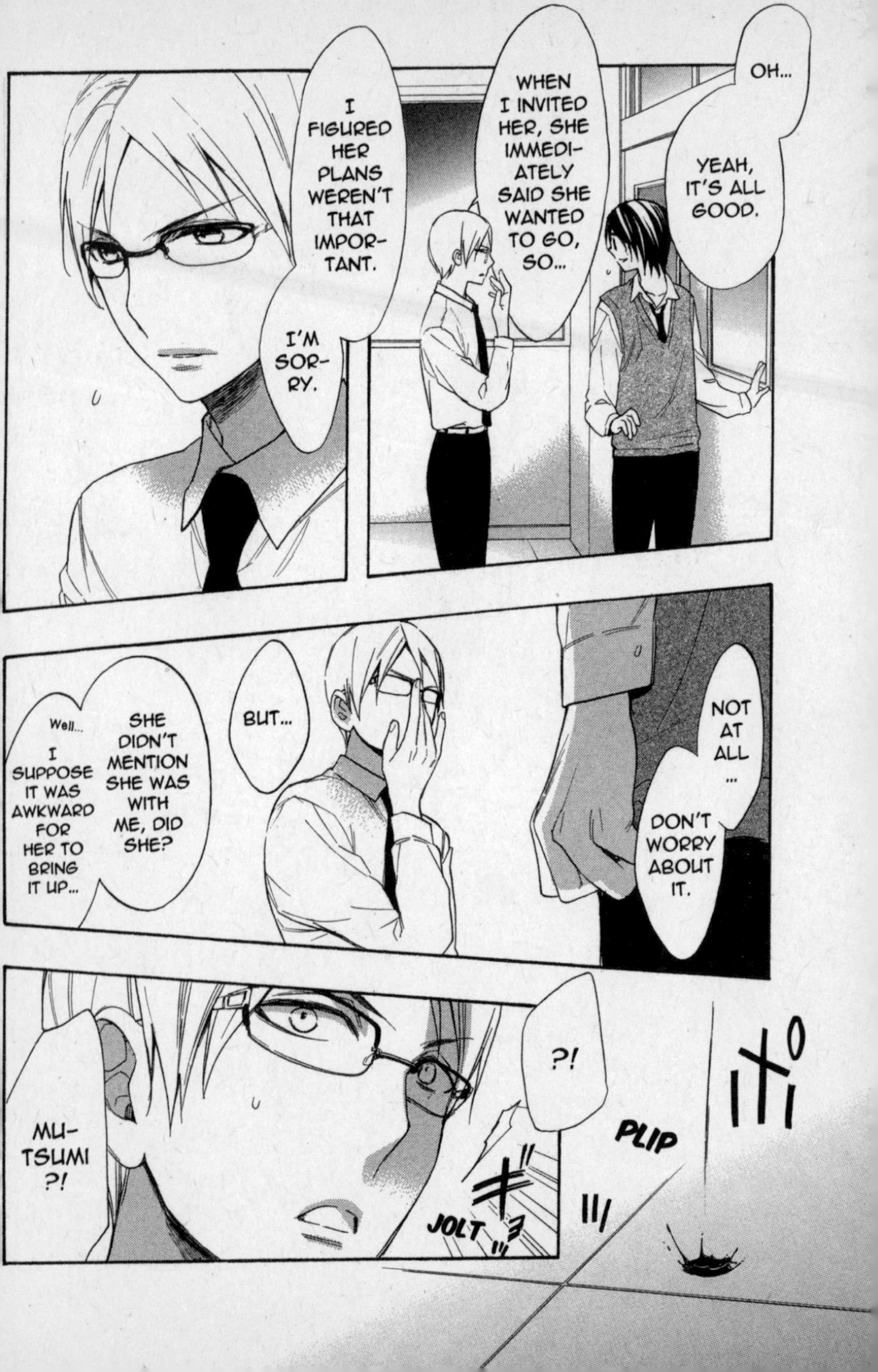
OH...
YEAH, IT'S ALL GOOD.
WHEN I INVITED HER, SHE IMMEDIATELY SAID SHE WANTED TO GO, SO...
I FIGURED HER PLANS WEREN'T THAT IMPORTANT.
I'M SORRY.
NOT AT ALL...
DON'T WORRY ABOUT IT.
BUT...
SHE DIDN'T MENTION SHE WAS WITH ME, DID SHE?
Well... I SUPPOSE IT WAS AWKWARD FOR HER TO BRING IT UP...
PLIP
?!
JOLT
MUTSUMI?!

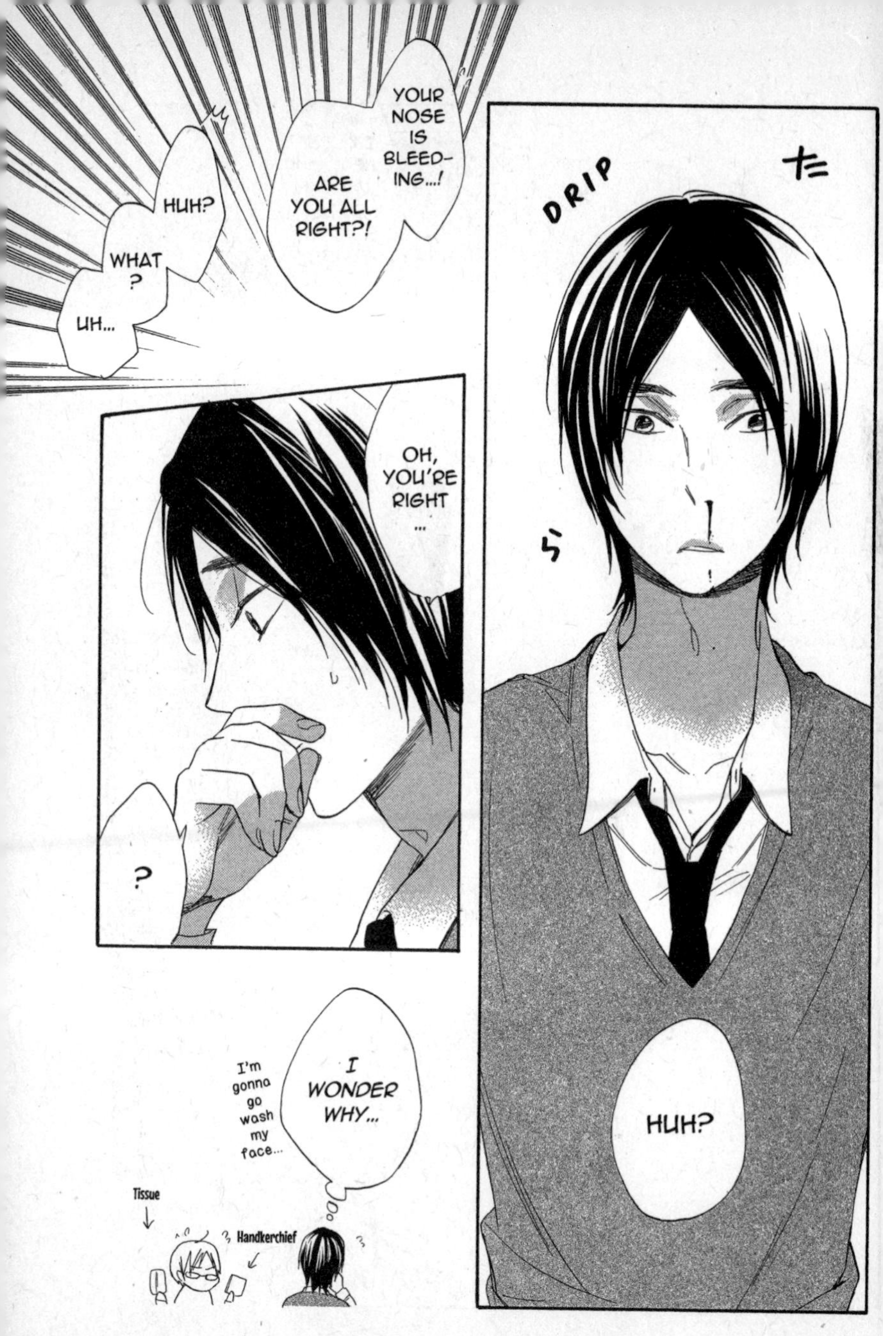

DRIP
HUH?
YOUR NOSE IS BLEED-ING...!
ARE YOU ALL RIGHT?!
HUH?
WHAT?
UH...
OH, YOU'RE RIGHT...
?
I WONDER WHY...
I'm gonna go wash my face...
Handkerchief
Tissue

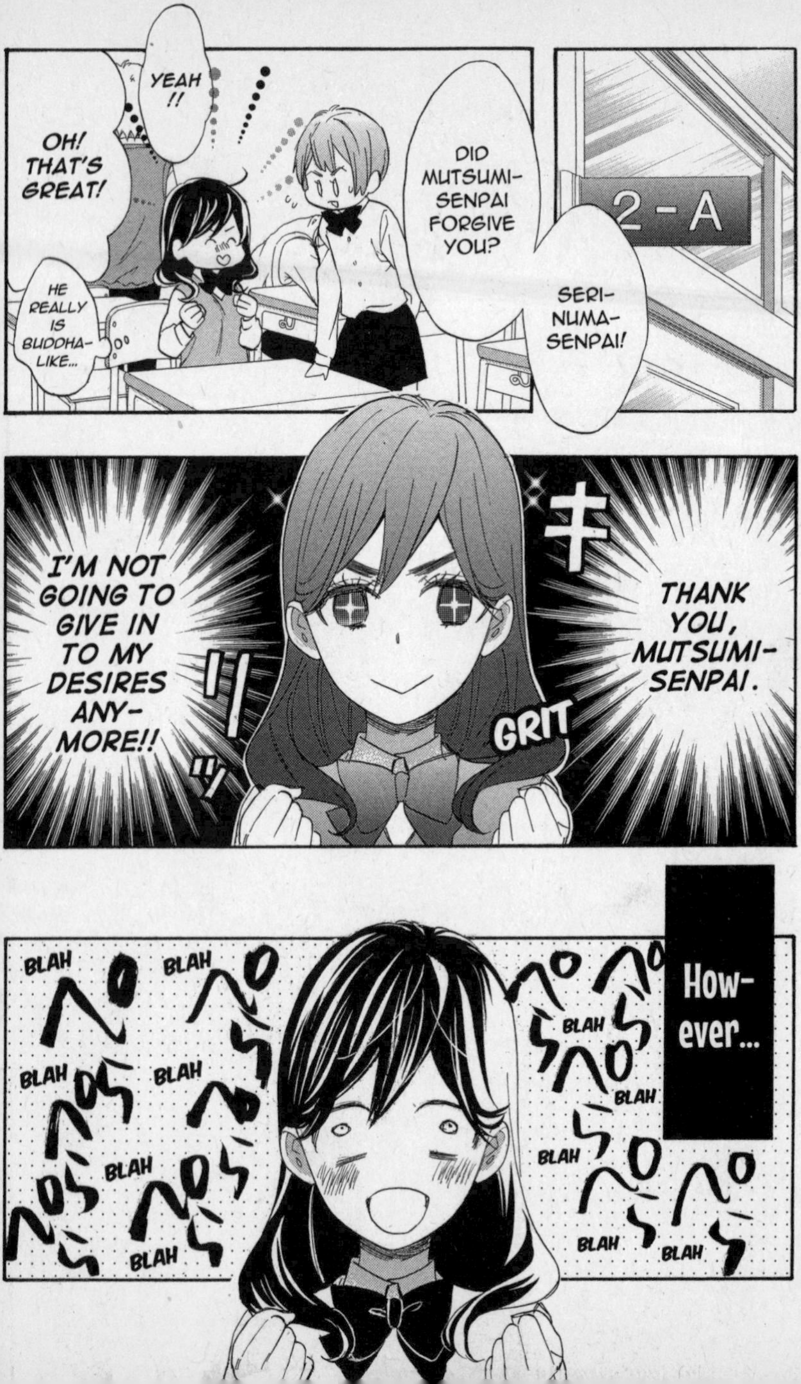
SERI-NUMA-SENPAI!
DID MUTSUMI-SENPAI FORGIVE YOU?
YEAH!!
OH! THAT'S GREAT!
HE REALLY IS BUDDHA-LIKE...
THANK YOU, MUTSUMI-SENPAI.
GRIT
I'M NOT GOING TO GIVE IN TO MY DESIRES ANYMORE!!
How-ever...
BLAH BLAH BLAH BLAH BLAH BLAH BLAH BLAH BLAH BLAH BLAH BLAH

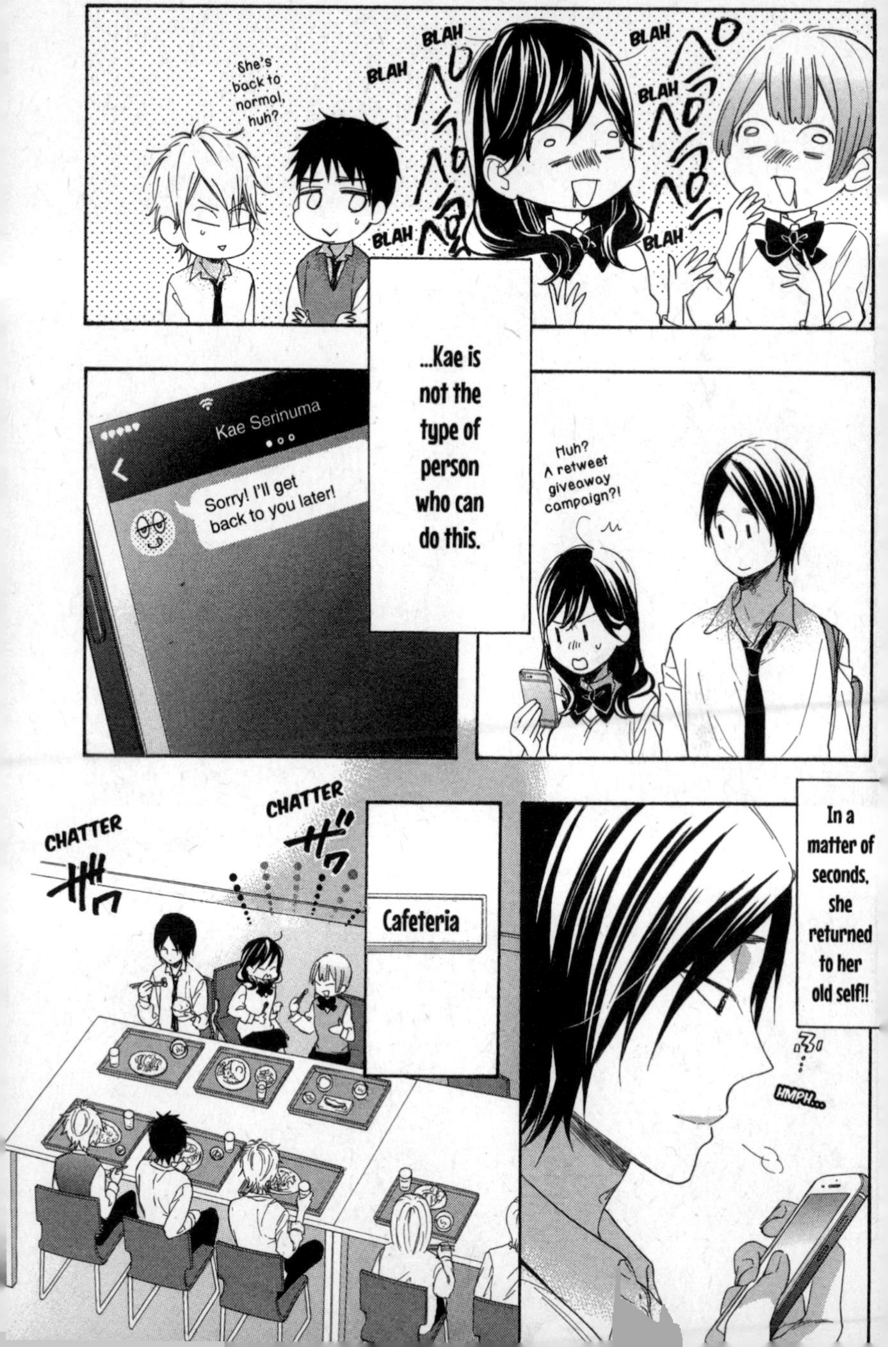
BLAH
BLAH
BLAH
BLAH
She's back to normal, huh?
BLAH
BLAH
Huh? A retweet giveaway campaign?!
...Kae is not the type of person who can do this.
Kae Serinuma
Sorry! I'll get back to you later!
In a matter of seconds, she returned to her old self!!
HMPH...
CHATTER
Cafeteria
CHATTER

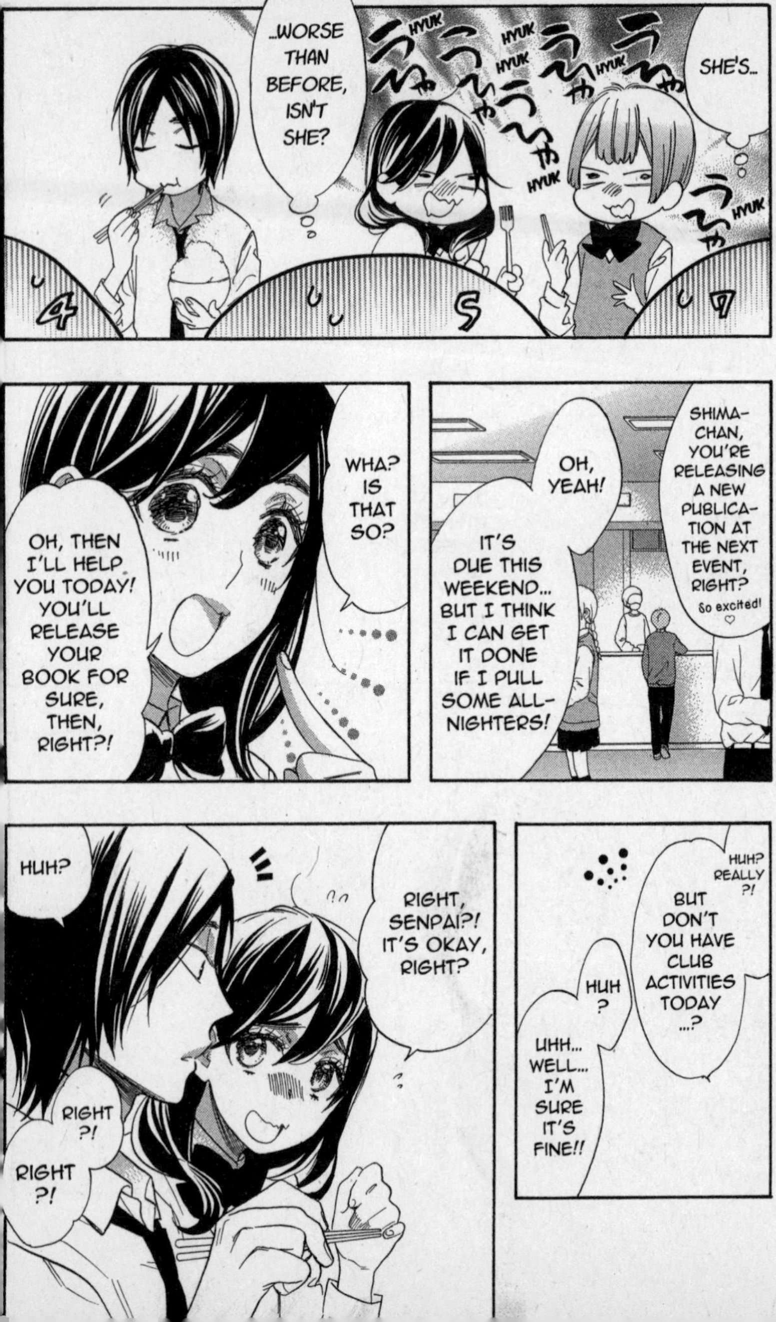
SHE'S...
HYUK
HYUK
HYUK
HYUK
HYUK
HYUK
...WORSE THAN BEFORE, ISN'T SHE?
SHIMA-CHAN, YOU'RE RELEASING A NEW PUBLICATION AT THE NEXT EVENT, RIGHT?
So excited! ♡
OH, YEAH!
IT'S DUE THIS WEEKEND... BUT I THINK I CAN GET IT DONE IF I PULL SOME ALL-NIGHTERS!
WHA? IS THAT SO?
OH, THEN I'LL HELP YOU TODAY! YOU'LL RELEASE YOUR BOOK FOR SURE, THEN, RIGHT?!
HUH? REALLY?!
BUT DON'T YOU HAVE CLUB ACTIVITIES TODAY...?
HUH?
UHH... WELL... I'M SURE IT'S FINE!!
RIGHT, SENPAI?! IT'S OKAY, RIGHT?
HUH?
RIGHT?!
RIGHT?!

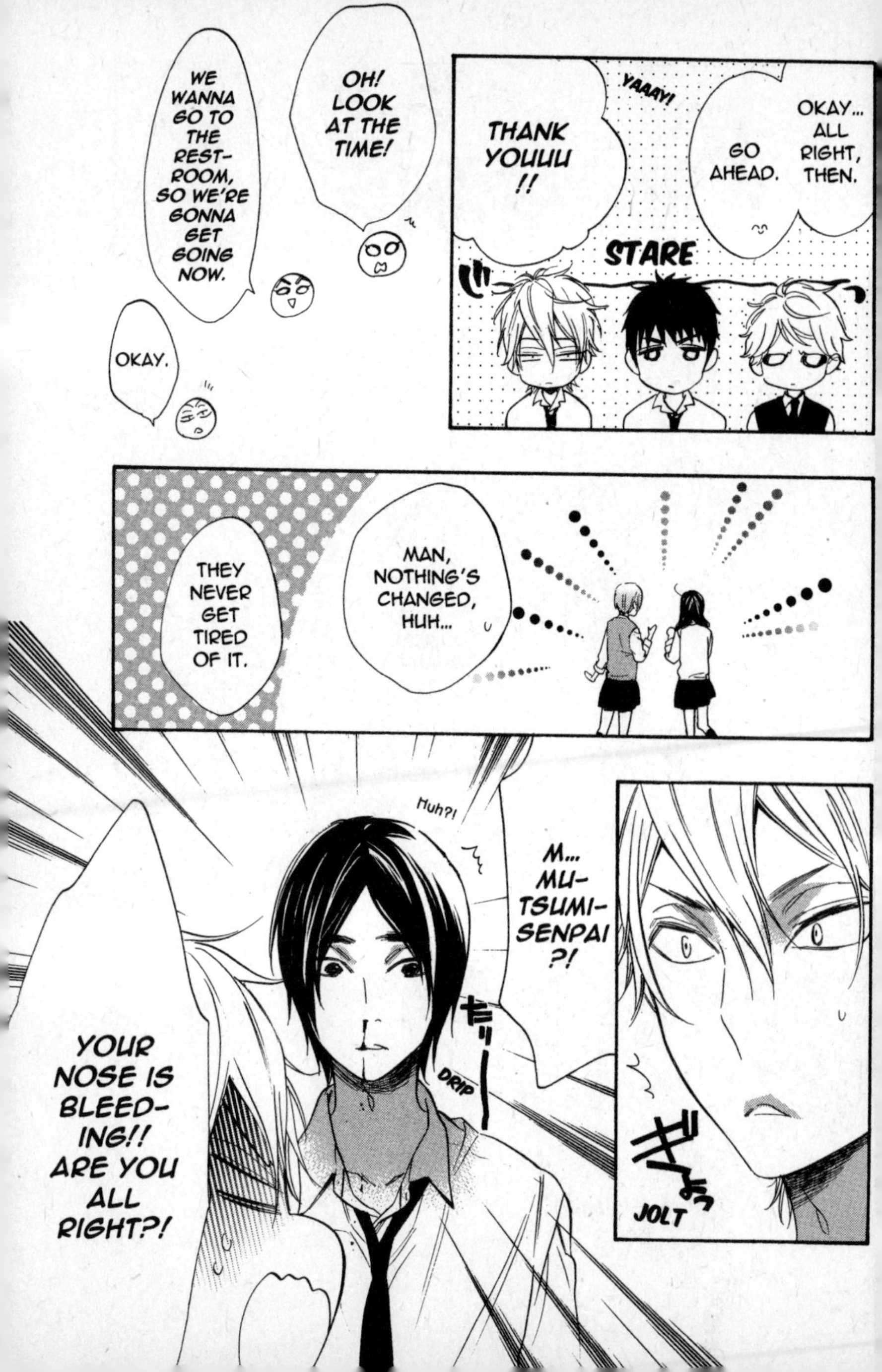
OKAY... ALL RIGHT, THEN.
GO AHEAD.
YAAAY!
THANK YOUUU!!
STARE
OH! LOOK AT THE TIME!
WE WANNA GO TO THE RESTROOM, SO WE'RE GONNA GET GOING NOW.
OKAY.
MAN, NOTHING'S CHANGED, HUH...
THEY NEVER GET TIRED OF IT.
M... MU-TSUMI-SENPAI?!
JOLT
Huh?!
DRIP
YOUR NOSE IS BLEEDING!! ARE YOU ALL RIGHT?!

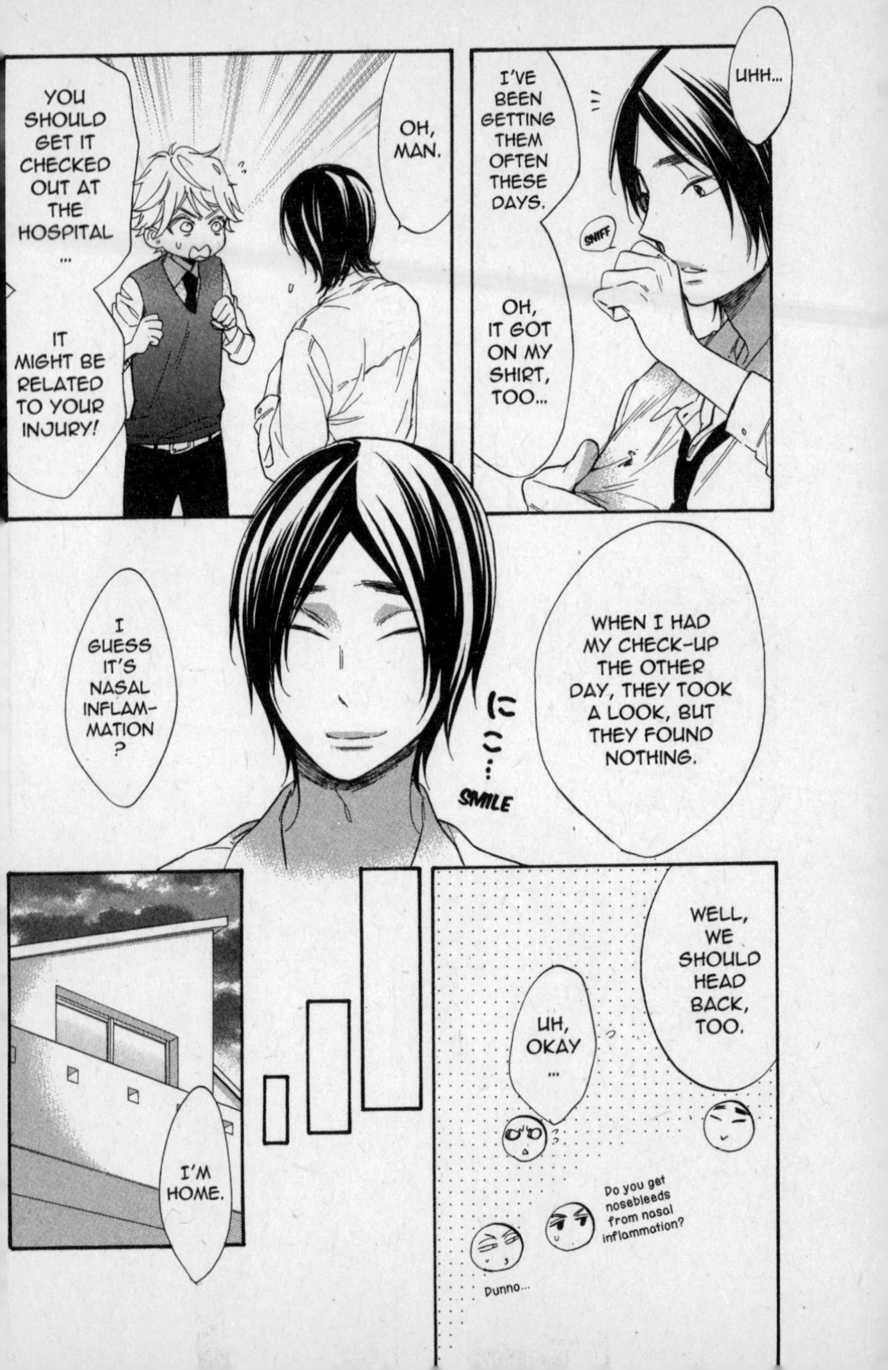
UHH...
I'VE BEEN GETTING THEM OFTEN THESE DAYS.
SNIFF
OH, IT GOT ON MY SHIRT, TOO...
OH, MAN.
YOU SHOULD GET IT CHECKED OUT AT THE HOSPITAL...
IT MIGHT BE RELATED TO YOUR INJURY!
WHEN I HAD MY CHECK-UP THE OTHER DAY, THEY TOOK A LOOK, BUT THEY FOUND NOTHING.
にこ...
SMILE
I GUESS IT'S NASAL INFLAMMATION?
WELL, WE SHOULD HEAD BACK, TOO.
UH, OKAY...
Do you get nosebleeds from nasal inflammation?
Dunno...
I'M HOME.

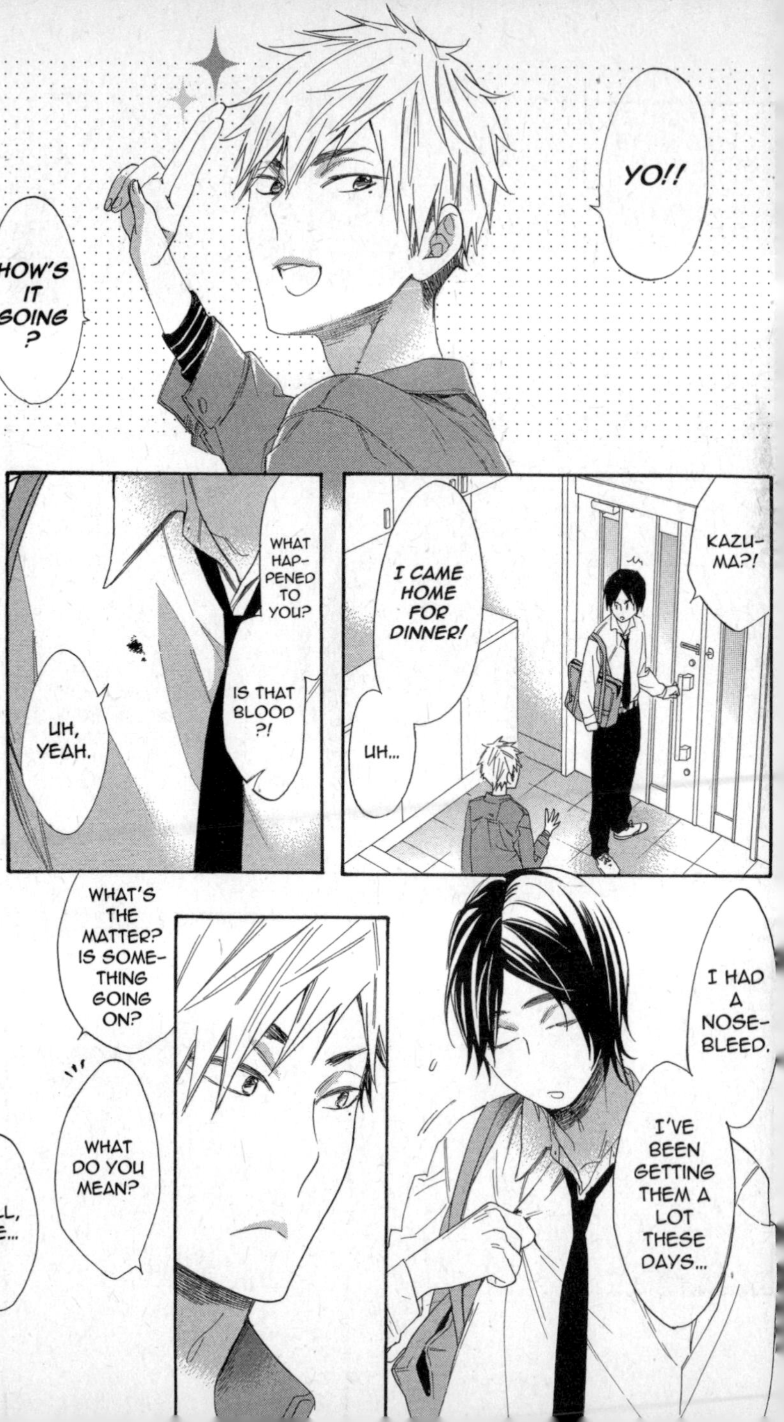

YO!!
HOW'S IT GOING?
KAZUMA?!
I CAME HOME FOR DINNER!
UH...
WHAT HAPPENED TO YOU?
IS THAT BLOOD?!
UH, YEAH.
I HAD A NOSEBLEED.
I'VE BEEN GETTING THEM A LOT THESE DAYS...
WHAT'S THE MATTER? IS SOMETHING GOING ON?
WHAT DO YOU MEAN?
WELL, LIKE...

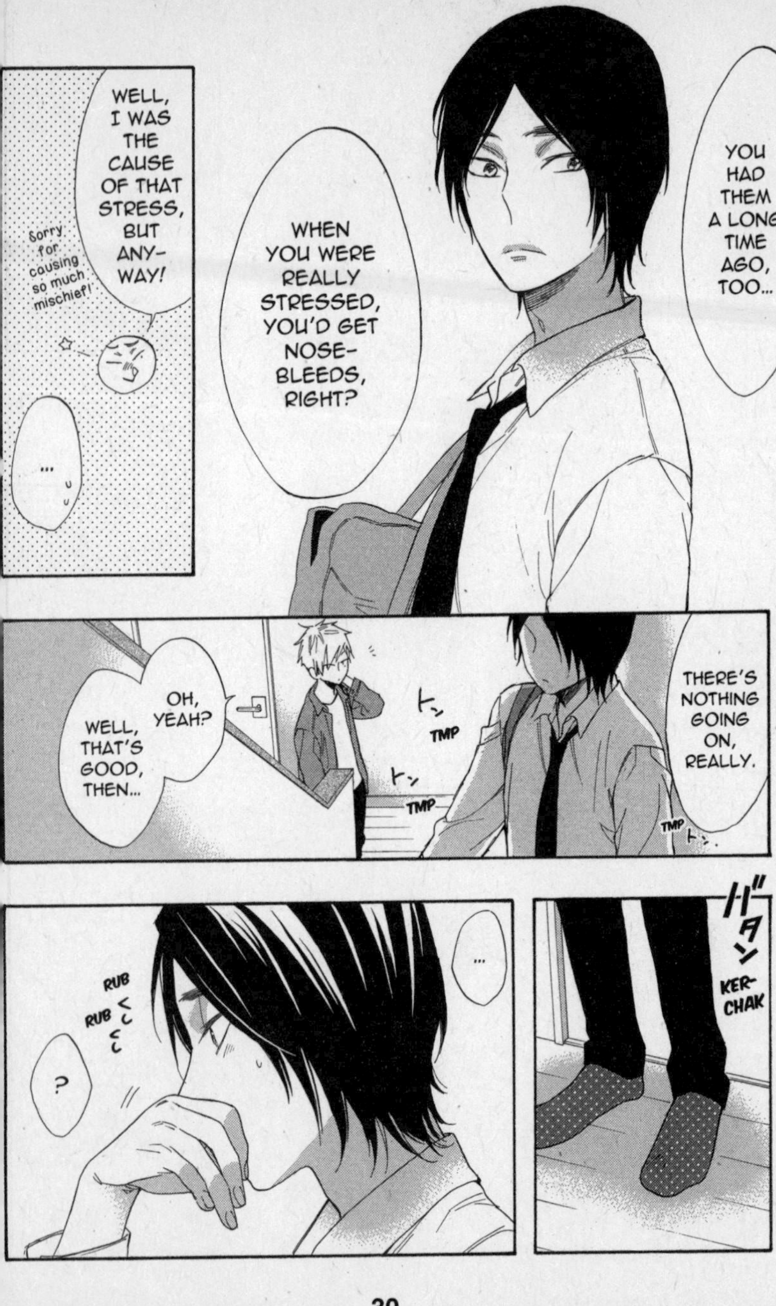
YOU HAD THEM A LONG TIME AGO, TOO...
WHEN YOU WERE REALLY STRESSED, YOU'D GET NOSE-BLEEDS, RIGHT?
WELL, I WAS THE CAUSE OF THAT STRESS, BUT ANY-WAY!
Sorry for causing so much mischief!
......
THERE'S NOTHING GOING ON, REALLY.
トン TMP
トン TMP
トン TMP
OH, YEAH?
WELL, THAT'S GOOD, THEN...
ガタン KER-CHAK
...
RUB RUB
?

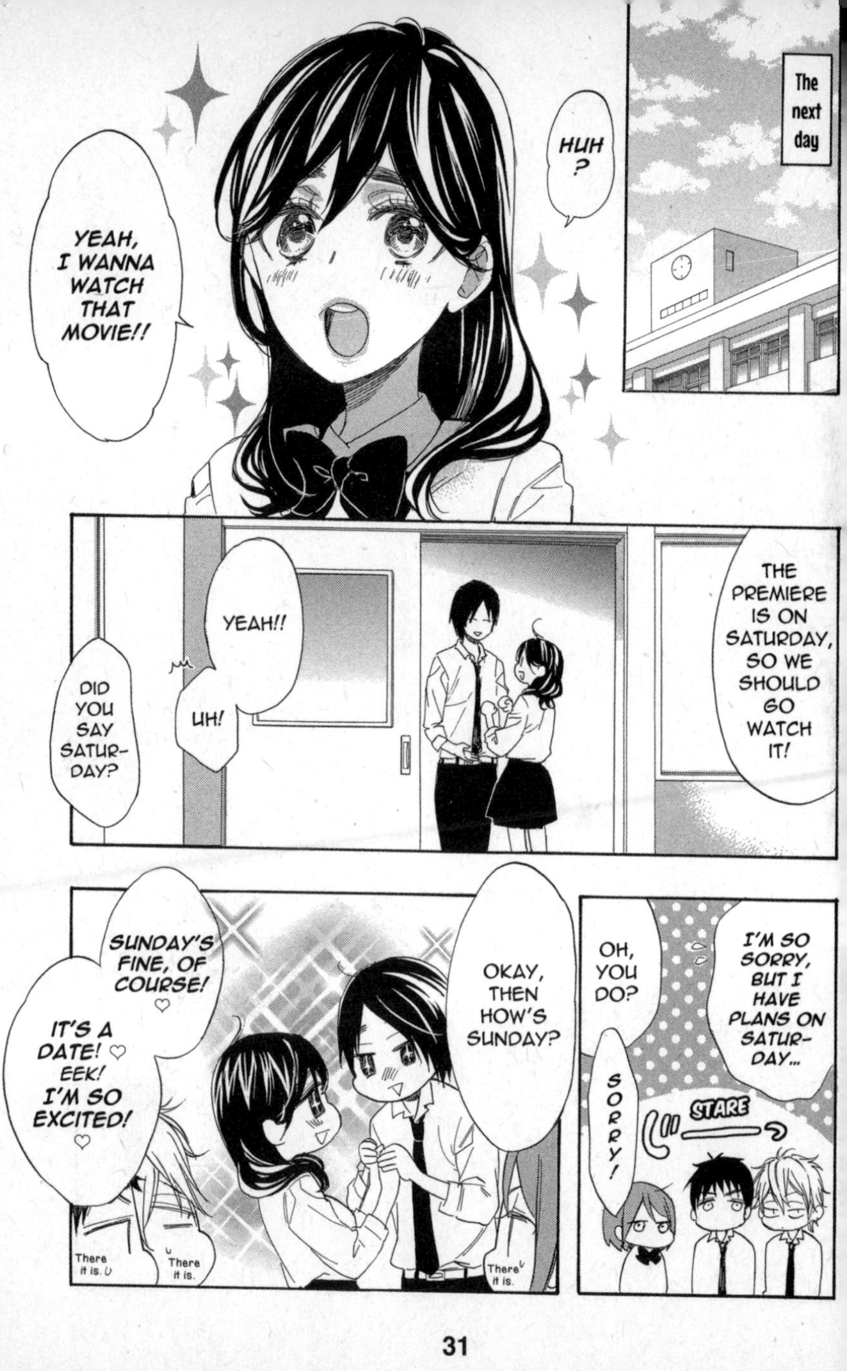
The next day
HUH?
YEAH, I WANNA WATCH THAT MOVIE!!
THE PREMIERE IS ON SATURDAY, SO WE SHOULD GO WATCH IT!
YEAH!!
UH!
DID YOU SAY SATURDAY?
I'M SO SORRY, BUT I HAVE PLANS ON SATURDAY...
OH, YOU DO?
SORRY!
STARE
OKAY, THEN HOW'S SUNDAY?
SUNDAY'S FINE, OF COURSE! ♡
IT'S A DATE! ♡ EEK! I'M SO EXCITED! ♡
There it is.
There it is.
There it is.

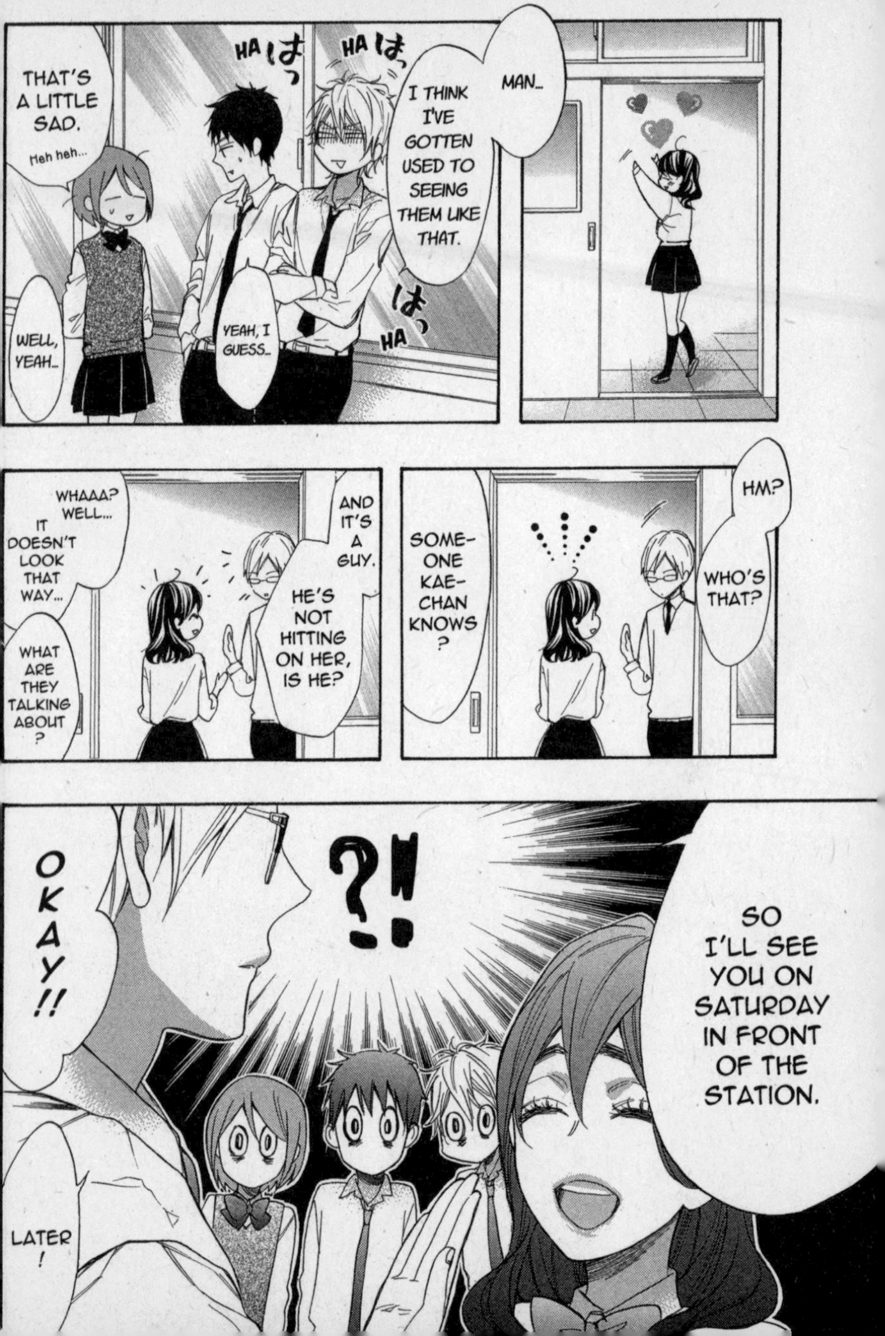
MAN...
I THINK I'VE GOTTEN USED TO SEEING THEM LIKE THAT.
HA はっ
HA はっ
YEAH, I GUESS..
はっ HA
THAT'S A LITTLE SAD.
Heh heh...
WELL, YEAH...
HM?
WHO'S THAT?
SOME-ONE KAE-CHAN KNOWS?
AND IT'S A GUY.
HE'S NOT HITTING ON HER, IS HE?
WHAAA? WELL... IT DOESN'T LOOK THAT WAY...
WHAT ARE THEY TALKING ABOUT?
SO I'LL SEE YOU ON SATURDAY IN FRONT OF THE STATION.
?!!
OKAY!!
LATER!

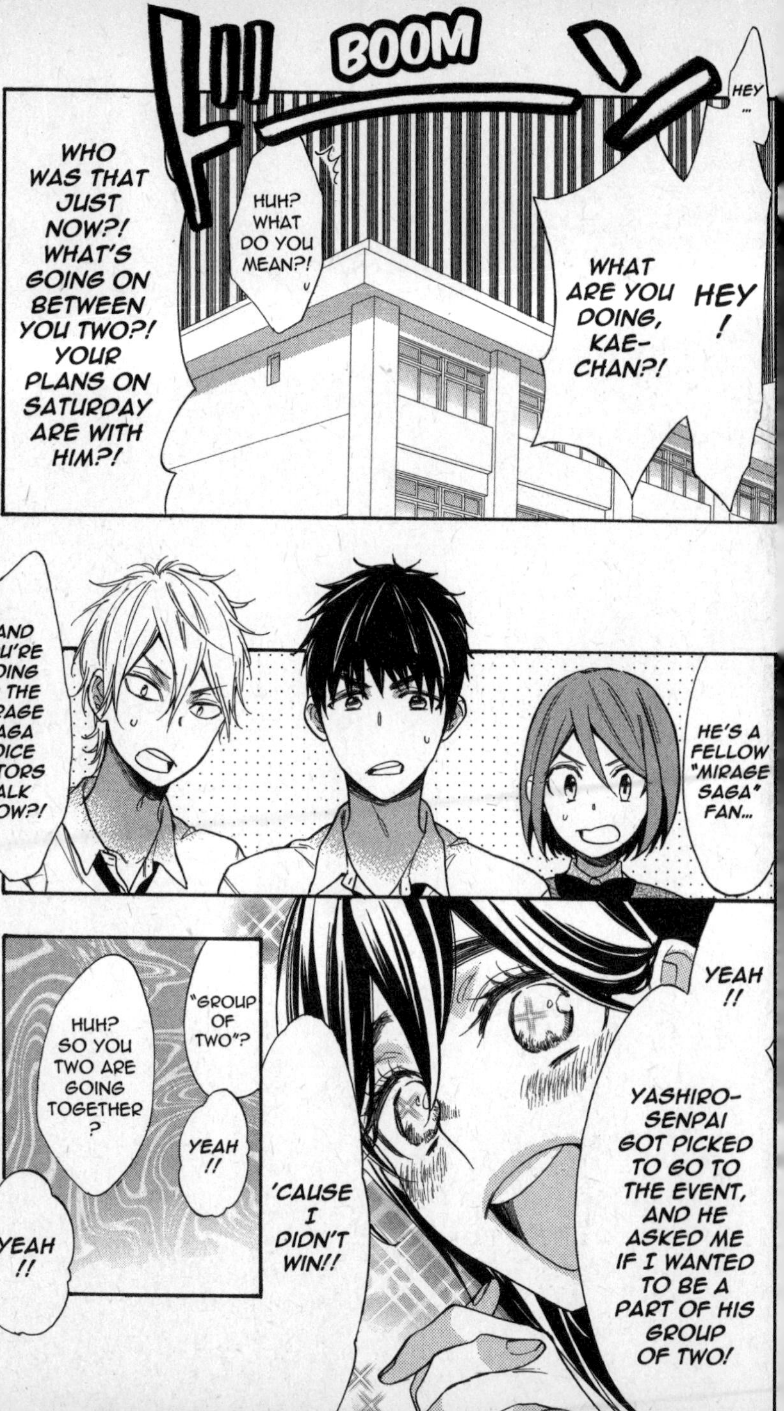
BOOM
HEY...
HEY!
WHAT ARE YOU DOING, KAE-CHAN?!
HUH? WHAT DO YOU MEAN?!
WHO WAS THAT JUST NOW?! WHAT'S GOING ON BETWEEN YOU TWO?! YOUR PLANS ON SATURDAY ARE WITH HIM?!
HE'S A FELLOW "MIRAGE SAGA" FAN...
...AND YOU'RE GOING TO THE MIRAGE SAGA VOICE ACTORS TALK SHOW?!
YEAH!!
YASHIRO-SENPAI GOT PICKED TO GO TO THE EVENT, AND HE ASKED ME IF I WANTED TO BE A PART OF HIS GROUP OF TWO!
'CAUSE I DIDN'T WIN!!
"GROUP OF TWO"?
HUH? SO YOU TWO ARE GOING TOGETHER?
YEAH!!
YEAH!!

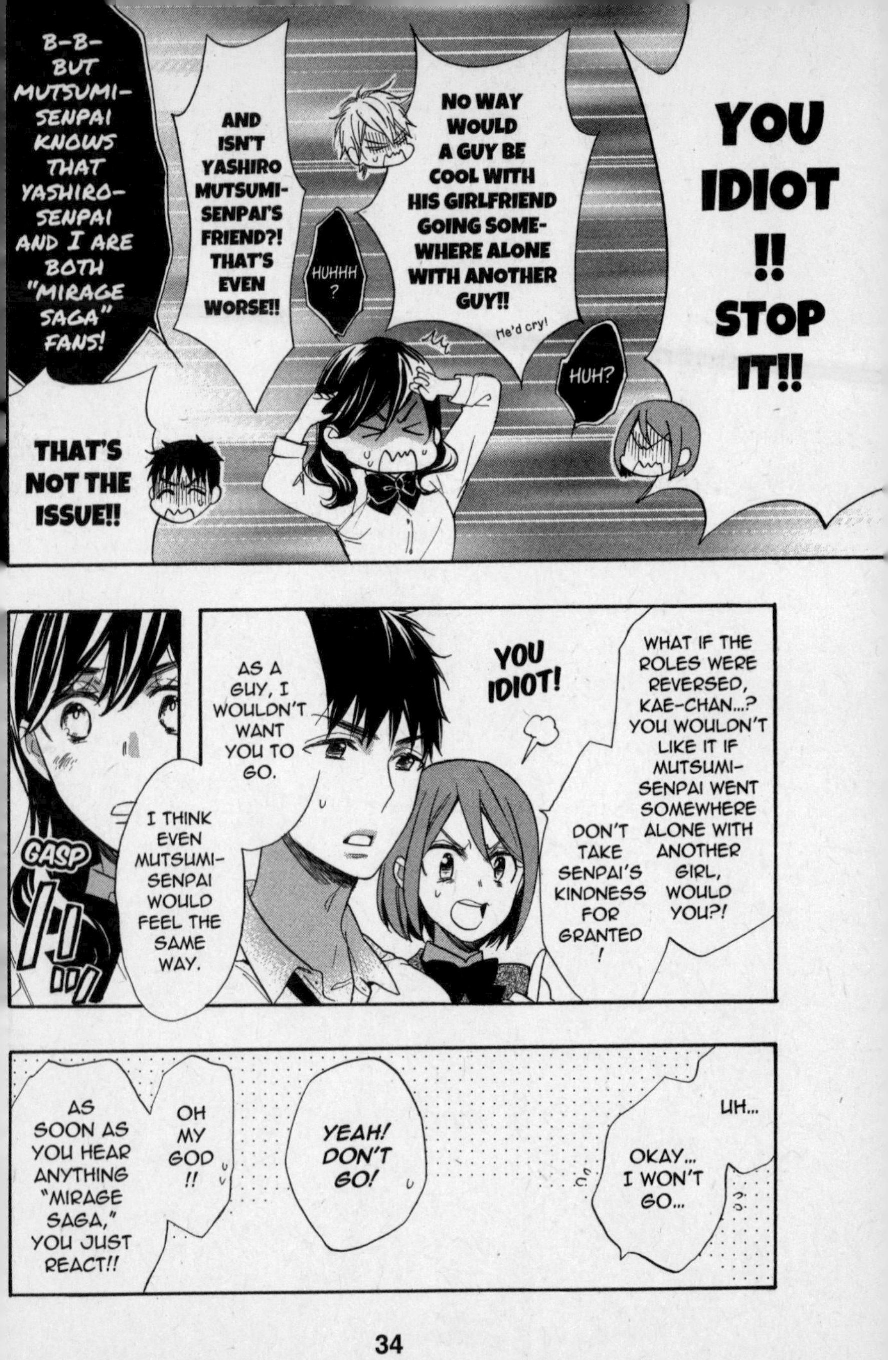
YOU IDIOT!! STOP IT!!
NO WAY WOULD A GUY BE COOL WITH HIS GIRLFRIEND GOING SOME-WHERE ALONE WITH ANOTHER GUY!!
He'd cry!
HUH?
HUHHH?
AND ISN'T YASHIRO MUTSUMI-SENPAI'S FRIEND?! THAT'S EVEN WORSE!!
B-B-BUT MUTSUMI-SENPAI KNOWS THAT YASHIRO-SENPAI AND I ARE BOTH "MIRAGE SAGA" FANS!
THAT'S NOT THE ISSUE!!
WHAT IF THE ROLES WERE REVERSED, KAE-CHAN...? YOU WOULDN'T LIKE IT IF MUTSUMI-SENPAI WENT SOMEWHERE ALONE WITH ANOTHER GIRL, WOULD YOU?!
DON'T TAKE SENPAI'S KINDNESS FOR GRANTED!
YOU IDIOT!
AS A GUY, I WOULDN'T WANT YOU TO GO.
I THINK EVEN MUTSUMI-SENPAI WOULD FEEL THE SAME WAY.
GASP
UH...
OKAY... I WON'T GO...
YEAH! DON'T GO!
OH MY GOD!!
AS SOON AS YOU HEAR ANYTHING "MIRAGE SAGA," YOU JUST REACT!!

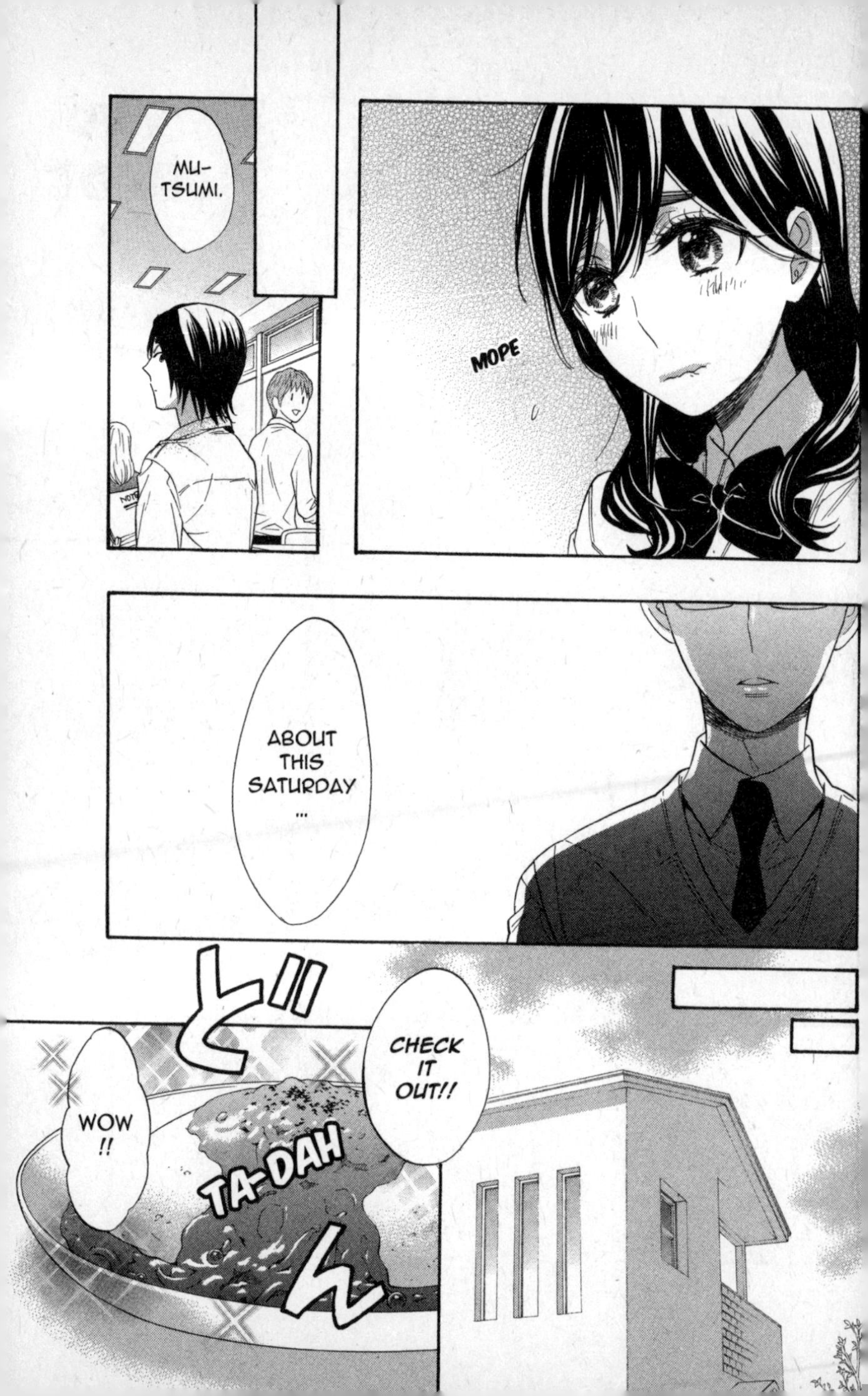
MOPE
MU-TSUMI.
ABOUT THIS SATURDAY ...
CHECK IT OUT!!
WOW !!
TA-DAH

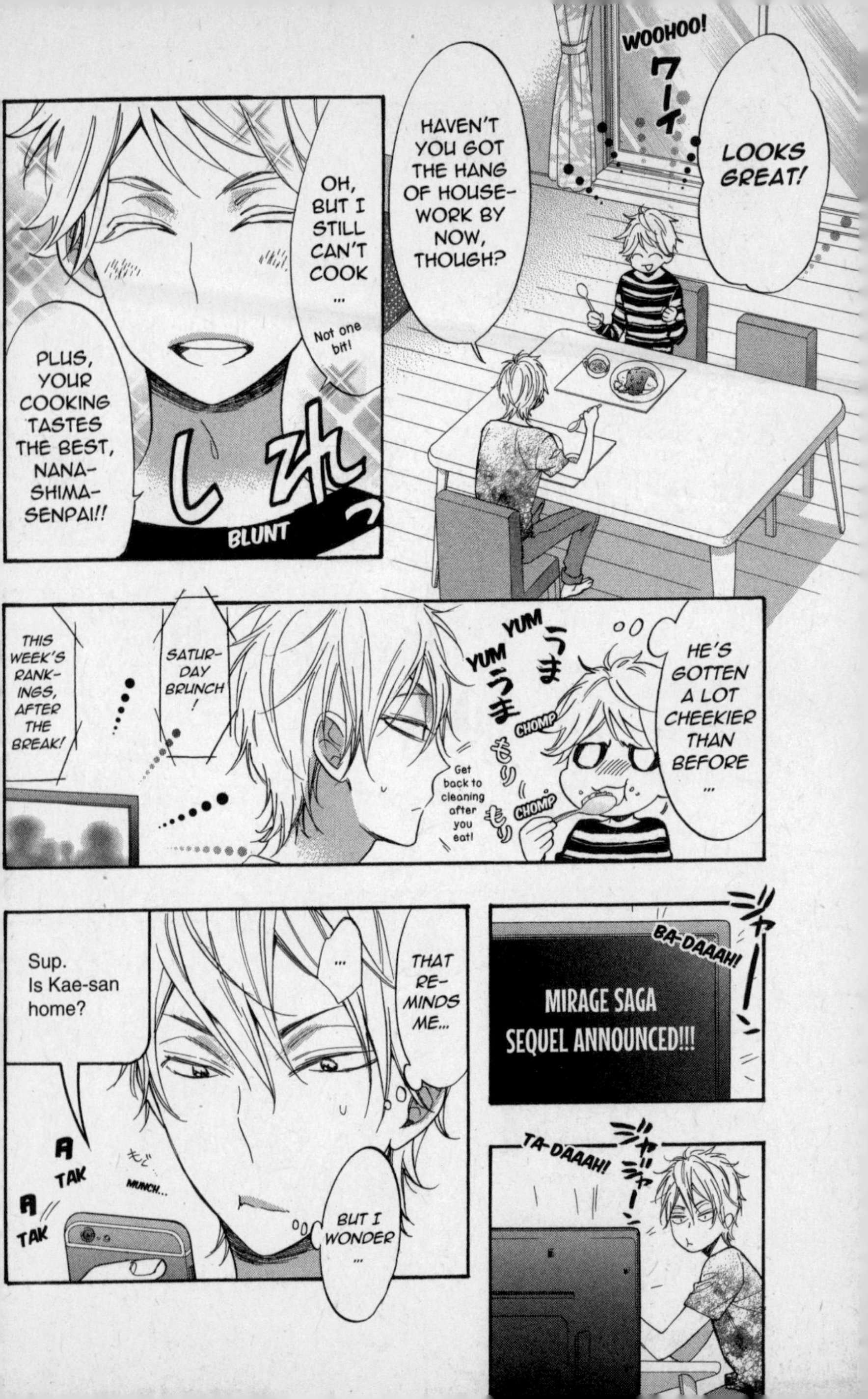
WOOHOO!
ワーイ
LOOKS GREAT!
HAVEN'T YOU GOT THE HANG OF HOUSE-WORK BY NOW, THOUGH?
OH, BUT I STILL CAN'T COOK ...
Not one bit!
PLUS, YOUR COOKING TASTES THE BEST, NANA-SHIMA-SENPAI!!
しれっ
BLUNT
HE'S GOTTEN A LOT CHEEKIER THAN BEFORE ...
うま うま
YUM YUM
もり もり
CHOMP CHOMP
Get back to cleaning after you eat!
SATUR-DAY BRUNCH!
THIS WEEK'S RANK-INGS, AFTER THE BREAK!
ジャーン
BA-DAAAH!
MIRAGE SAGA SEQUEL ANNOUNCED!!!
ジャジャーン
TA-DAAAH!
THAT RE-MINDS ME...
...
BUT I WONDER ...
Sup. Is Kae-san home?
TAK TAK
もぐ
MUNCH...

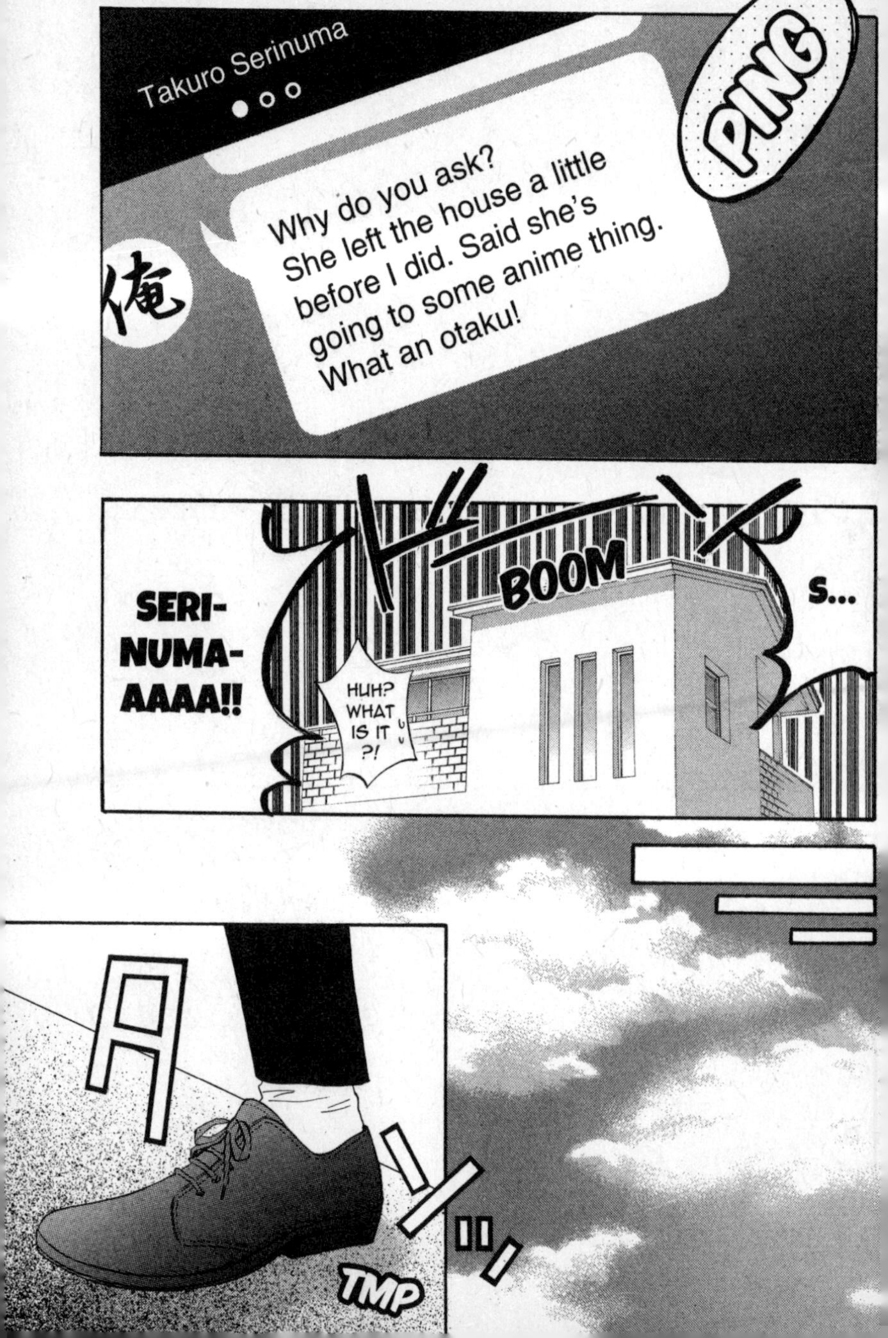
PING
Takuro Serinuma
俺
Why do you ask?
She left the house a little before I did. Said she's going to some anime thing.
What an otaku!
S...
BOOM
HUH? WHAT IS IT ?!
SERI-NUMA-AAAA!!
TMP

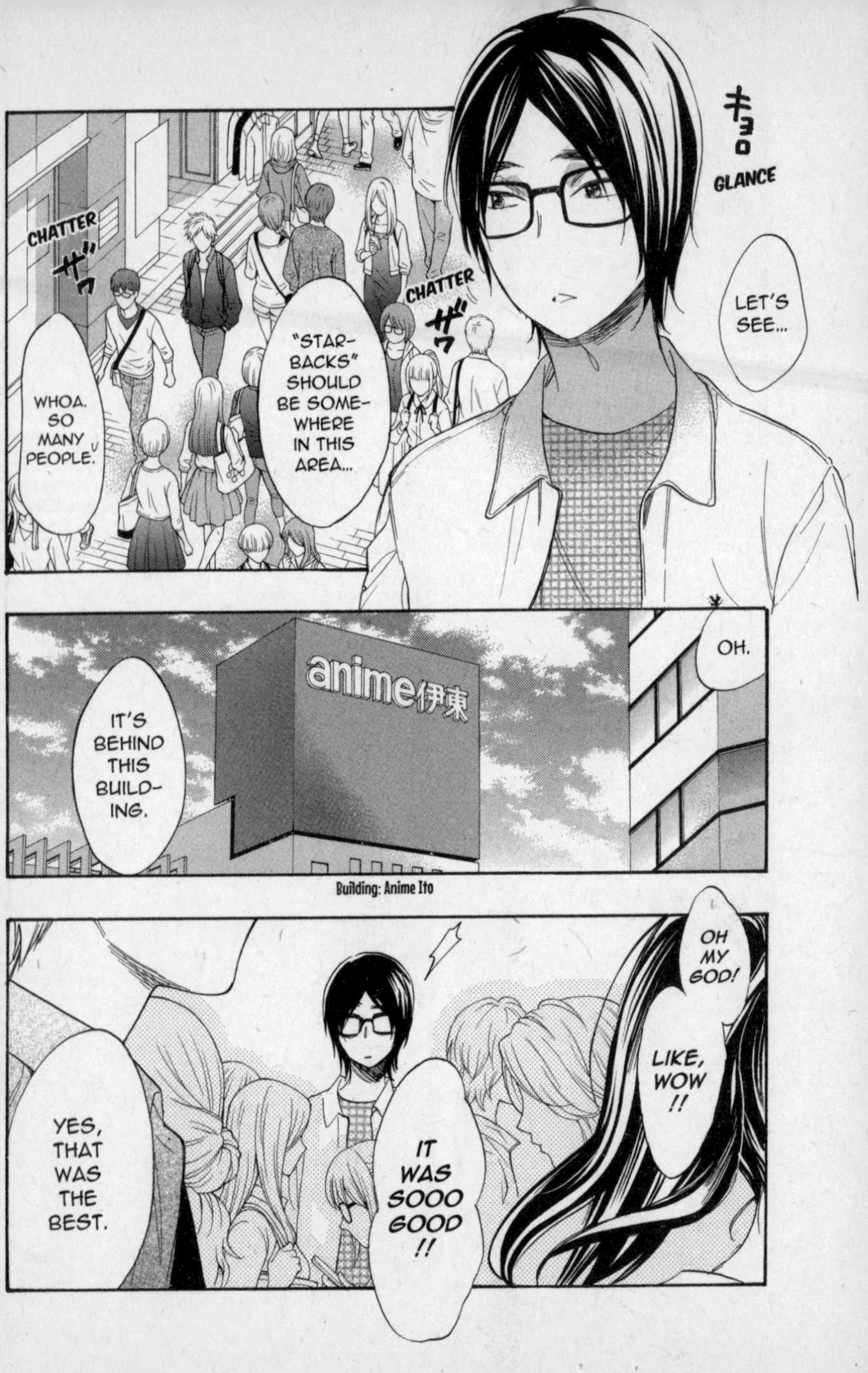
キョロ
GLANCE
LET'S SEE...
CHATTER
ザワ
"STAR-BACKS" SHOULD BE SOME-WHERE IN THIS AREA...
CHATTER
ザワ
WHOA. SO MANY PEOPLE.
OH.
anime伊東
IT'S BEHIND THIS BUILD-ING.
Building: Anime Ito
OH MY GOD!
LIKE, WOW!!
IT WAS SOOO GOOD!!
YES, THAT WAS THE BEST.

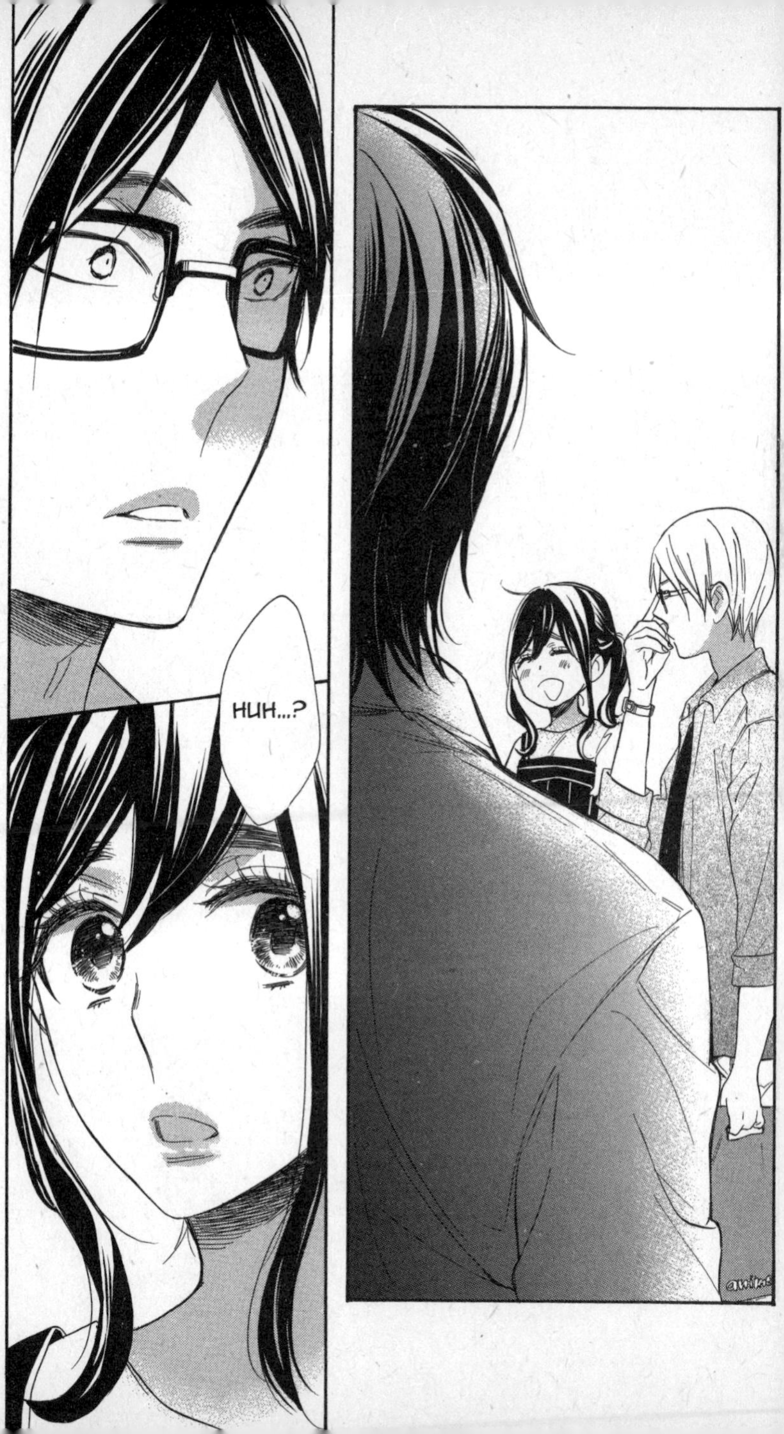
HUH...?

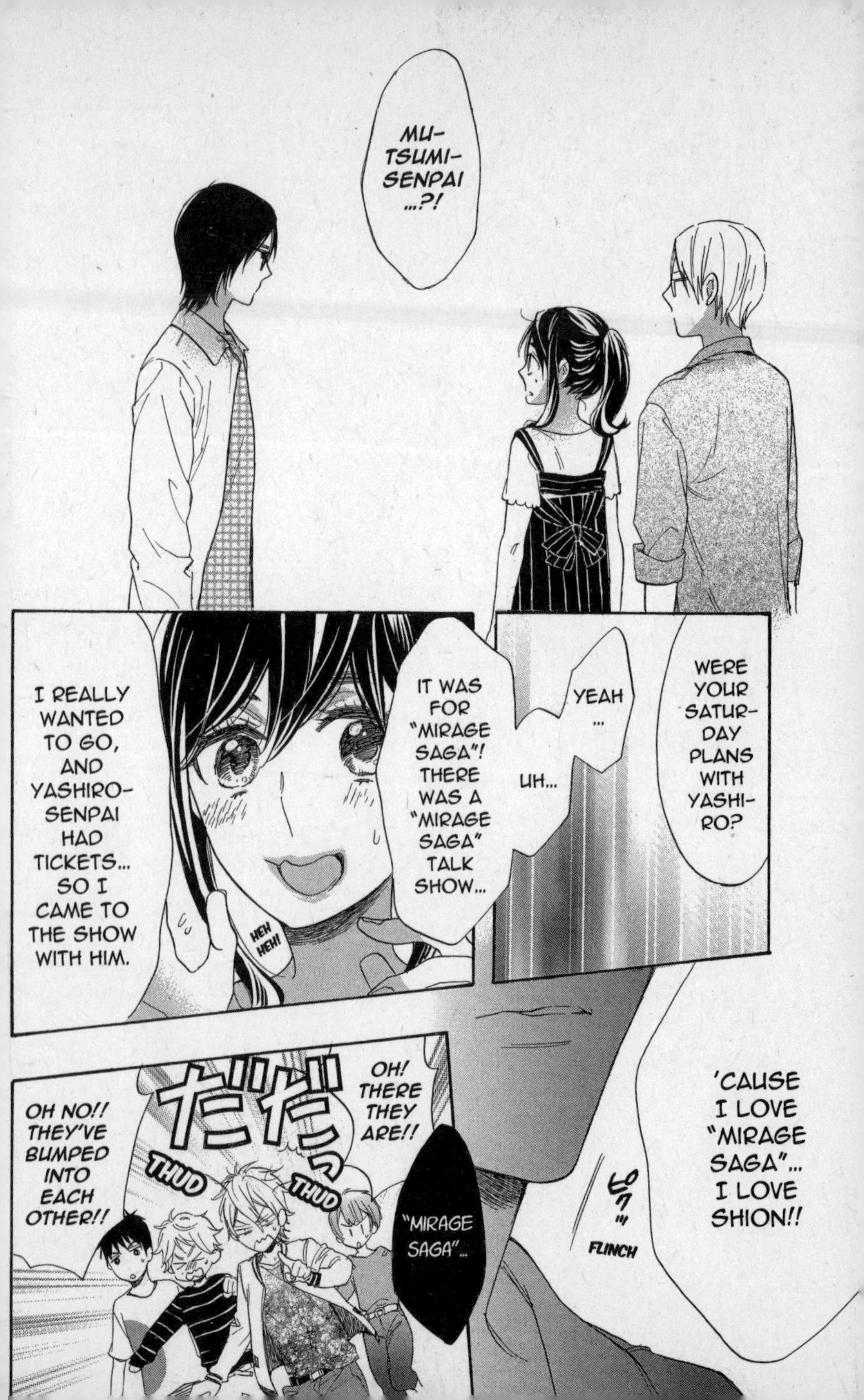
MU-TSUMI-SENPAI ...?!
WERE YOUR SATUR-DAY PLANS WITH YASHI-RO?
YEAH ...
UH...
IT WAS FOR "MIRAGE SAGA"! THERE WAS A "MIRAGE SAGA" TALK SHOW...
I REALLY WANTED TO GO, AND YASHIRO-SENPAI HAD TICKETS... SO I CAME TO THE SHOW WITH HIM.
HEH HEH!
'CAUSE I LOVE "MIRAGE SAGA"... I LOVE SHION!!
ピク
FLINCH
"MIRAGE SAGA"...
OH! THERE THEY ARE!!
だだっ
THUD THUD
OH NO!! THEY'VE BUMPED INTO EACH OTHER!!

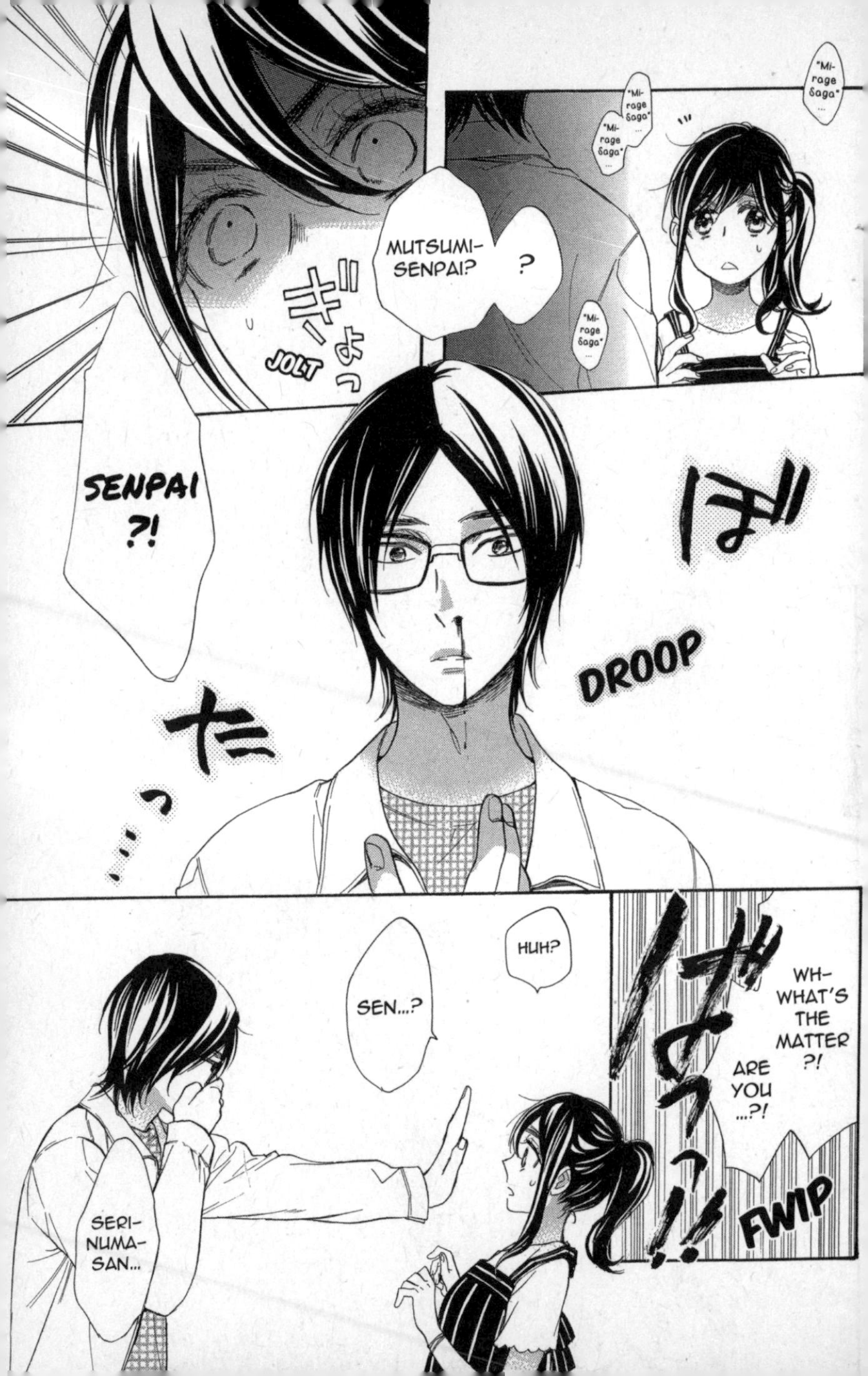
"Mi-rage Saga" ...
"Mi-rage Saga" ...
"Mi-rage Saga" ...
"Mi-rage Saga" ...
?
MUTSUMI-SENPAI?
ぎょっ
JOLT
ぼ
DROOP
SENPAI ?!
たっ...
げほっ!!
FWIP
WH-WHAT'S THE MATTER ?!
ARE YOU ...?!
HUH?
SEN...?
SERI-NUMA-SAN...

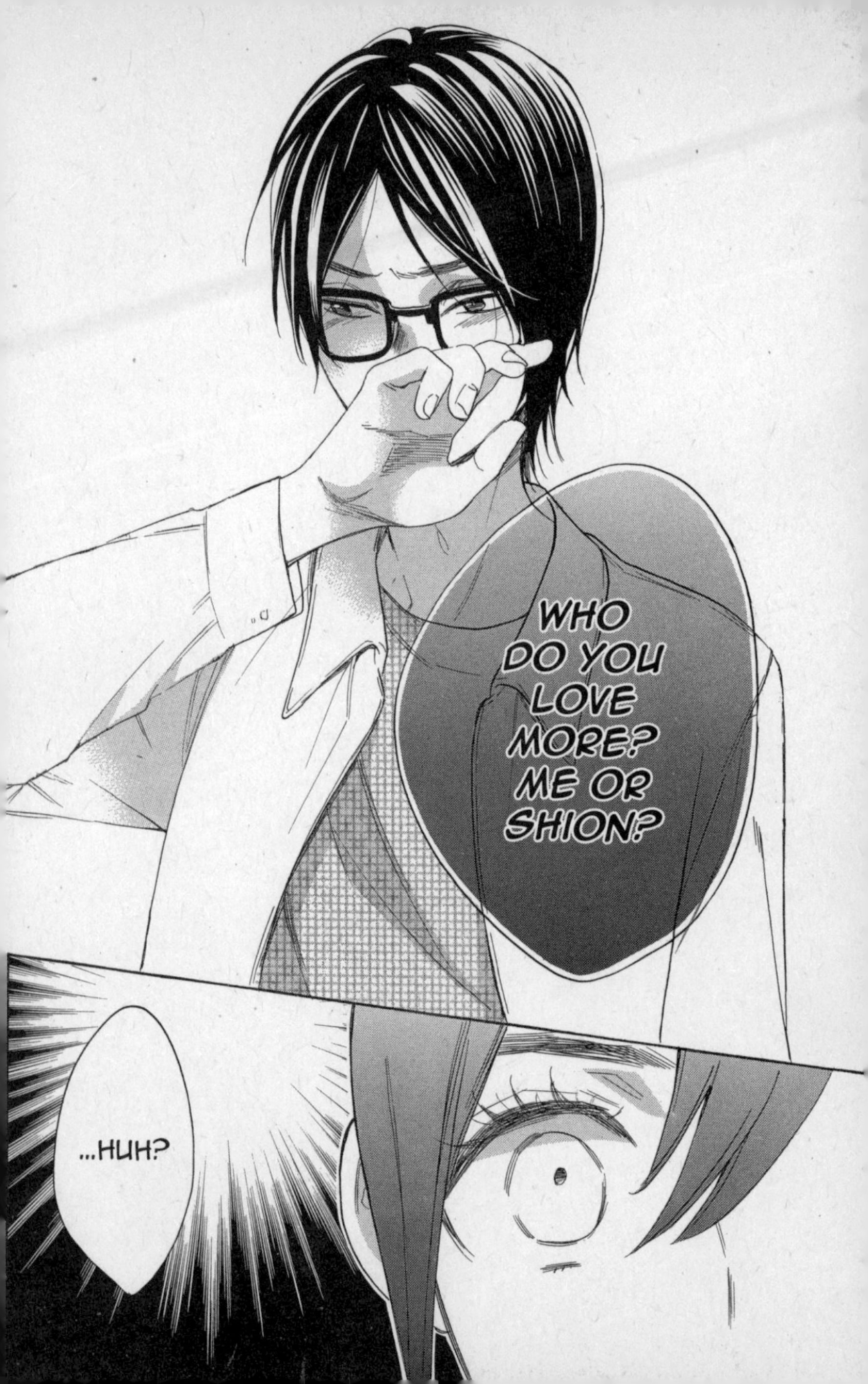
WHO DO YOU LOVE MORE? ME OR SHION?
...HUH?

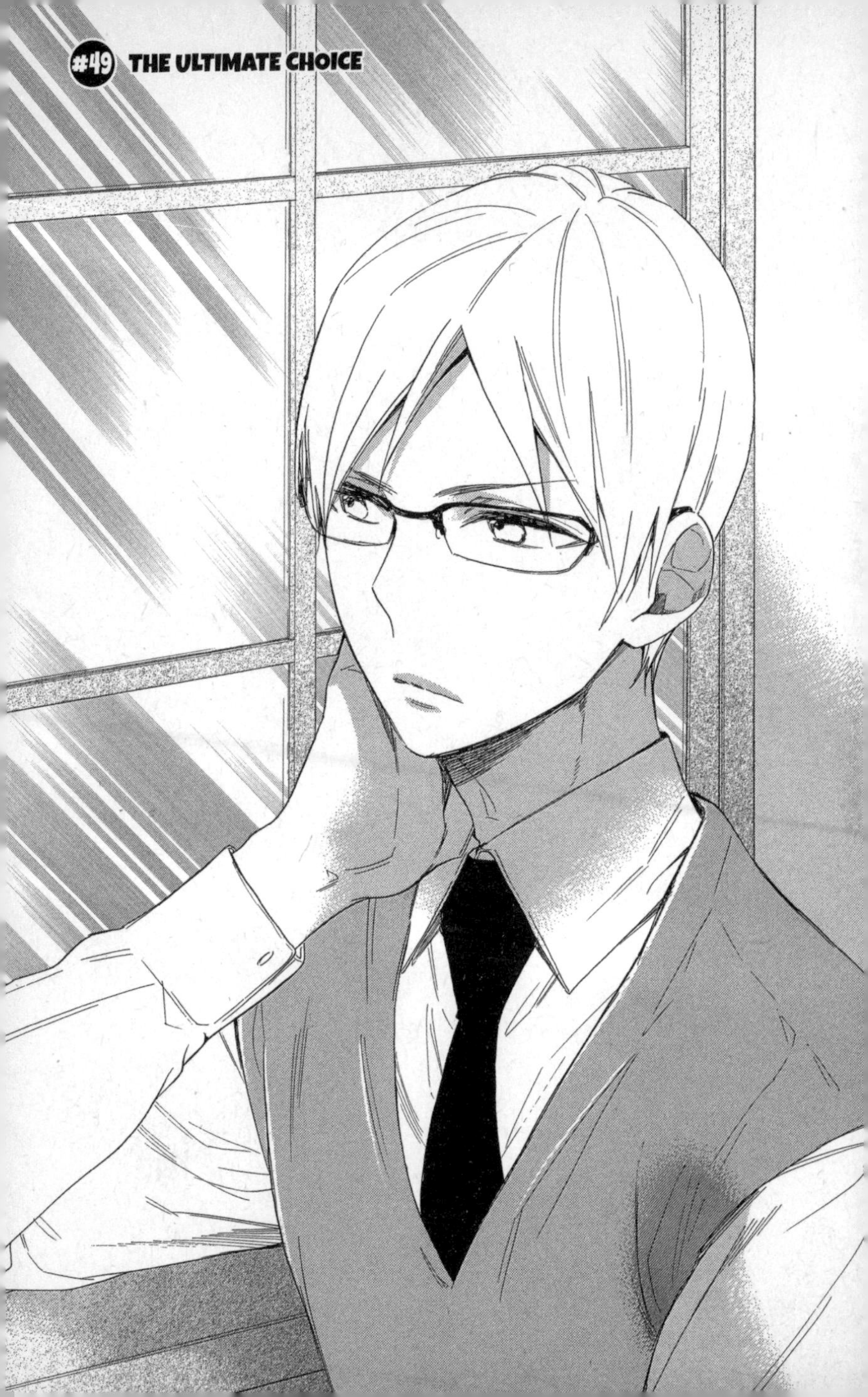
#49 THE ULTIMATE CHOICE

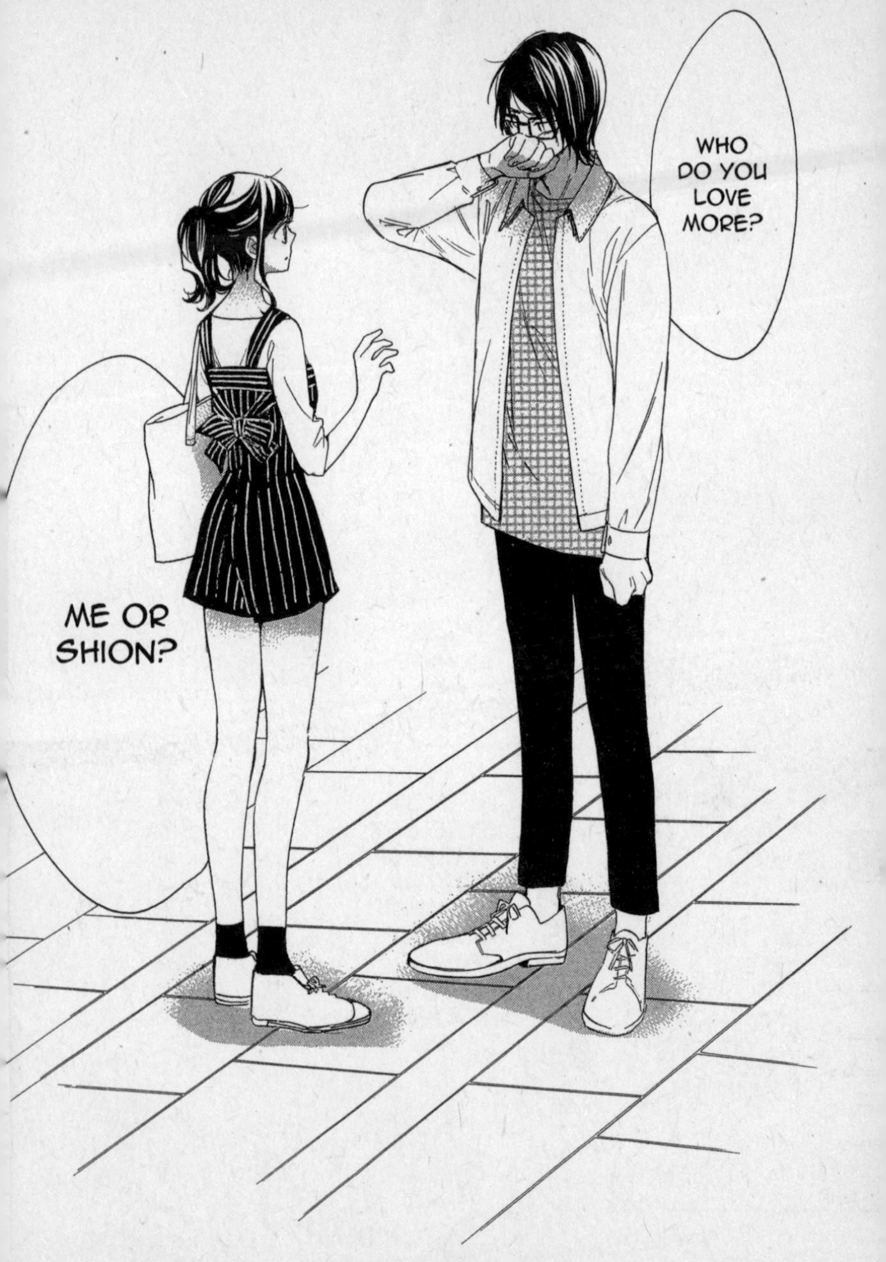
WHO DO YOU LOVE MORE?
ME OR SHION?

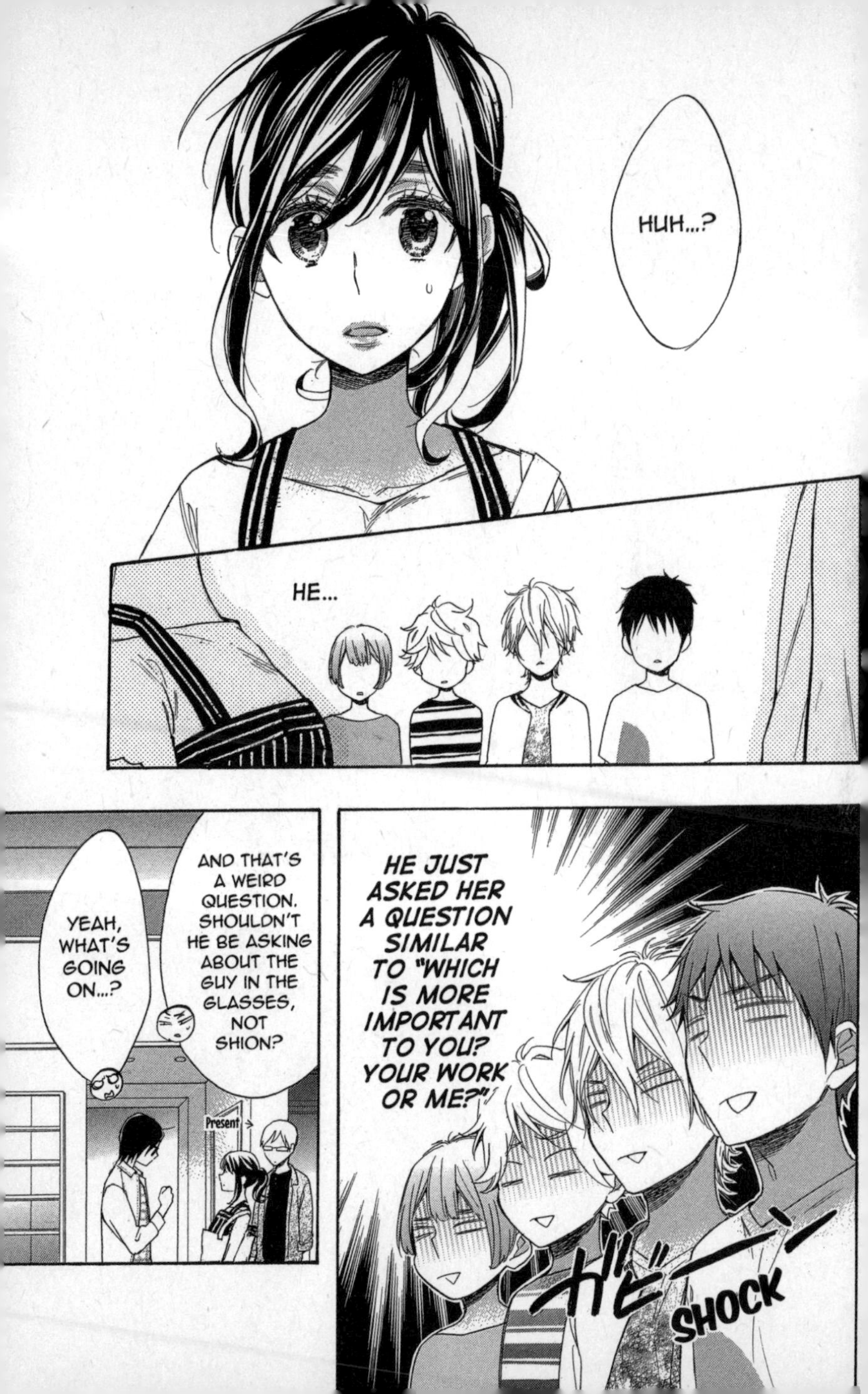
HUH...?
HE...
HE JUST ASKED HER A QUESTION SIMILAR TO "WHICH IS MORE IMPORTANT TO YOU? YOUR WORK OR ME?"
SHOCK
AND THAT'S A WEIRD QUESTION. SHOULDN'T HE BE ASKING ABOUT THE GUY IN THE GLASSES, NOT SHION?
YEAH, WHAT'S GOING ON...?
Present

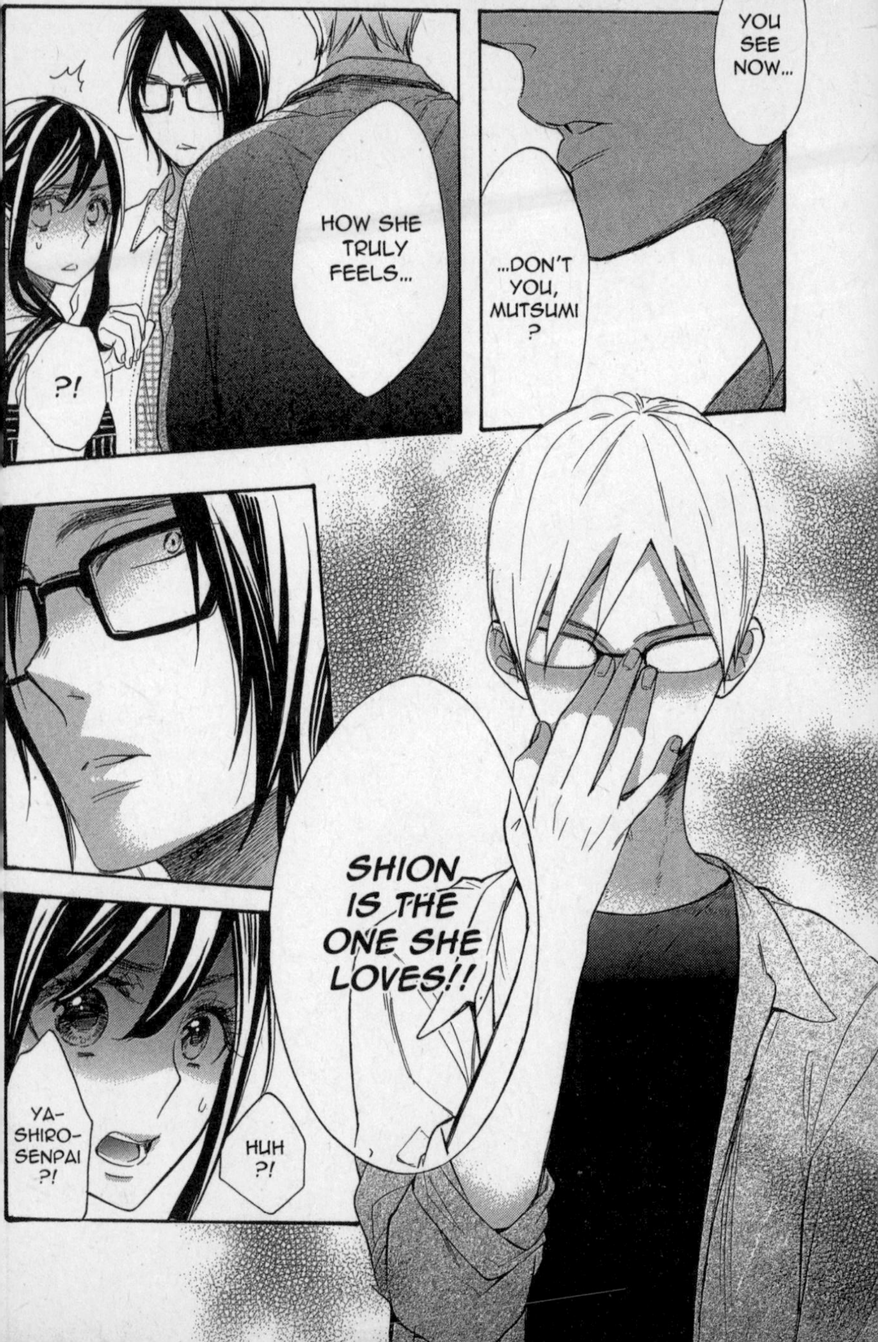
YOU SEE NOW...
...DON'T YOU, MUTSUMI?
HOW SHE TRULY FEELS...
?!
SHION IS THE ONE SHE LOVES!!
HUH?!
YA-SHIRO-SENPAI?!

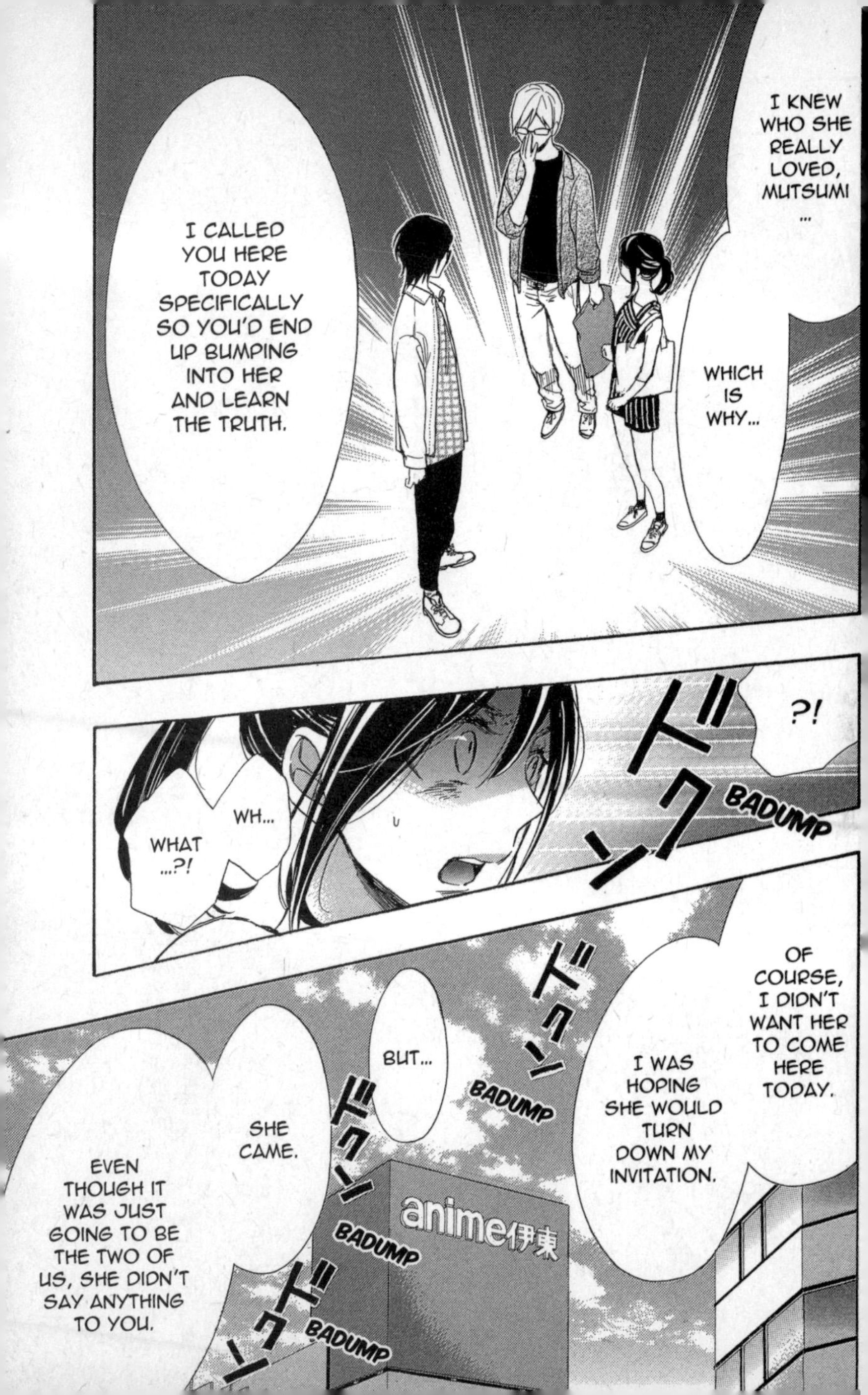
I KNEW WHO SHE REALLY LOVED, MUTSUMI ...
WHICH IS WHY...
I CALLED YOU HERE TODAY SPECIFICALLY SO YOU'D END UP BUMPING INTO HER AND LEARN THE TRUTH.
?!
ドクン
BADUMP
WH...
WHAT ...?!
OF COURSE, I DIDN'T WANT HER TO COME HERE TODAY.
I WAS HOPING SHE WOULD TURN DOWN MY INVITATION.
ドクン
BADUMP
BUT...
SHE CAME.
ドクン
BADUMP
EVEN THOUGH IT WAS JUST GOING TO BE THE TWO OF US, SHE DIDN'T SAY ANYTHING TO YOU.
anime伊東
ドクン
BADUMP

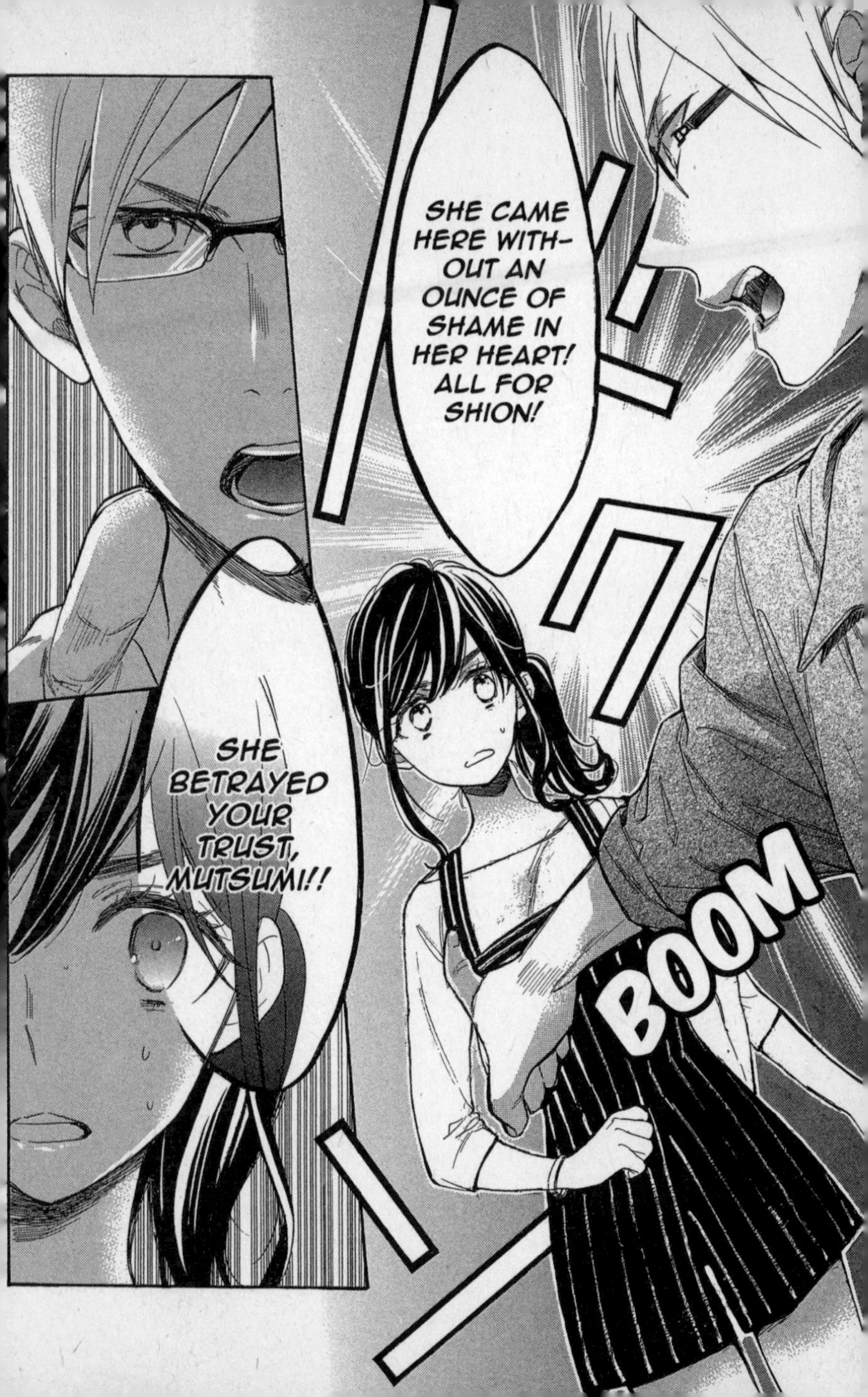
SHE CAME HERE WITH-OUT AN OUNCE OF SHAME IN HER HEART! ALL FOR SHION!
SHE BETRAYED YOUR TRUST, MUTSUMI!!
BOOM

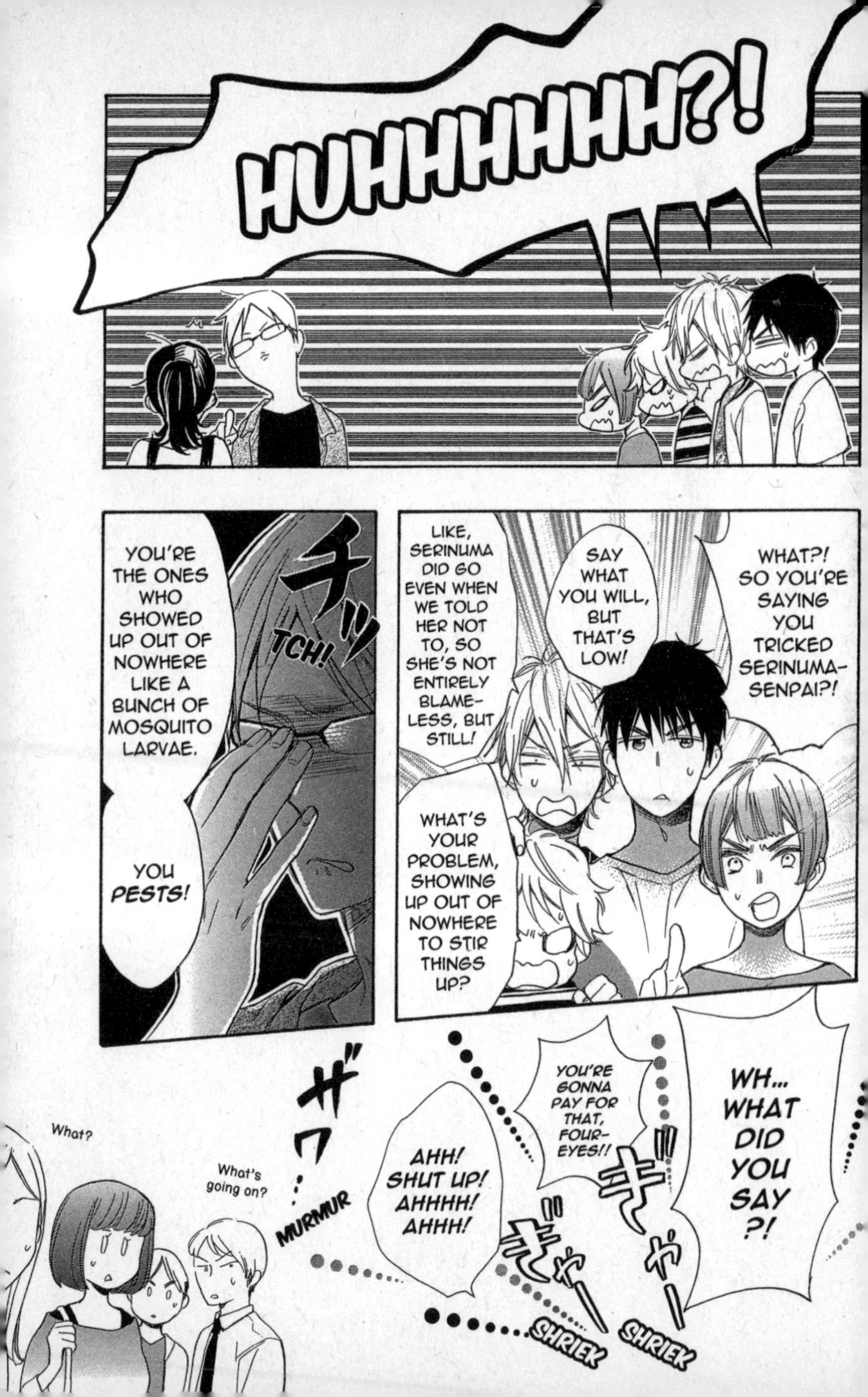
HUHHHHHHH?!
WHAT?! SO YOU'RE SAYING YOU TRICKED SERINUMA-SENPAI?!
SAY WHAT YOU WILL, BUT THAT'S LOW!
LIKE, SERINUMA DID GO EVEN WHEN WE TOLD HER NOT TO, SO SHE'S NOT ENTIRELY BLAMELESS, BUT STILL!
WHAT'S YOUR PROBLEM, SHOWING UP OUT OF NOWHERE TO STIR THINGS UP?
チッ
TCH!
YOU'RE THE ONES WHO SHOWED UP OUT OF NOWHERE LIKE A BUNCH OF MOSQUITO LARVAE.
YOU PESTS!
WH... WHAT DID YOU SAY?!
YOU'RE GONNA PAY FOR THAT, FOUR-EYES!!
ぎゃー
SHRIEK
AHH! SHUT UP! AHHHH! AHHH!
ぎゃー
SHRIEK
ザワ
MURMUR
What's going on?
What?

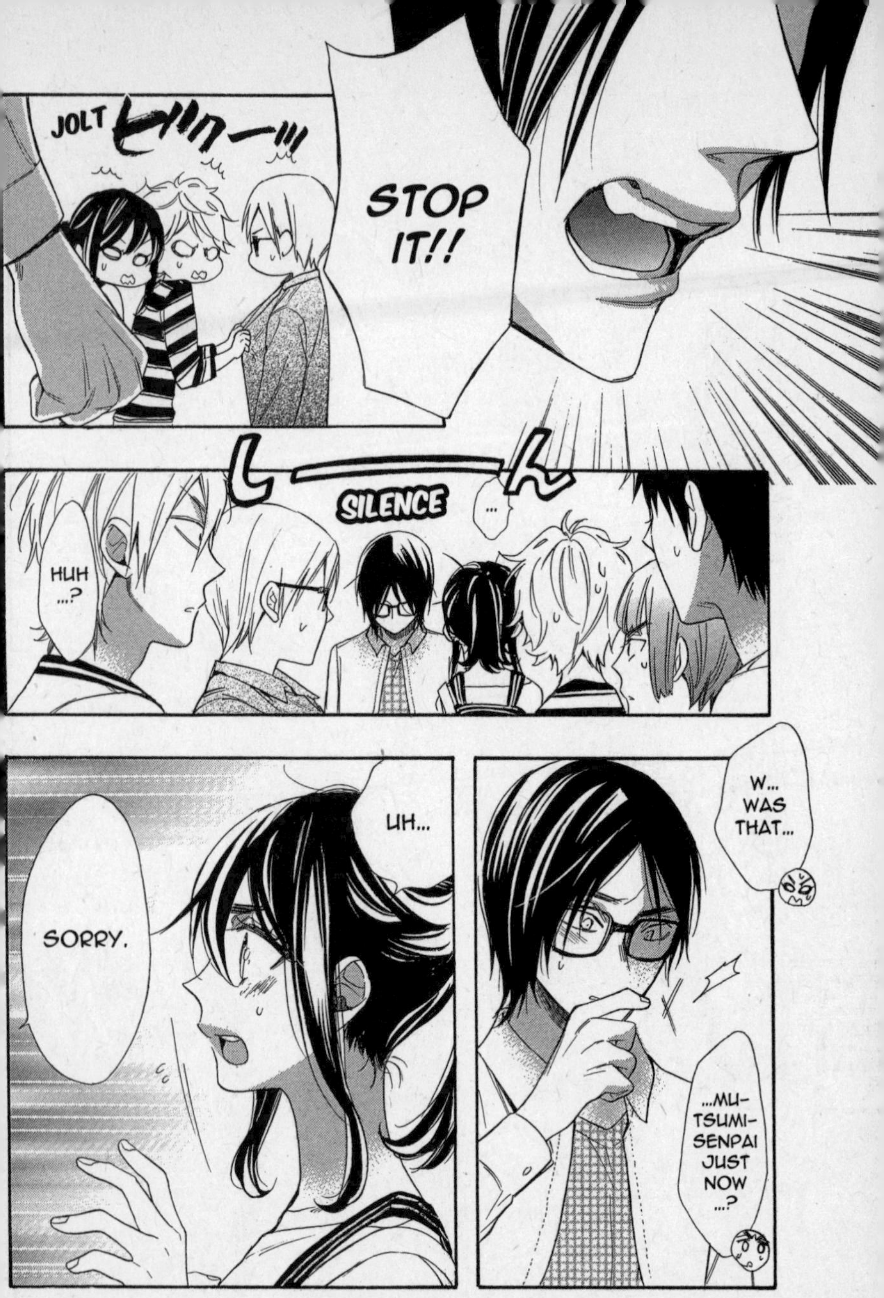
STOP IT!!
JOLT
ビリクー!!!
しーーん
SILENCE
...
HUH ...?
W... WAS THAT...
...MU-TSUMI-SENPAI JUST NOW ...?
UH...
SORRY.

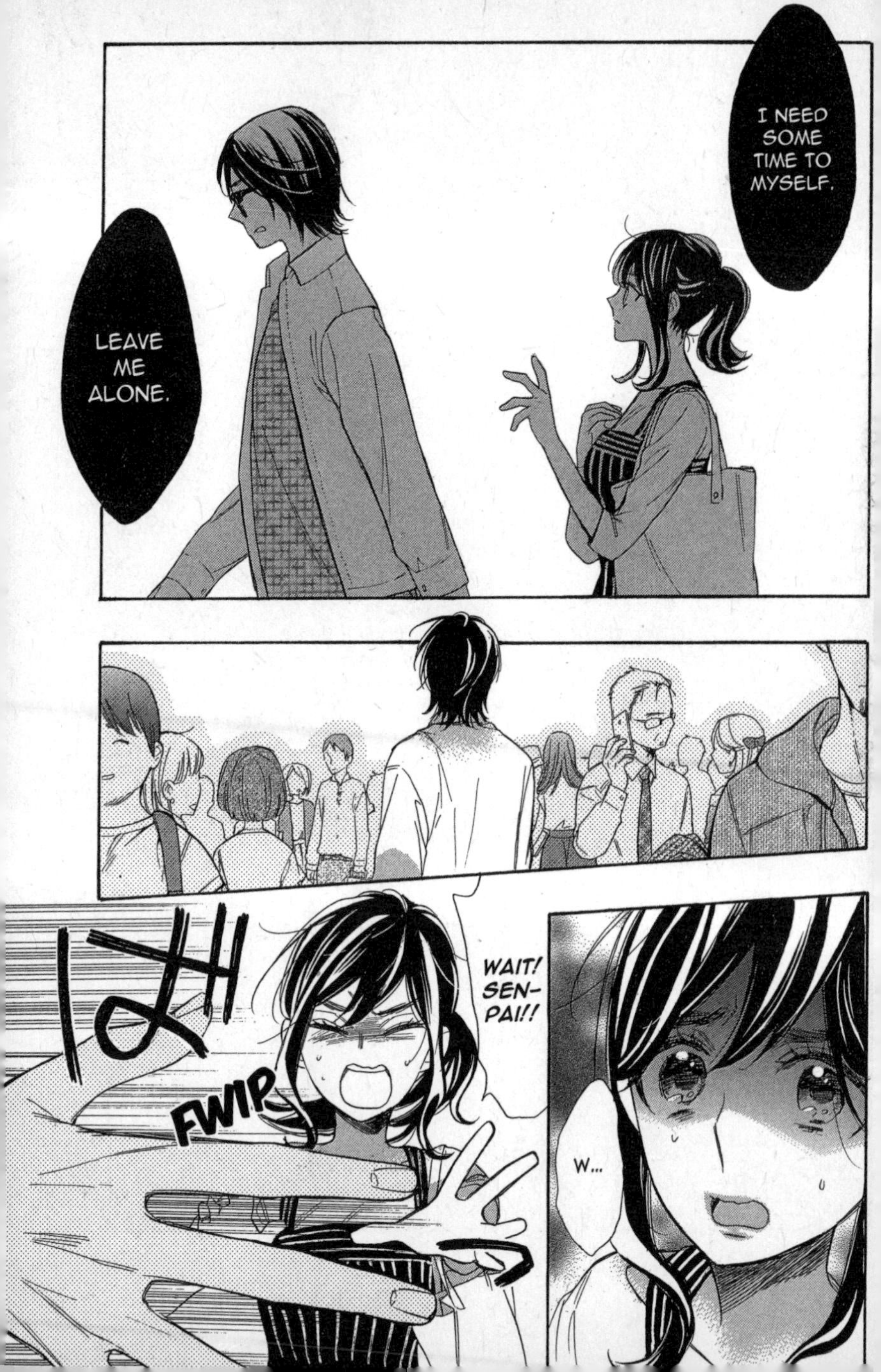
I NEED SOME TIME TO MYSELF.
LEAVE ME ALONE.
W...
WAIT! SEN-PAI!!
FWIP

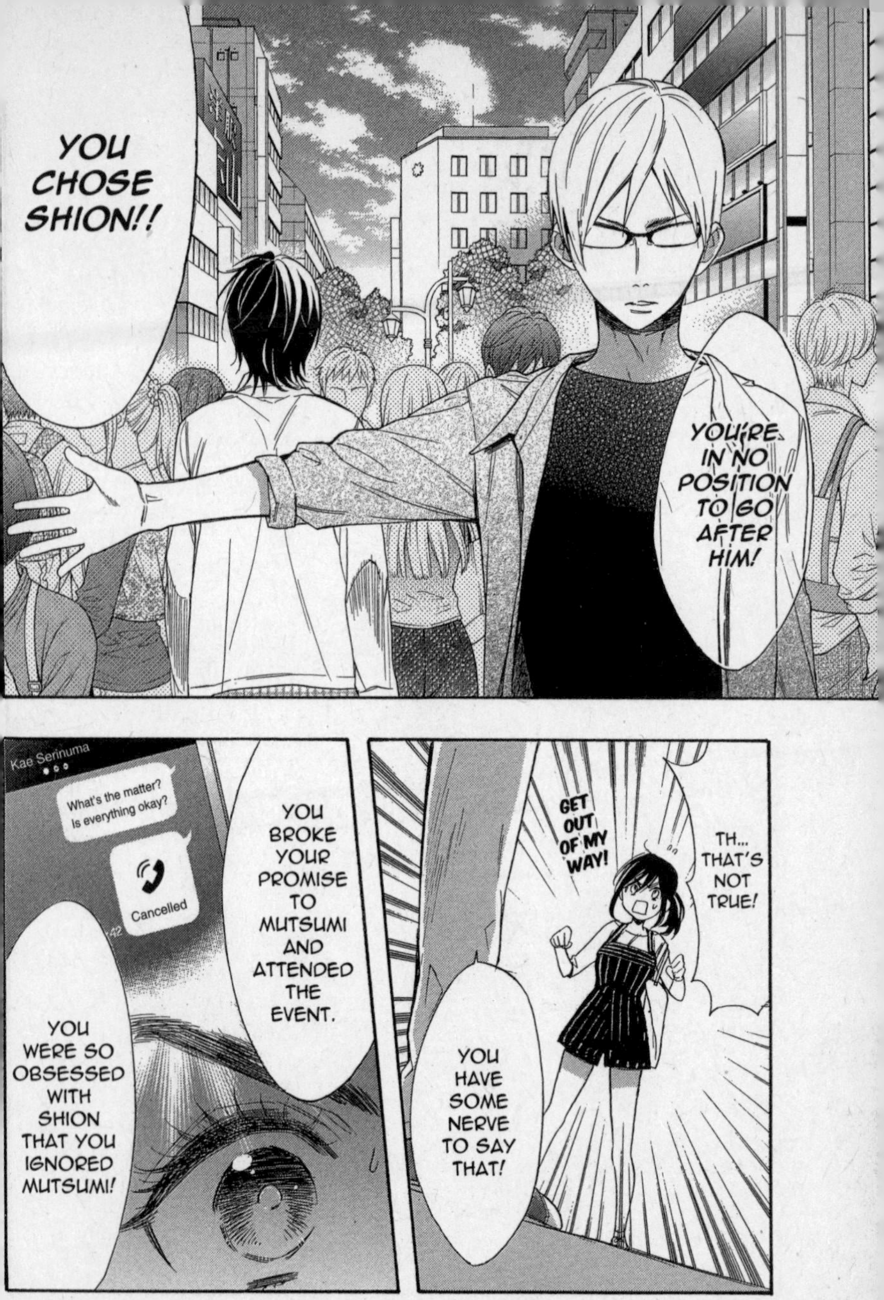
YOU'RE IN NO POSITION TO GO AFTER HIM!
YOU CHOSE SHION!!
TH... THAT'S NOT TRUE!
GET OUT OF MY WAY!
YOU HAVE SOME NERVE TO SAY THAT!
YOU BROKE YOUR PROMISE TO MUTSUMI AND ATTENDED THE EVENT.
Kae Serinuma
What's the matter? Is everything okay?
Cancelled
YOU WERE SO OBSESSED WITH SHION THAT YOU IGNORED MUTSUMI!

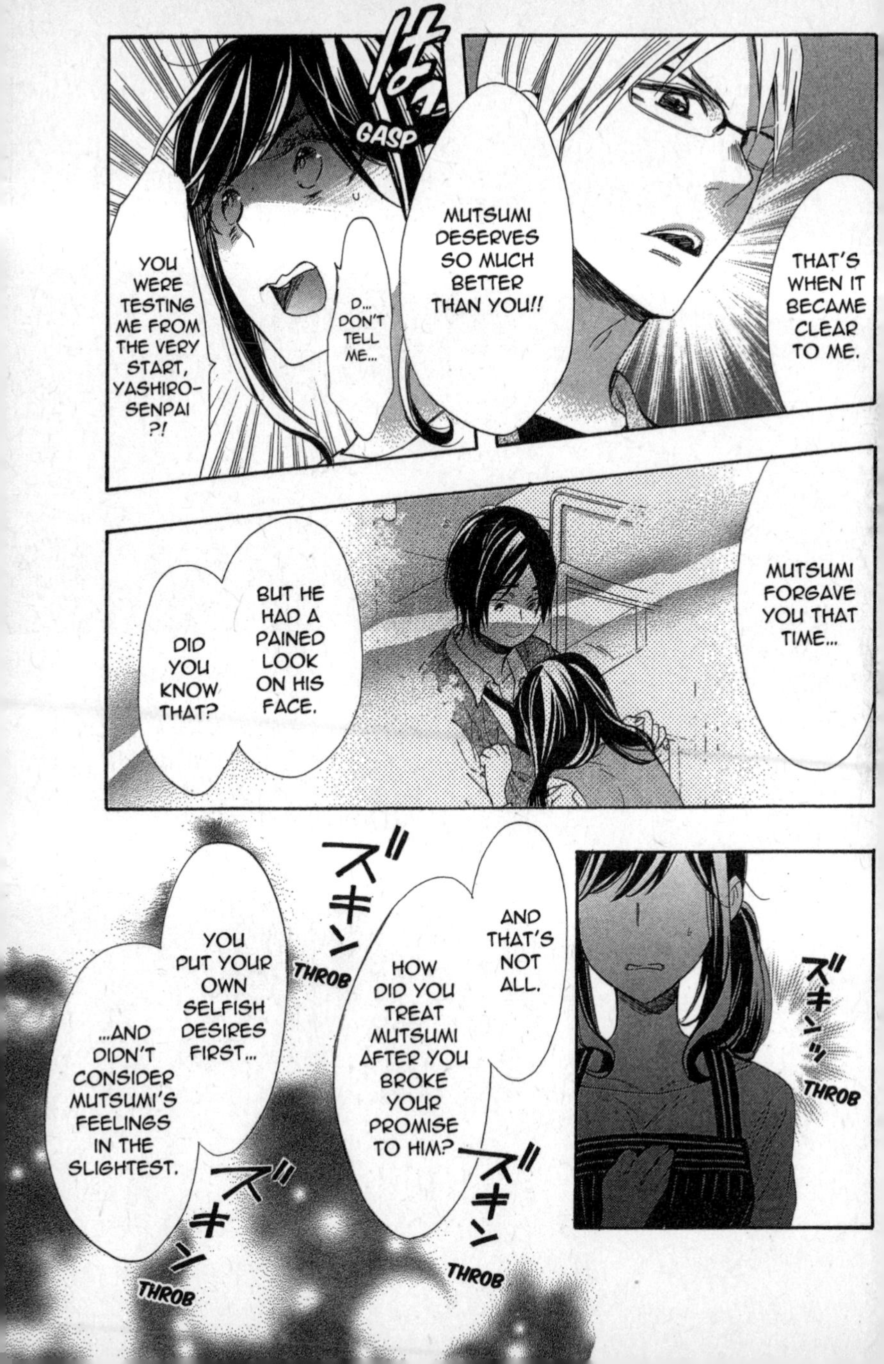
THAT'S WHEN IT BECAME CLEAR TO ME.
MUTSUMI DESERVES SO MUCH BETTER THAN YOU!!
はっ
GASP
D... DON'T TELL ME...
YOU WERE TESTING ME FROM THE VERY START, YASHIRO-SENPAI?!
MUTSUMI FORGAVE YOU THAT TIME...
BUT HE HAD A PAINED LOOK ON HIS FACE.
DID YOU KNOW THAT?
ズキンッ
THROB
AND THAT'S NOT ALL.
HOW DID YOU TREAT MUTSUMI AFTER YOU BROKE YOUR PROMISE TO HIM?
ズキン
THROB
ズキン
THROB
YOU PUT YOUR OWN SELFISH DESIRES FIRST...
...AND DIDN'T CONSIDER MUTSUMI'S FEELINGS IN THE SLIGHTEST.
ズキン
THROB

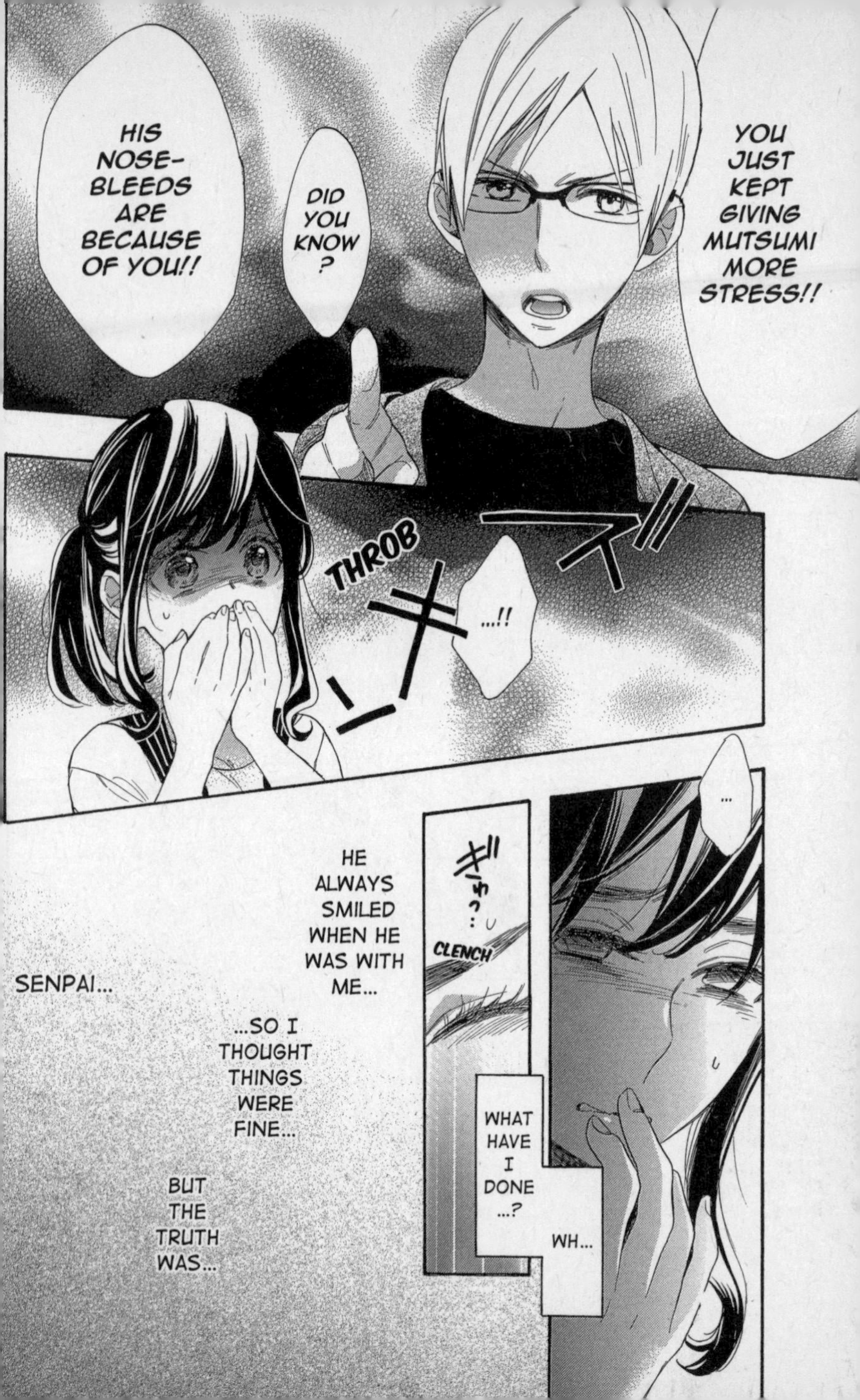
YOU JUST KEPT GIVING MUTSUMI MORE STRESS!!
DID YOU KNOW?
HIS NOSE-BLEEDS ARE BECAUSE OF YOU!!
THROB
...!!
...
CLENCH
WH...
WHAT HAVE I DONE...?
HE ALWAYS SMILED WHEN HE WAS WITH ME...
...SO I THOUGHT THINGS WERE FINE...
BUT THE TRUTH WAS...
SENPAI...

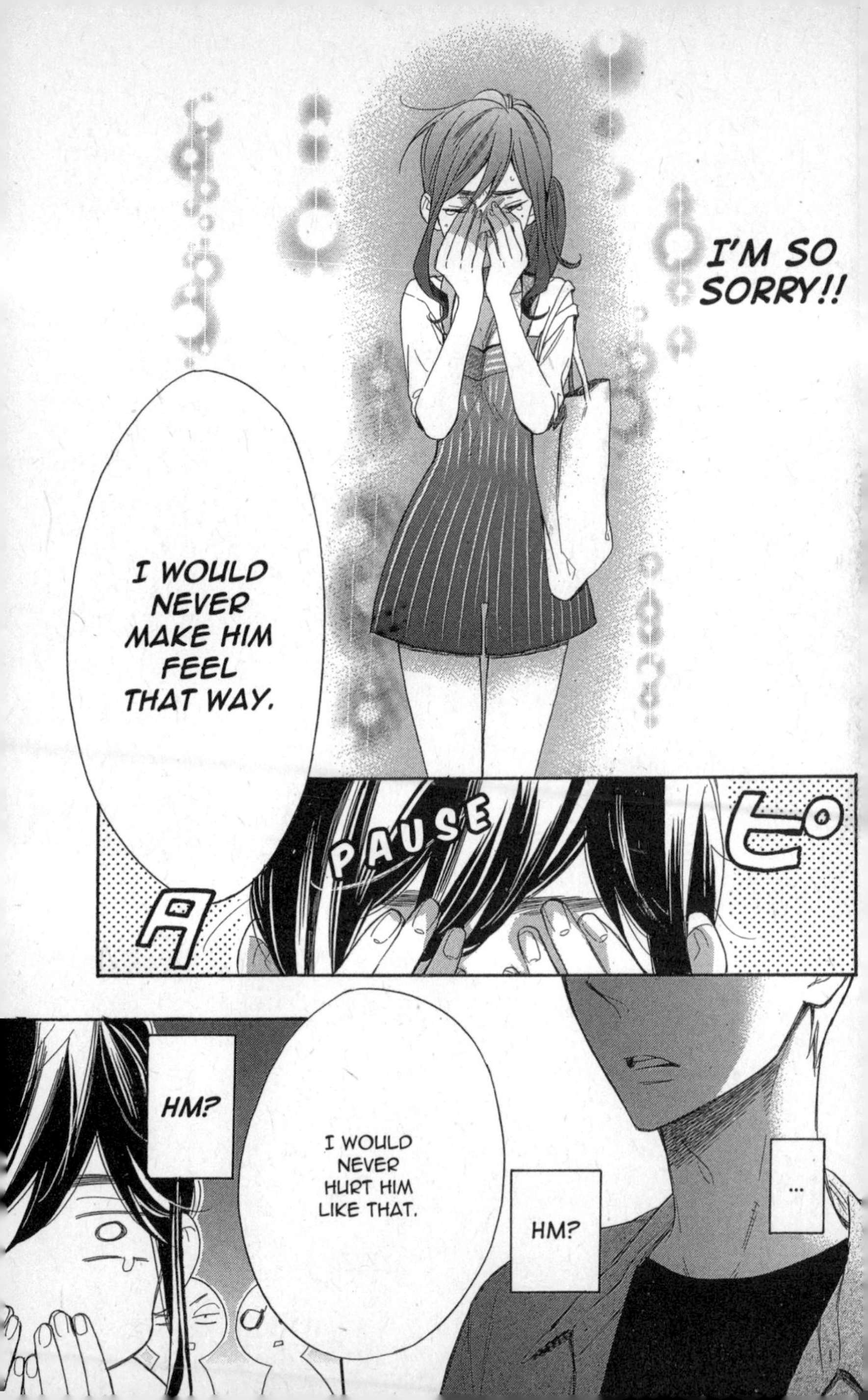
I'M SO SORRY!!
I WOULD NEVER MAKE HIM FEEL THAT WAY.
ピ
PAUSE
タ
...
HM?
I WOULD NEVER HURT HIM LIKE THAT.
HM?

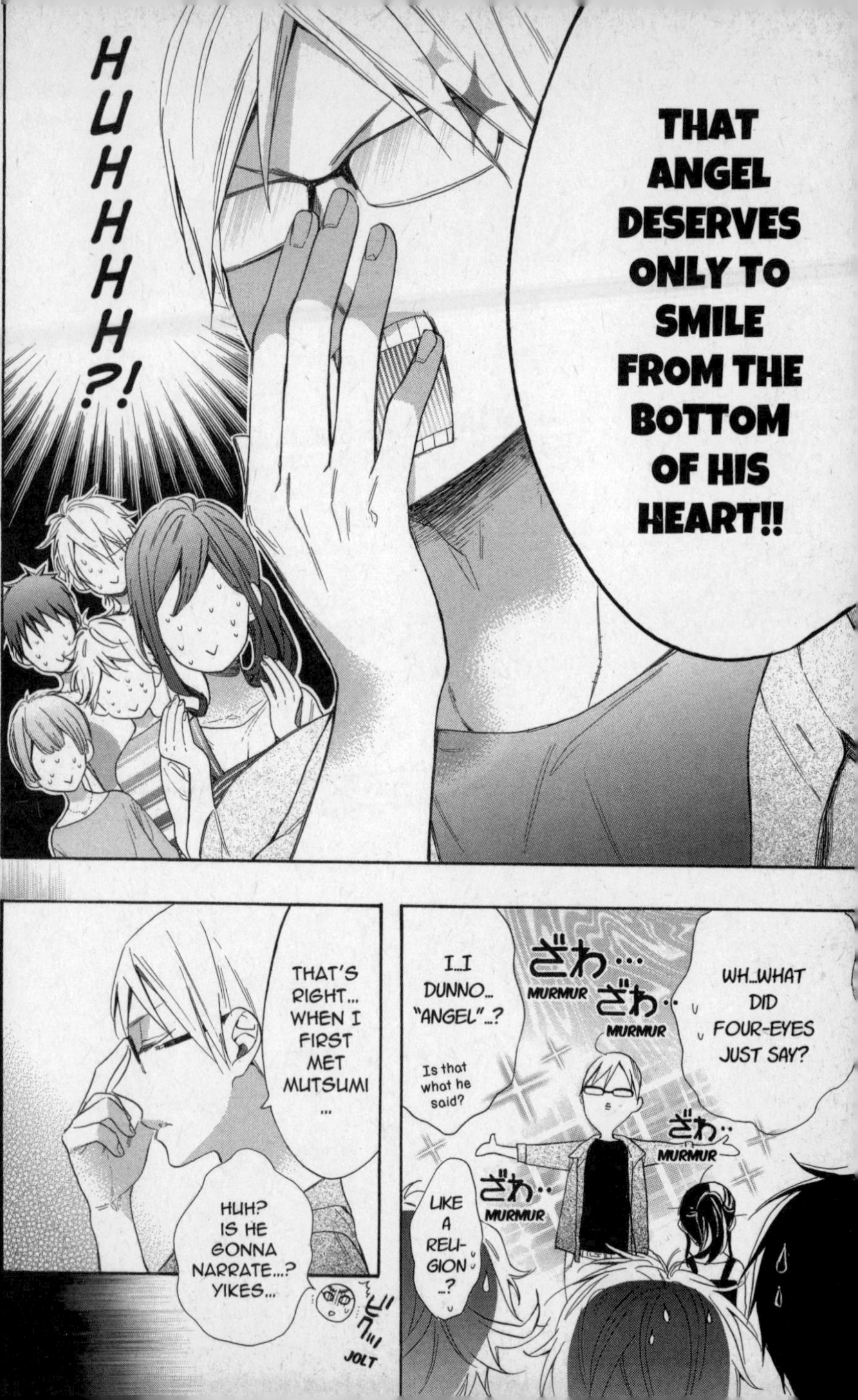
THAT ANGEL DESERVES ONLY TO SMILE FROM THE BOTTOM OF HIS HEART!!
HUHHHHH?!
WH...WHAT DID FOUR-EYES JUST SAY?
ざわ…
MURMUR
ざわ‥
MURMUR
I...I DUNNO... "ANGEL"...?
Is that what he said?
ざわ‥
MURMUR
ざわ‥
MURMUR
LIKE A RELIGION ...?
THAT'S RIGHT... WHEN I FIRST MET MUTSUMI ...
HUH? IS HE GONNA NARRATE...? YIKES...
JOLT

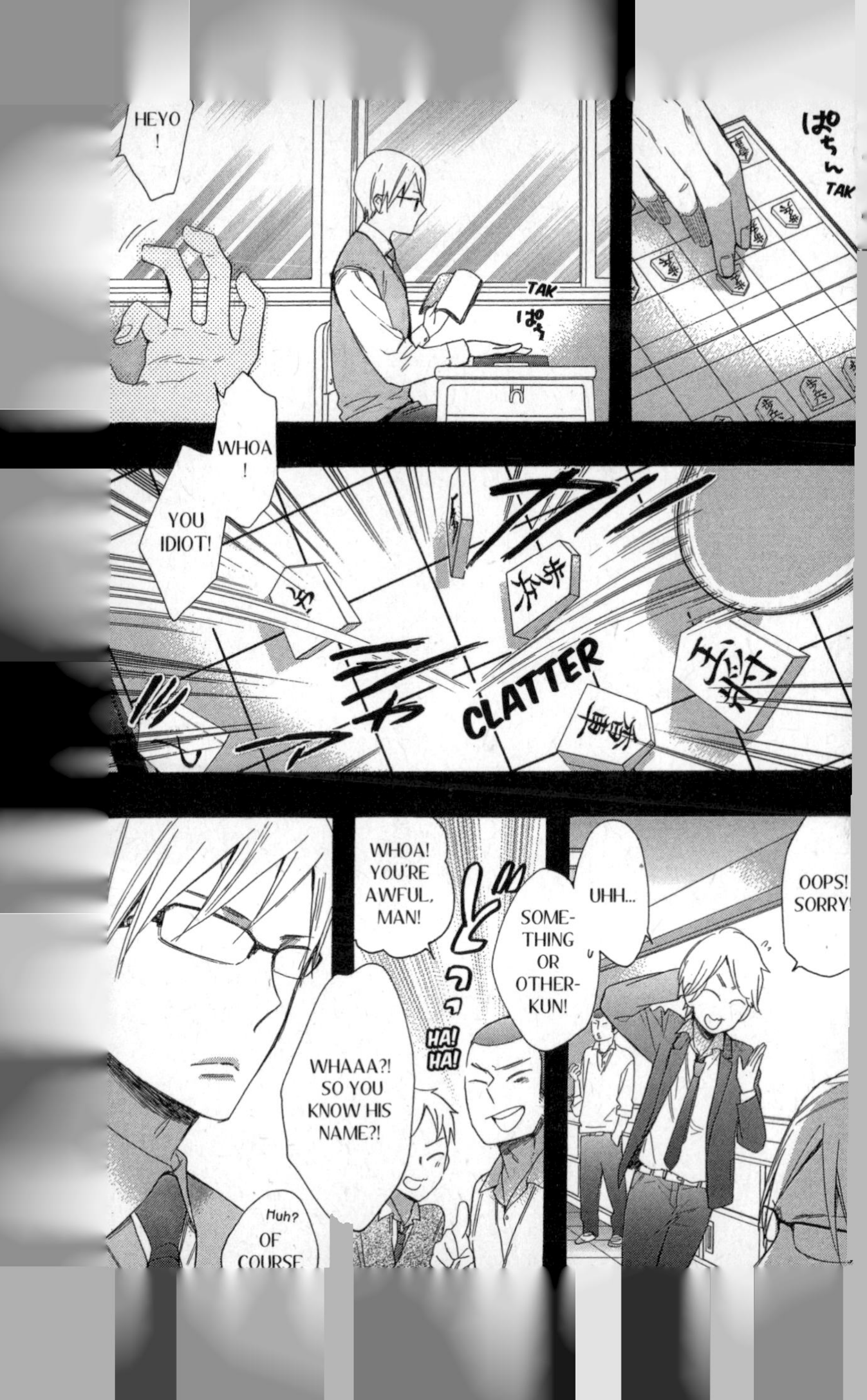
ぱちん
TAK
HEYO!
TAK
WHOA!
YOU IDIOT!
CLATTER
OOPS! SORRY!
UHH...
SOMETHING OR OTHER-KUN!
WHOA! YOU'RE AWFUL, MAN!
HA! HA!
WHAAA?! SO YOU KNOW HIS NAME?!
Huh?
OF COURSE.

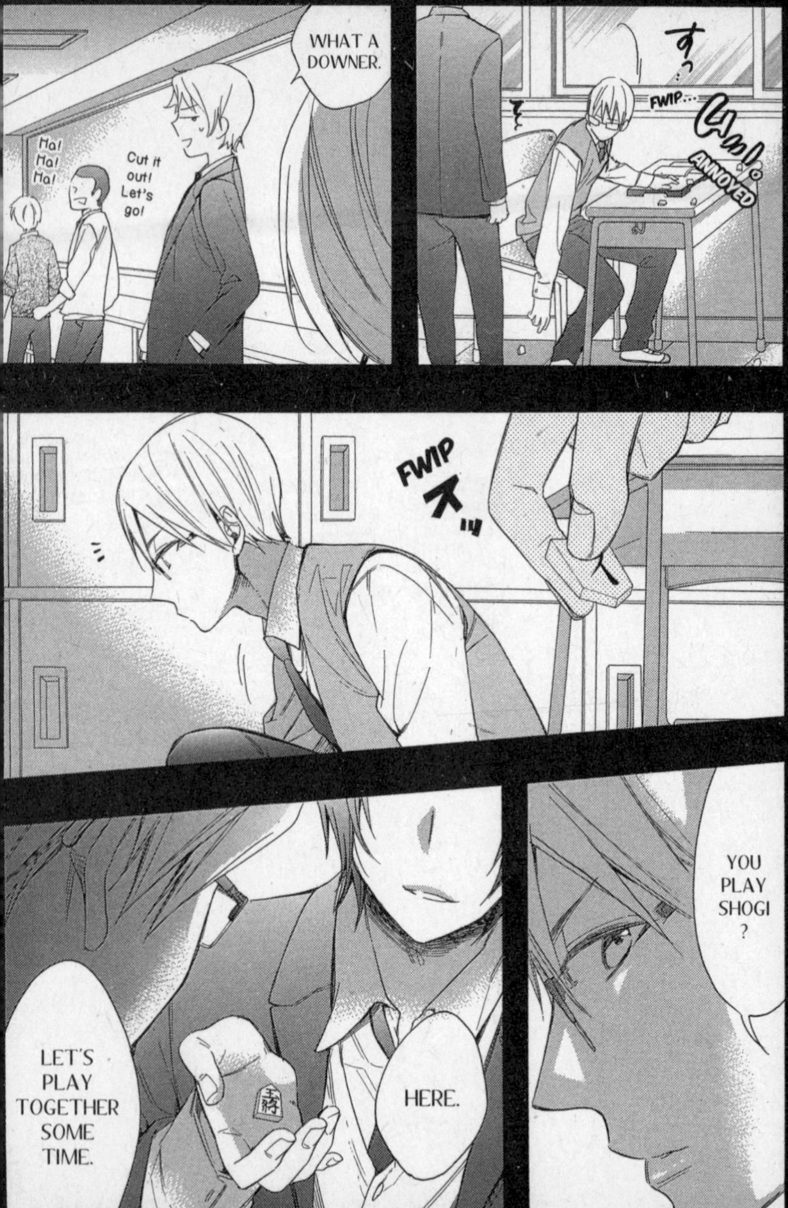
すっ
FWIP...
むっ
ANNOYED
WHAT A DOWNER.
Cut it out! Let's go!
Ha! Ha! Ha!
FWIP
スッ
YOU PLAY SHOGI?
HERE.
LET'S PLAY TOGETHER SOME TIME.

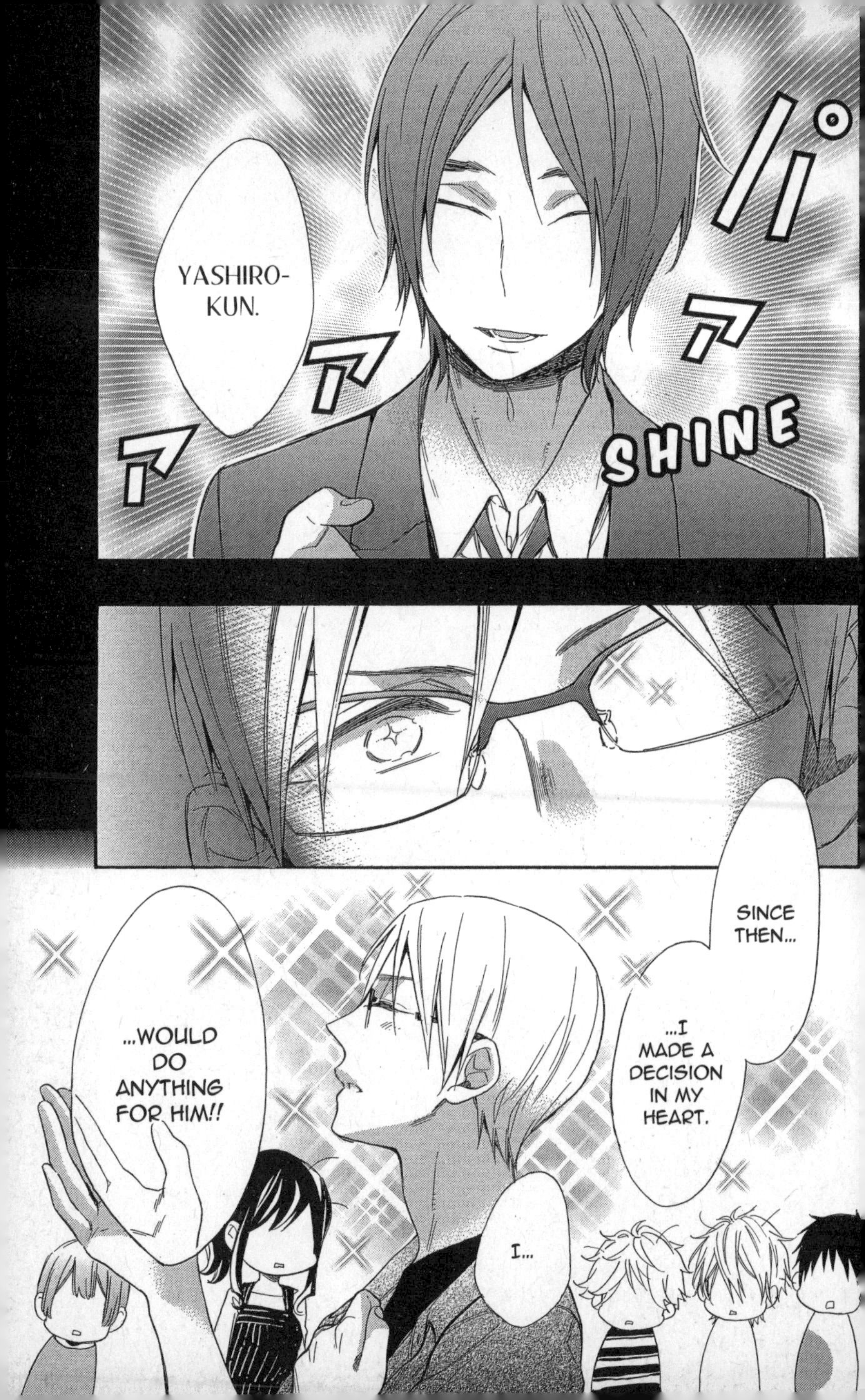
パァ
SHINE
YASHIRO-KUN.
ァァ
SINCE THEN...
...I MADE A DECISION IN MY HEART.
I...
...WOULD DO ANYTHING FOR HIM!!

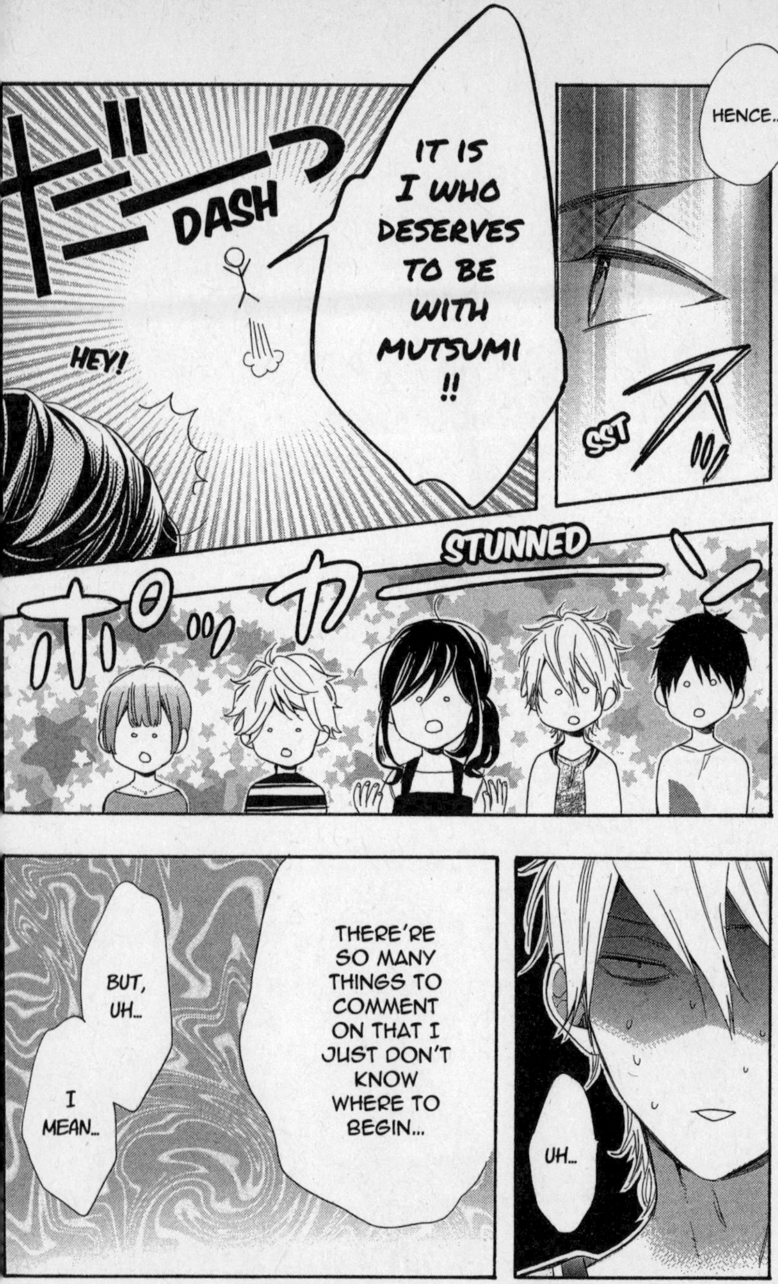
HENCE...
SST
IT IS I WHO DESERVES TO BE WITH MUTSUMI !!
DASH
HEY!
STUNNED
UH...
THERE'RE SO MANY THINGS TO COMMENT ON THAT I JUST DON'T KNOW WHERE TO BEGIN...
BUT, UH...
I MEAN...

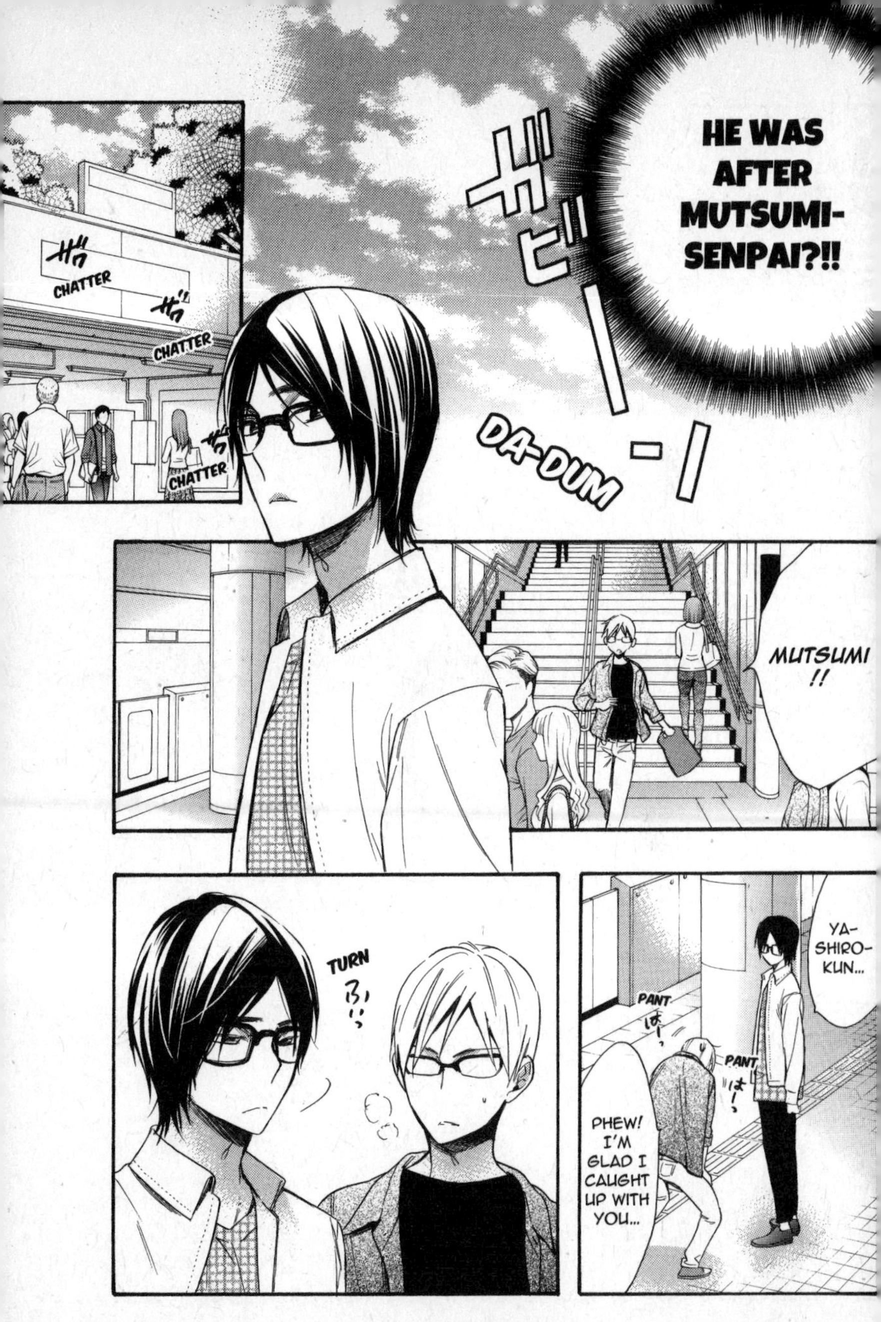
HE WAS AFTER MUTSUMI-SENPAI?!!
DA-DUM
CHATTER
CHATTER
CHATTER
MUTSUMI!!
YA-SHIRO-KUN...
PANT
PANT
PHEW! I'M GLAD I CAUGHT UP WITH YOU...
TURN

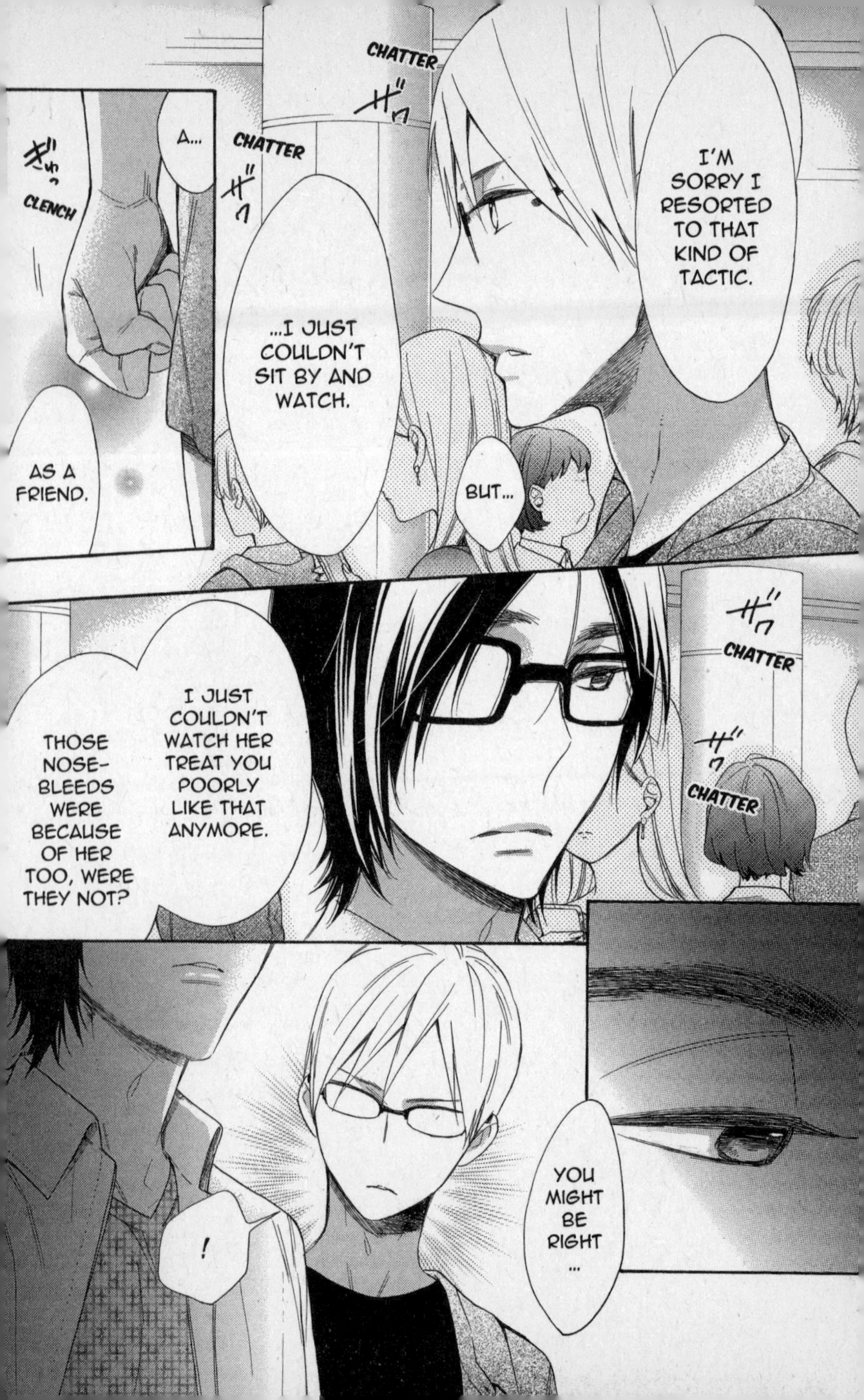
CHATTER
ザワ
CHATTER
ザワ
I'M SORRY I RESORTED TO THAT KIND OF TACTIC.
BUT...
...I JUST COULDN'T SIT BY AND WATCH.
A...
ギュッ
CLENCH
AS A FRIEND.
ザワ
CHATTER
ザワ
CHATTER
I JUST COULDN'T WATCH HER TREAT YOU POORLY LIKE THAT ANYMORE.
THOSE NOSE-BLEEDS WERE BECAUSE OF HER TOO, WERE THEY NOT?
YOU MIGHT BE RIGHT ...
!

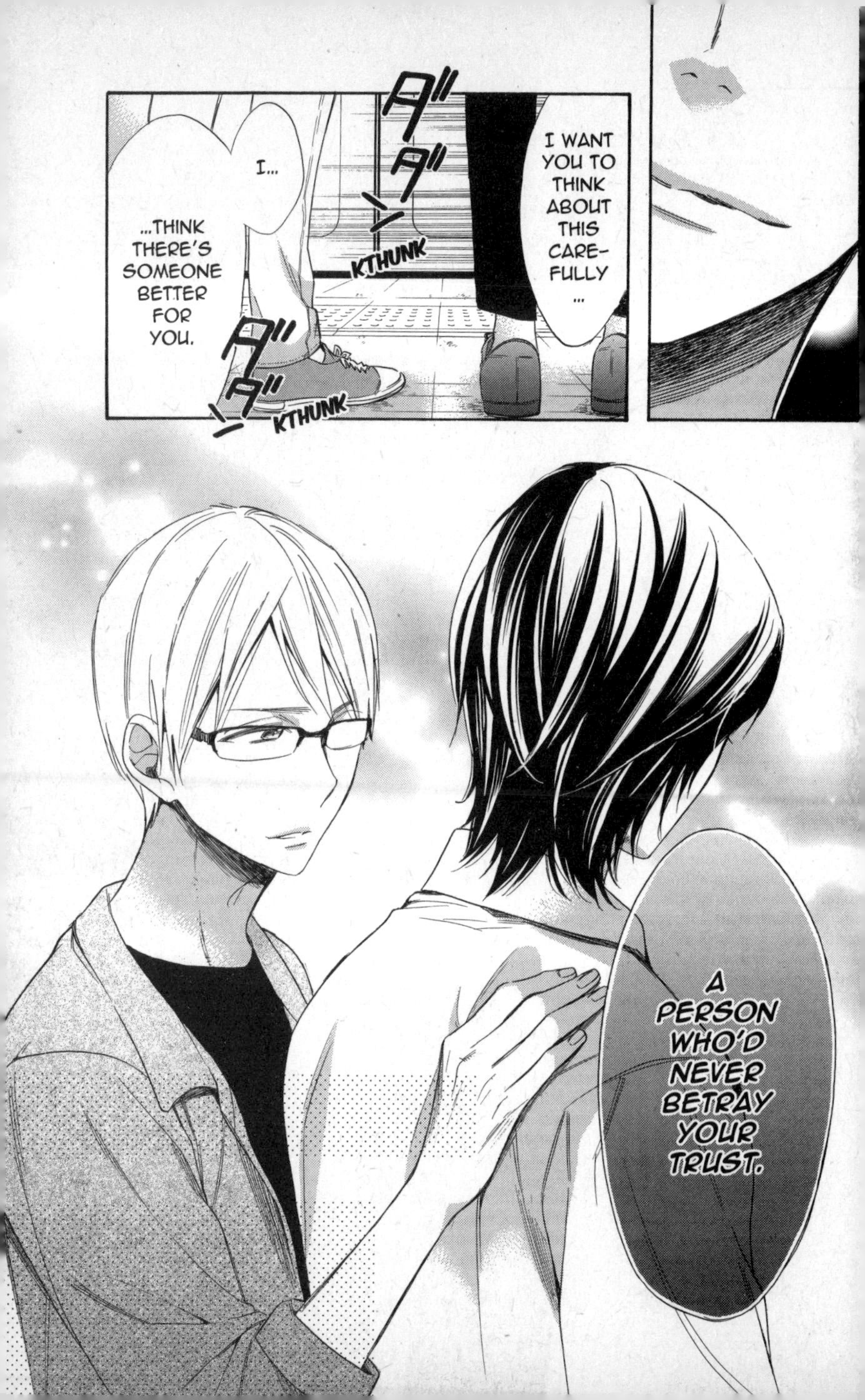
I WANT YOU TO THINK ABOUT THIS CARE-FULLY ...
ダダン
KTHUNK
I...
...THINK THERE'S SOMEONE BETTER FOR YOU.
ダダン
KTHUNK
A PERSON WHO'D NEVER BETRAY YOUR TRUST.

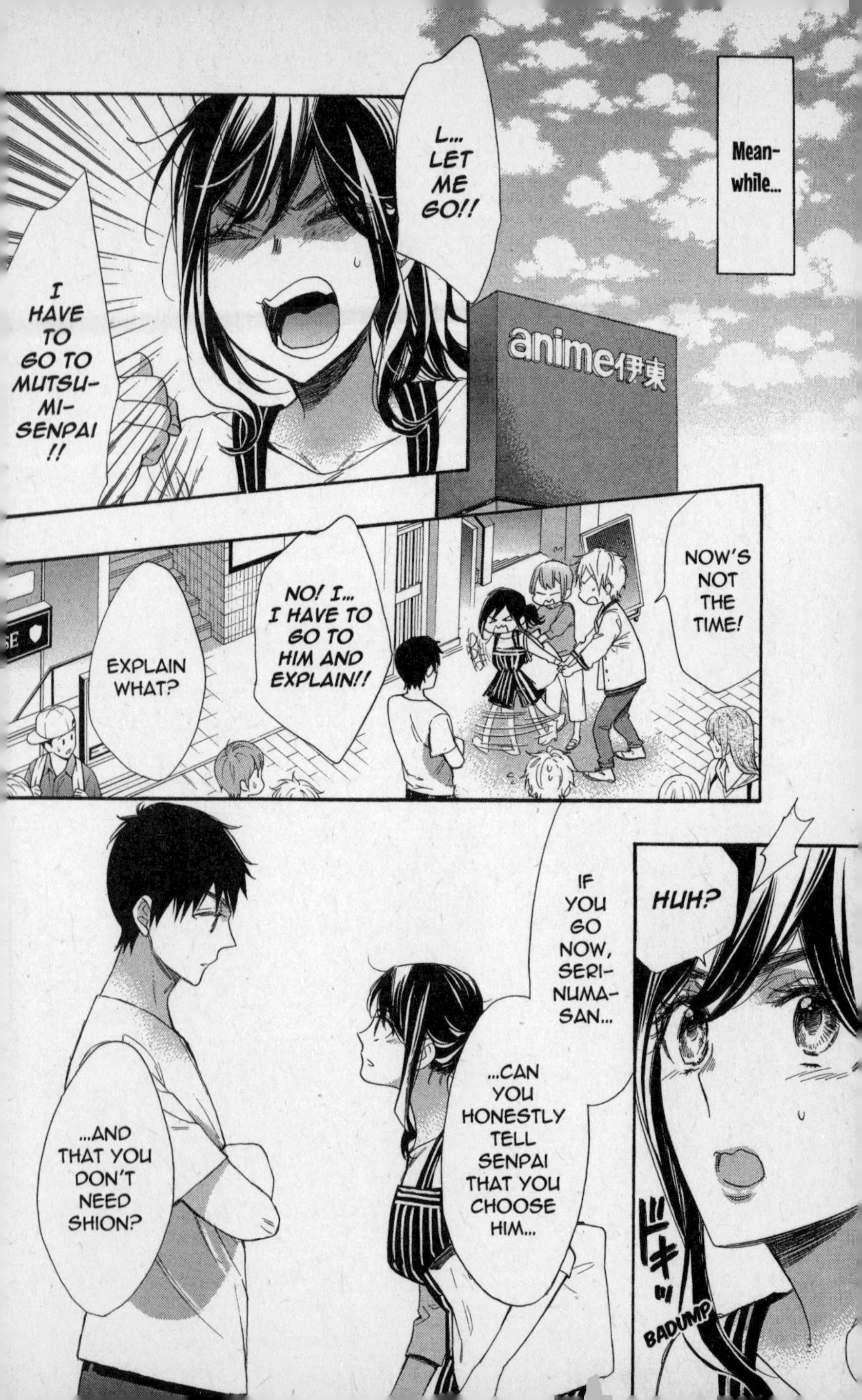
Mean-while...
L... LET ME GO!!
I HAVE TO GO TO MUTSU-MI-SENPAI!!
NOW'S NOT THE TIME!
NO! I... I HAVE TO GO TO HIM AND EXPLAIN!!
EXPLAIN WHAT?
anime伊東
IF YOU GO NOW, SERI-NUMA-SAN...
...CAN YOU HONESTLY TELL SENPAI THAT YOU CHOOSE HIM...
...AND THAT YOU DON'T NEED SHION?
HUH?
ドキッ
BADUMP

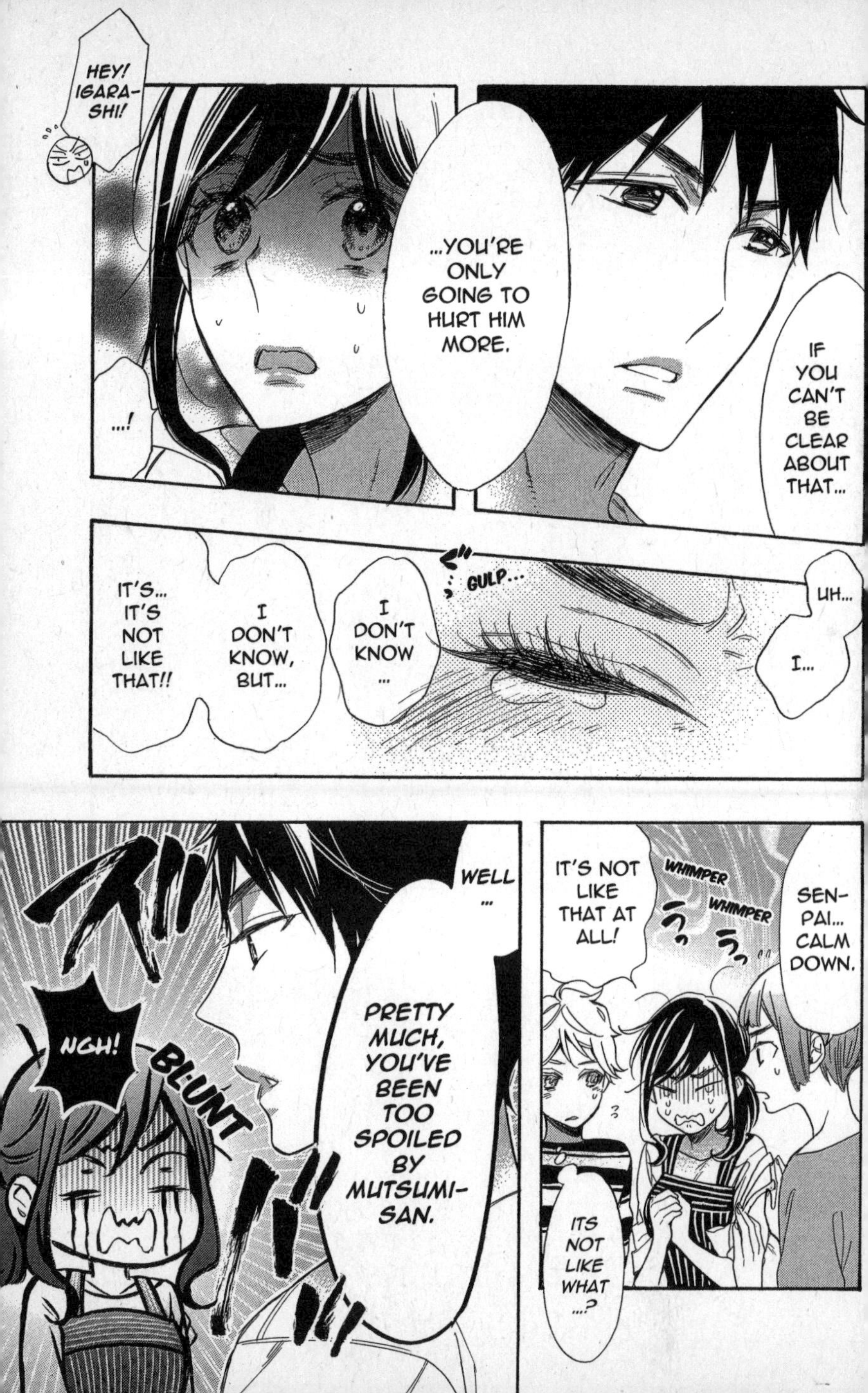
IF YOU CAN'T BE CLEAR ABOUT THAT...
...YOU'RE ONLY GOING TO HURT HIM MORE.
HEY! IGARA-SHI!
...!
UH... I...
GULP...
I DON'T KNOW ...
I DON'T KNOW, BUT...
IT'S... IT'S NOT LIKE THAT!!
SEN-PAI... CALM DOWN.
WHIMPER
WHIMPER
IT'S NOT LIKE THAT AT ALL!
ITS NOT LIKE WHAT ...?
WELL ...
PRETTY MUCH, YOU'VE BEEN TOO SPOILED BY MUTSUMI-SAN.
BLUNT
NGH!

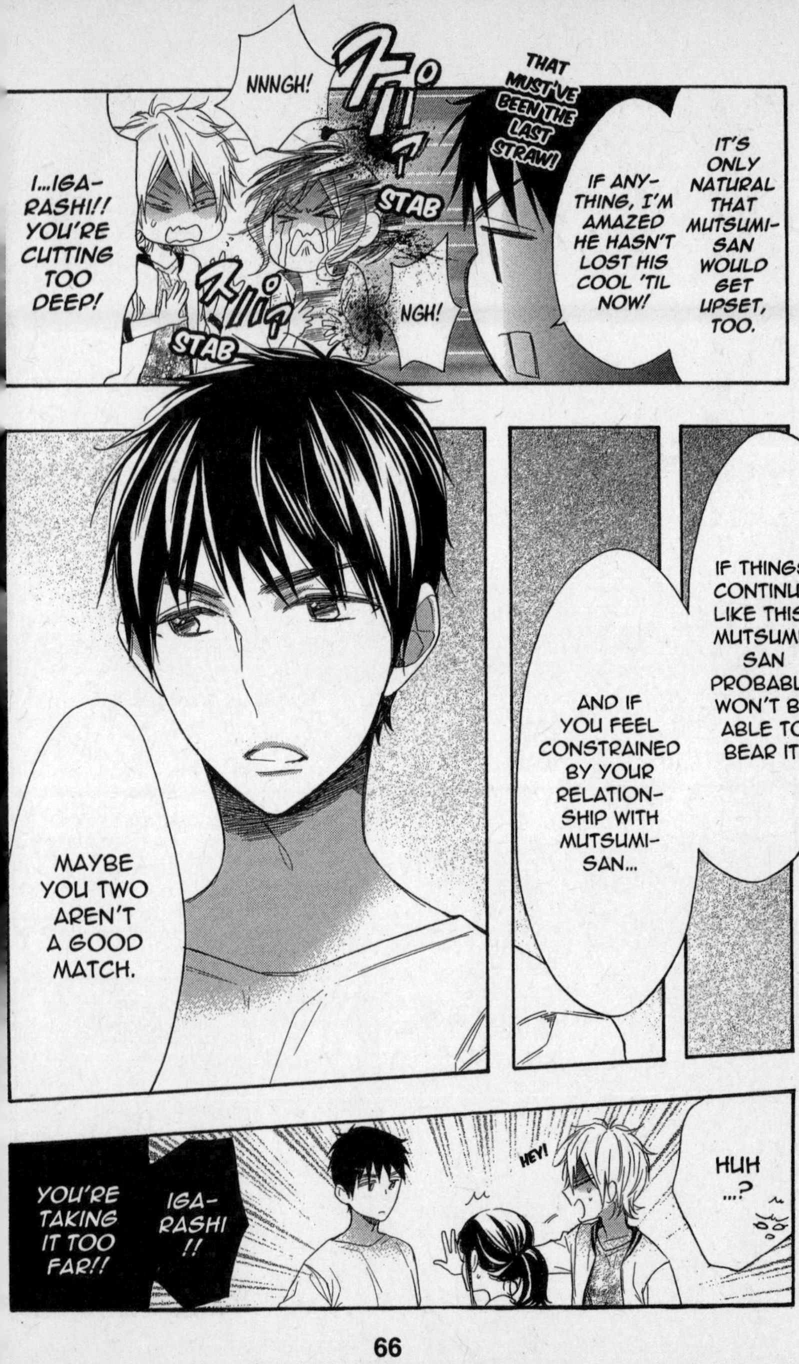
IT'S ONLY NATURAL THAT MUTSUMI-SAN WOULD GET UPSET, TOO.
IF ANYTHING, I'M AMAZED HE HASN'T LOST HIS COOL 'TIL NOW!
THAT MUST'VE BEEN THE LAST STRAW!
NNNGH!
STAB
NGH!
I...IGA-RASHI!! YOU'RE CUTTING TOO DEEP!
STAB
IF THINGS CONTINUE LIKE THIS, MUTSUMI-SAN PROBABLY WON'T BE ABLE TO BEAR IT.
AND IF YOU FEEL CONSTRAINED BY YOUR RELATION-SHIP WITH MUTSUMI-SAN...
MAYBE YOU TWO AREN'T A GOOD MATCH.
HUH ...?
HEY!
IGA-RASHI !!
YOU'RE TAKING IT TOO FAR!!

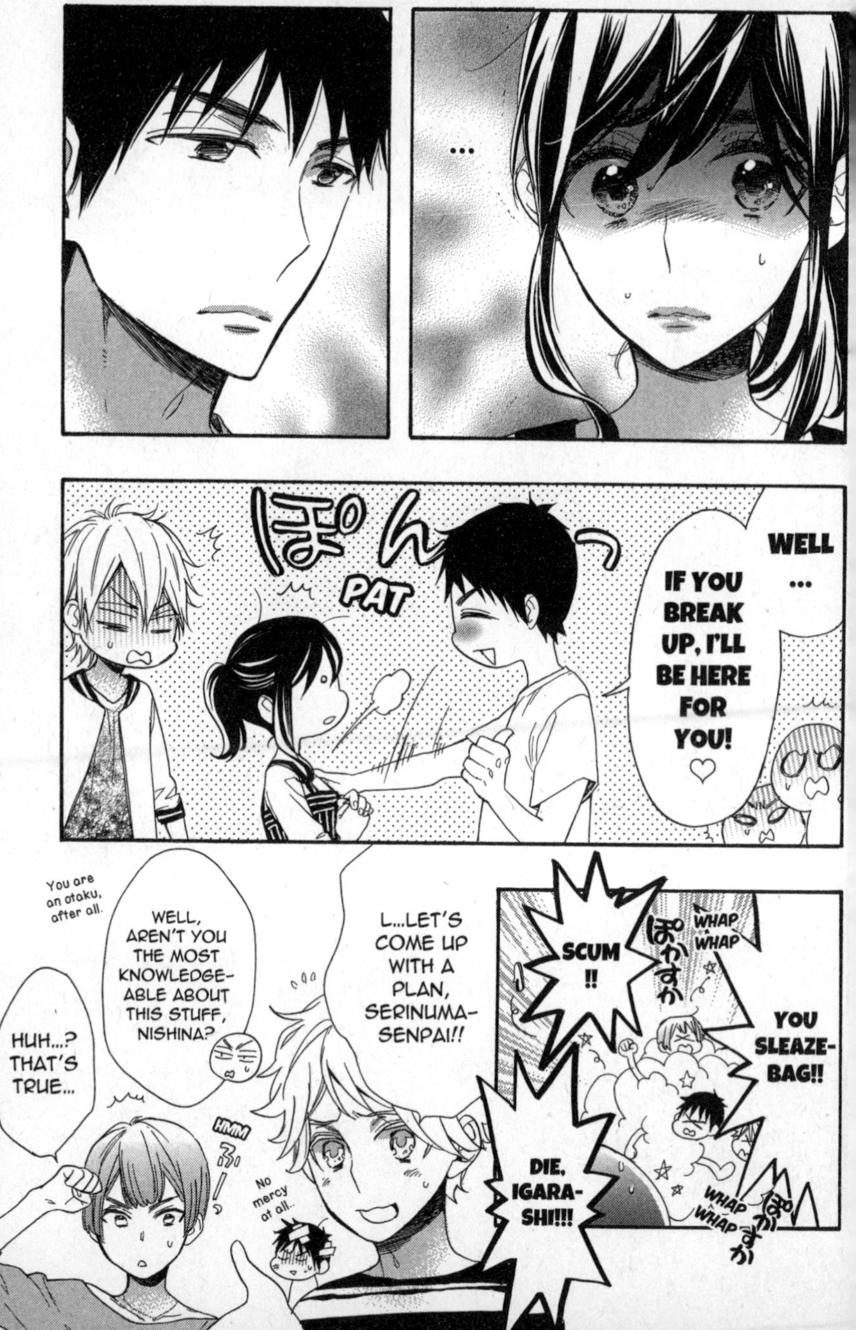
...
ぽんっ
PAT
WELL ...
IF YOU BREAK UP, I'LL BE HERE FOR YOU! ♡
SCUM !!
ぽかすか
WHAP WHAP
YOU SLEAZE-BAG!!
DIE, IGARA-SHI!!!
WHAP WHAP
ぽかすか
L...LET'S COME UP WITH A PLAN, SERINUMA-SENPAI!!
No mercy at all..
HMM
ふ!
WELL, AREN'T YOU THE MOST KNOWLEDGE-ABLE ABOUT THIS STUFF, NISHINA?
You are an otaku, after all.
HUH...? THAT'S TRUE...

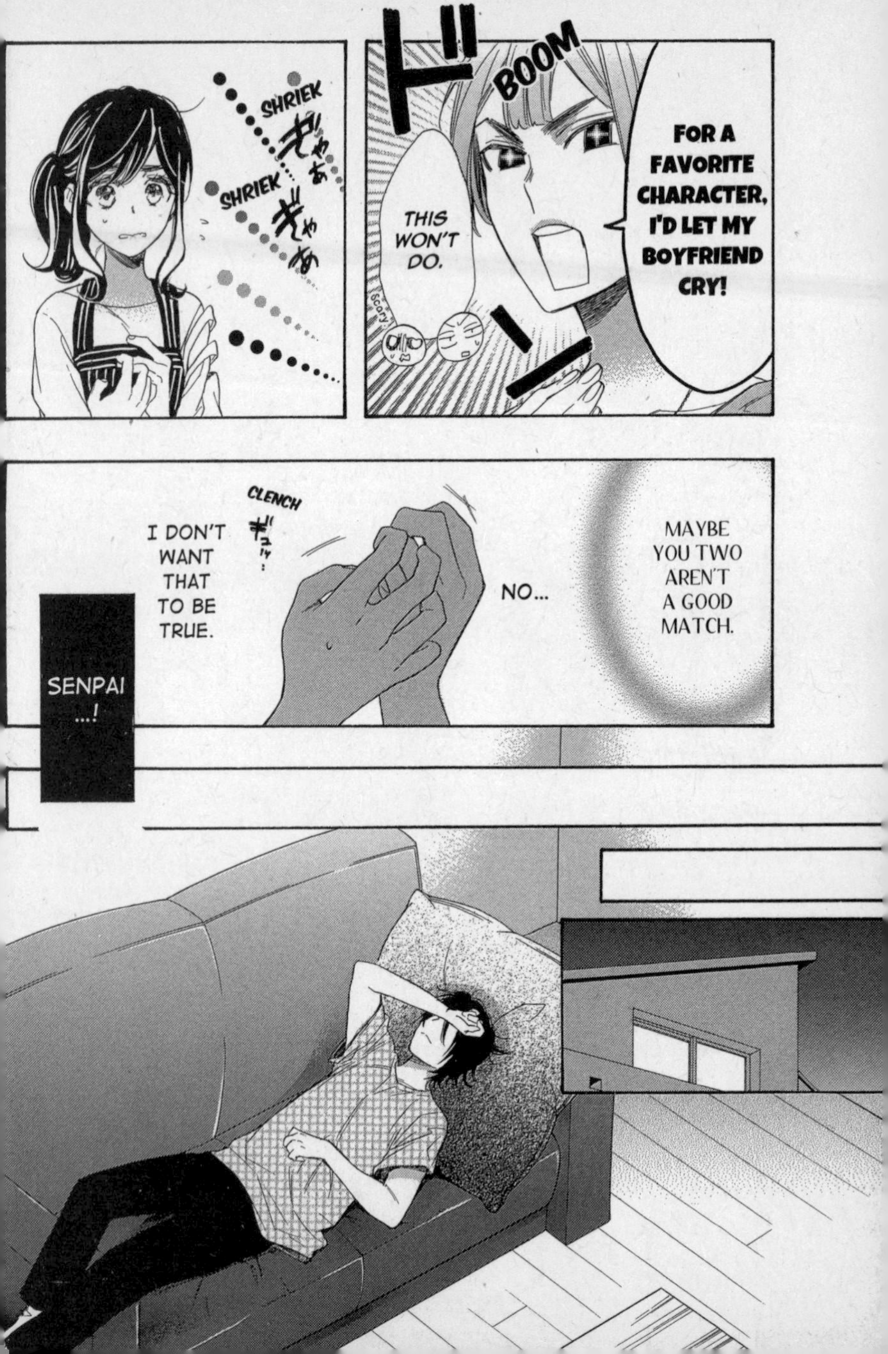
FOR A FAVORITE CHARACTER, I'D LET MY BOYFRIEND CRY!
BOOM
THIS WON'T DO.
Scary
SHRIEK
SHRIEK
MAYBE YOU TWO AREN'T A GOOD MATCH.
NO...
CLENCH
I DON'T WANT THAT TO BE TRUE.
SENPAI ...!

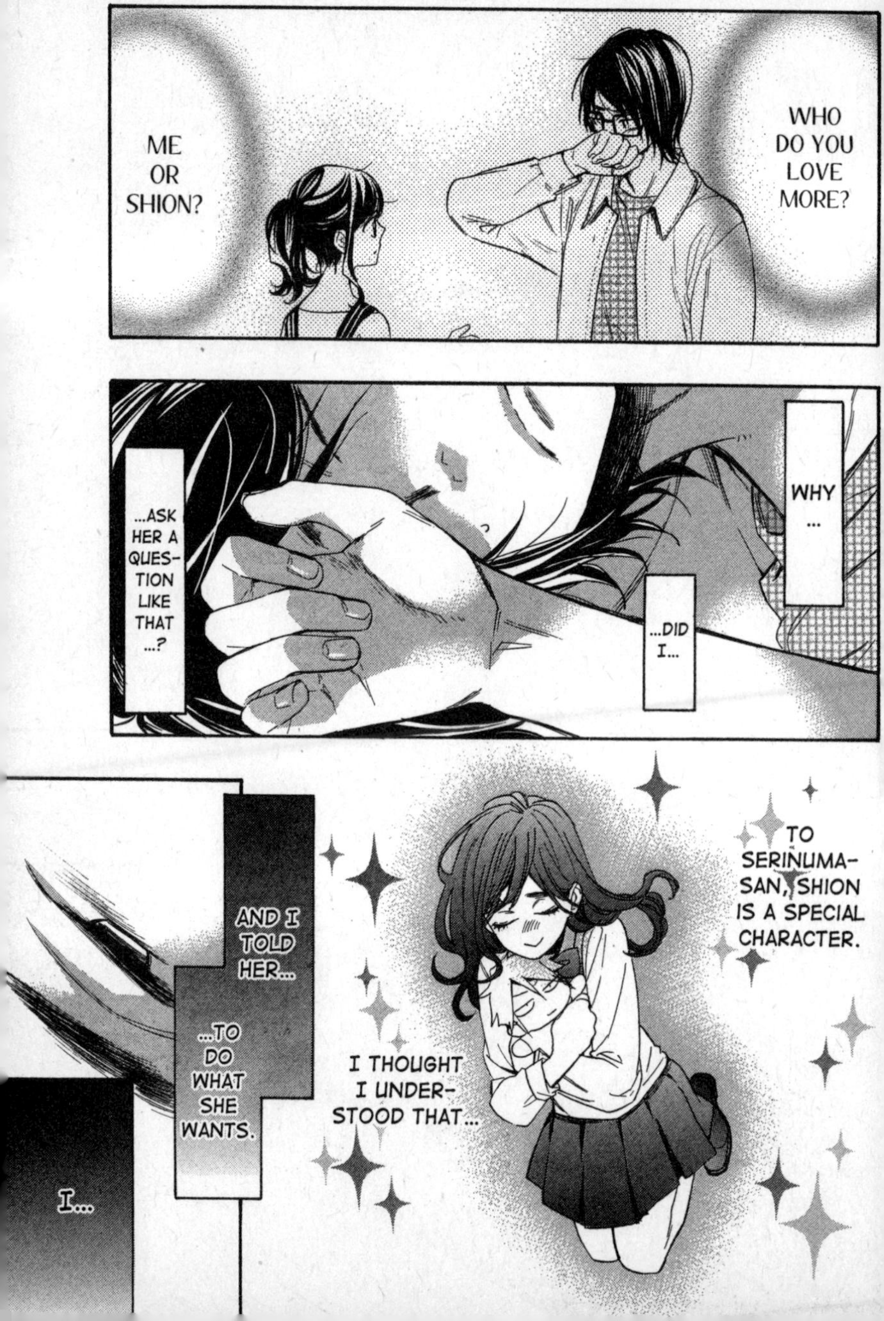
WHO DO YOU LOVE MORE?
ME OR SHION?
WHY...
...DID I...
...ASK HER A QUESTION LIKE THAT...?
TO SERINUMA-SAN, SHION IS A SPECIAL CHARACTER.
I THOUGHT I UNDERSTOOD THAT...
AND I TOLD HER...
...TO DO WHAT SHE WANTS.
I...

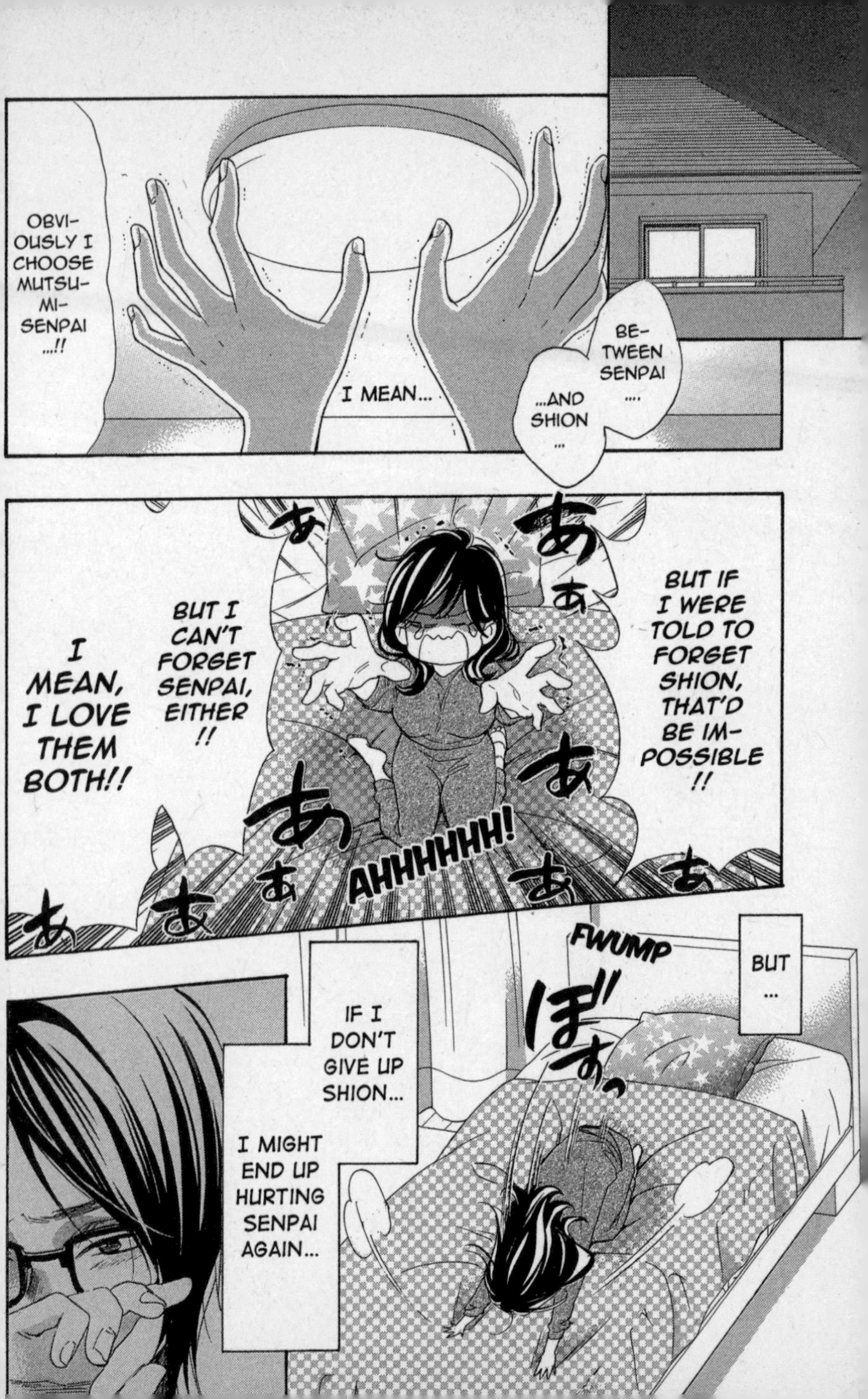
BE-TWEEN SENPAI....
...AND SHION...
I MEAN...
OBVI-OUSLY I CHOOSE MUTSU-MI-SENPAI...!!
BUT IF I WERE TOLD TO FORGET SHION, THAT'D BE IM-POSSIBLE!!
BUT I CAN'T FORGET SENPAI, EITHER!!
I MEAN, I LOVE THEM BOTH!!
AHHHHHH!
BUT...
FWUMP
IF I DON'T GIVE UP SHION...
I MIGHT END UP HURTING SENPAI AGAIN...

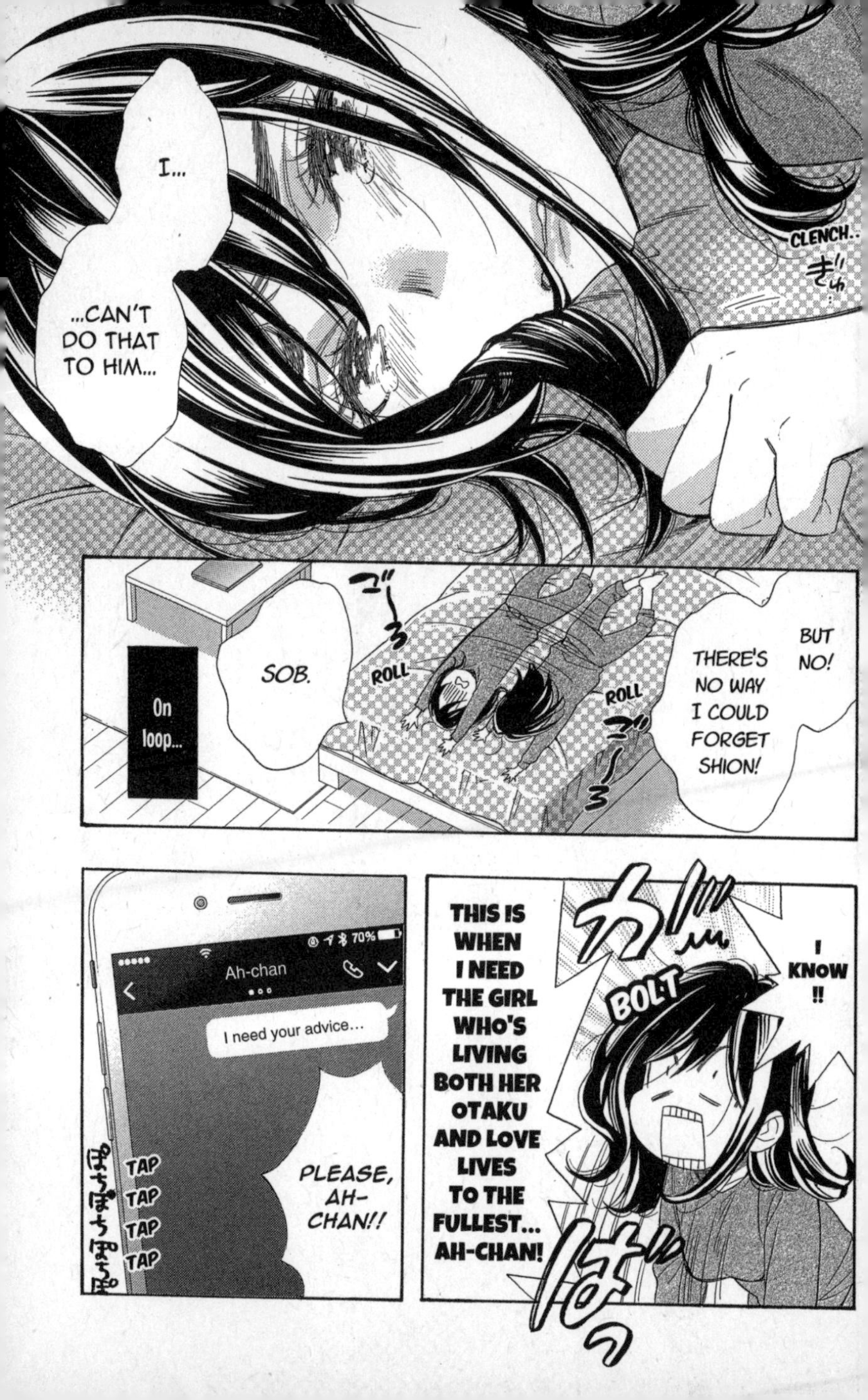
CLENCH..
ぎゅ
I...
...CAN'T DO THAT TO HIM...
BUT NO!
THERE'S NO WAY I COULD FORGET SHION!
ROLL
ごろ
ROLL
ごろ
SOB.
On loop...
I KNOW!!
BOLT
ガッ
THIS IS WHEN I NEED THE GIRL WHO'S LIVING BOTH HER OTAKU AND LOVE LIVES TO THE FULLEST... AH-CHAN!
はっ
70%
Ah-chan
I need your advice...
PLEASE, AH-CHAN!!
TAP
TAP
TAP
TAP
ぽちぽちぽちぽち

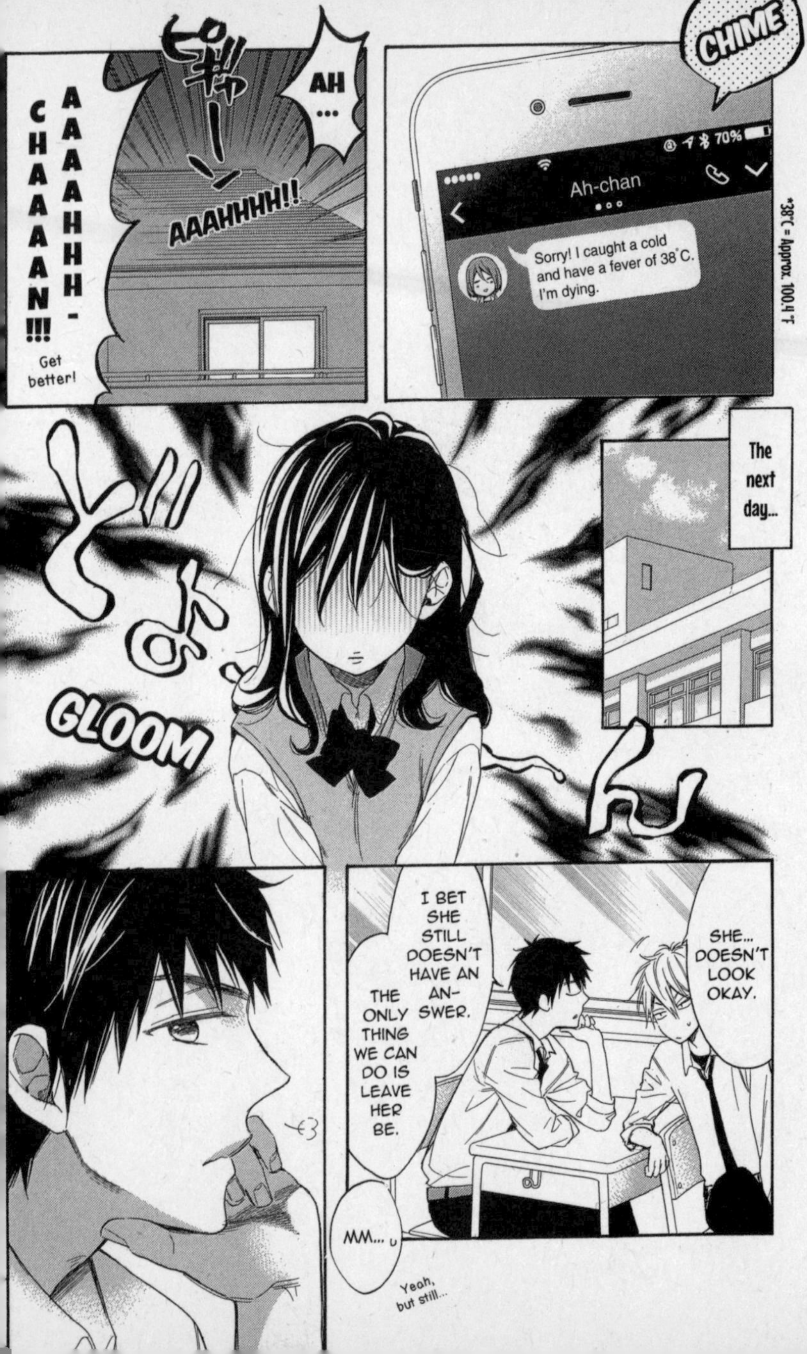
CHIME
Ah-chan
Sorry! I caught a cold and have a fever of 38°C. I'm dying.
*38°C = Approx. 100.4°F
AH...
AAAHHHH!!
AAAAAAHHH-CHAAAAAN!!!
Get better!
The next day...
GLOOM
SHE... DOESN'T LOOK OKAY.
I BET SHE STILL DOESN'T HAVE AN ANSWER.
THE ONLY THING WE CAN DO IS LEAVE HER BE.
MM...
Yeah, but still...

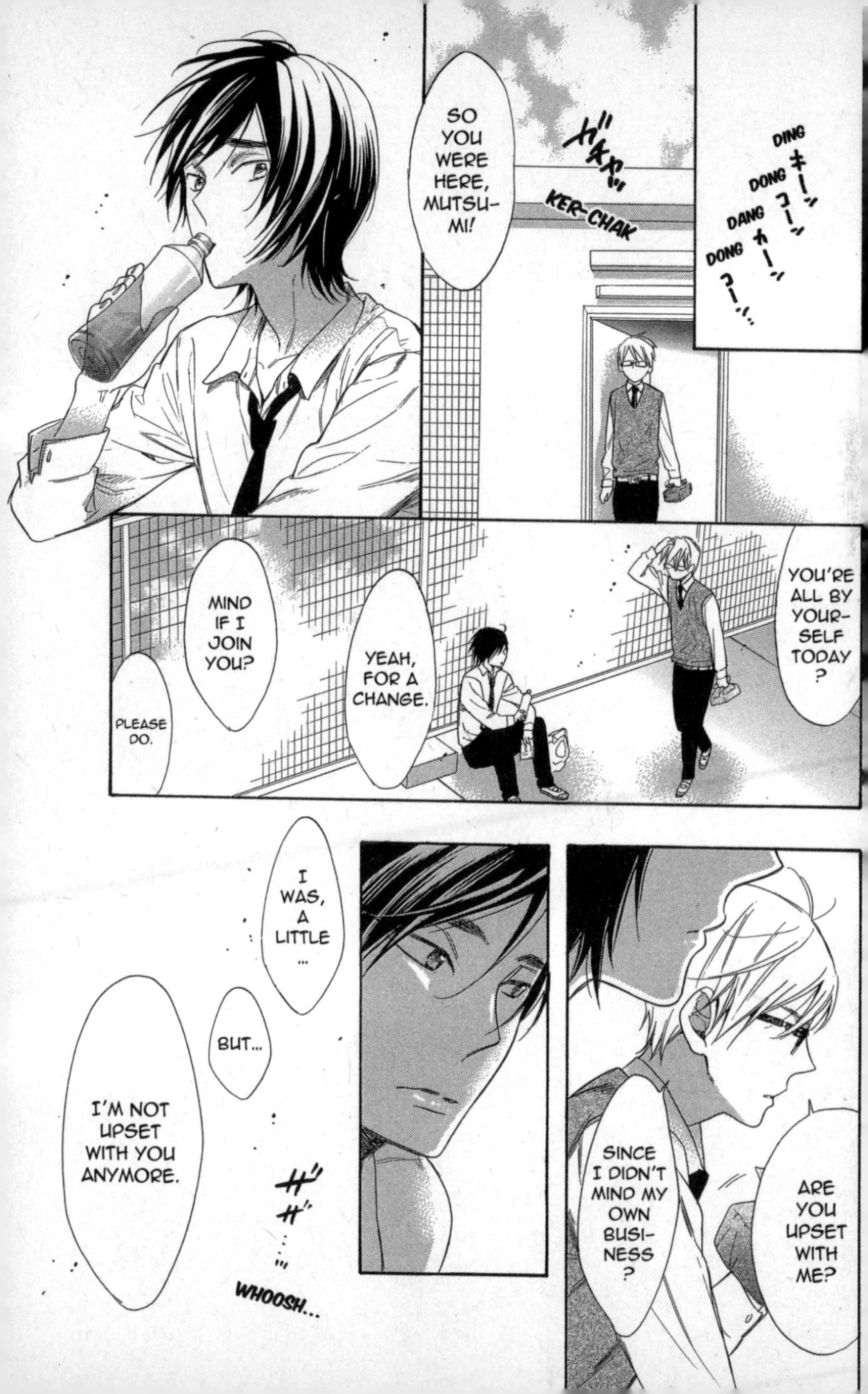

DING キーン
DONG コーン
DANG カーン
DONG コーン…
ガチャッ
KER-CHAK
SO YOU WERE HERE, MUTSU-MI!
YOU'RE ALL BY YOUR-SELF TODAY?
YEAH, FOR A CHANGE.
MIND IF I JOIN YOU?
PLEASE DO.
ARE YOU UPSET WITH ME?
SINCE I DIDN'T MIND MY OWN BUSI-NESS?
I WAS, A LITTLE ...
BUT...
I'M NOT UPSET WITH YOU ANYMORE.
ザザ
WHOOSH...

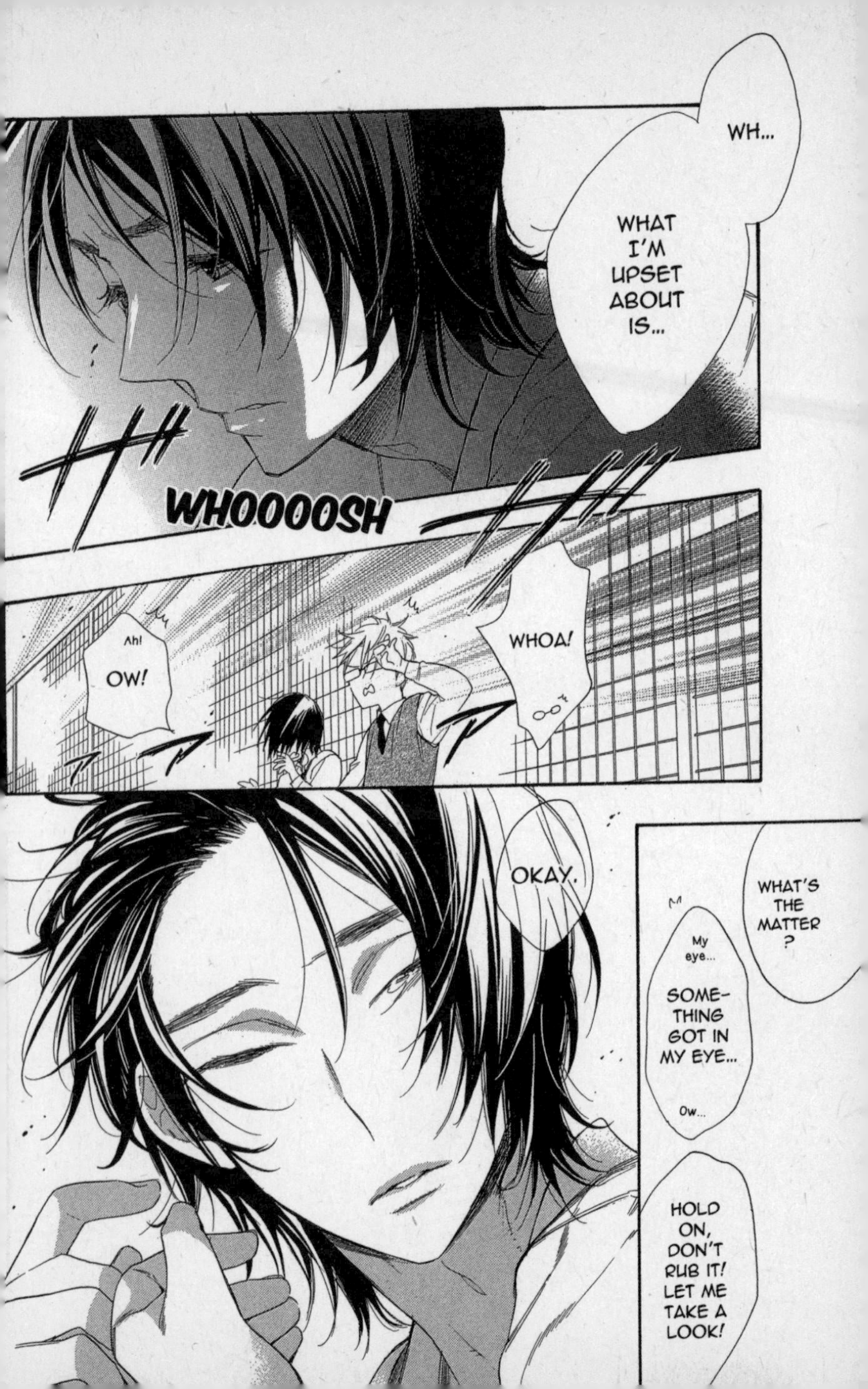
WH...
WHAT I'M UPSET ABOUT IS...
WHOOOOSH
WHOA!
Ah!
OW!
WHAT'S THE MATTER?
My eye...
SOME-THING GOT IN MY EYE...
Ow...
HOLD ON, DON'T RUB IT! LET ME TAKE A LOOK!
OKAY.

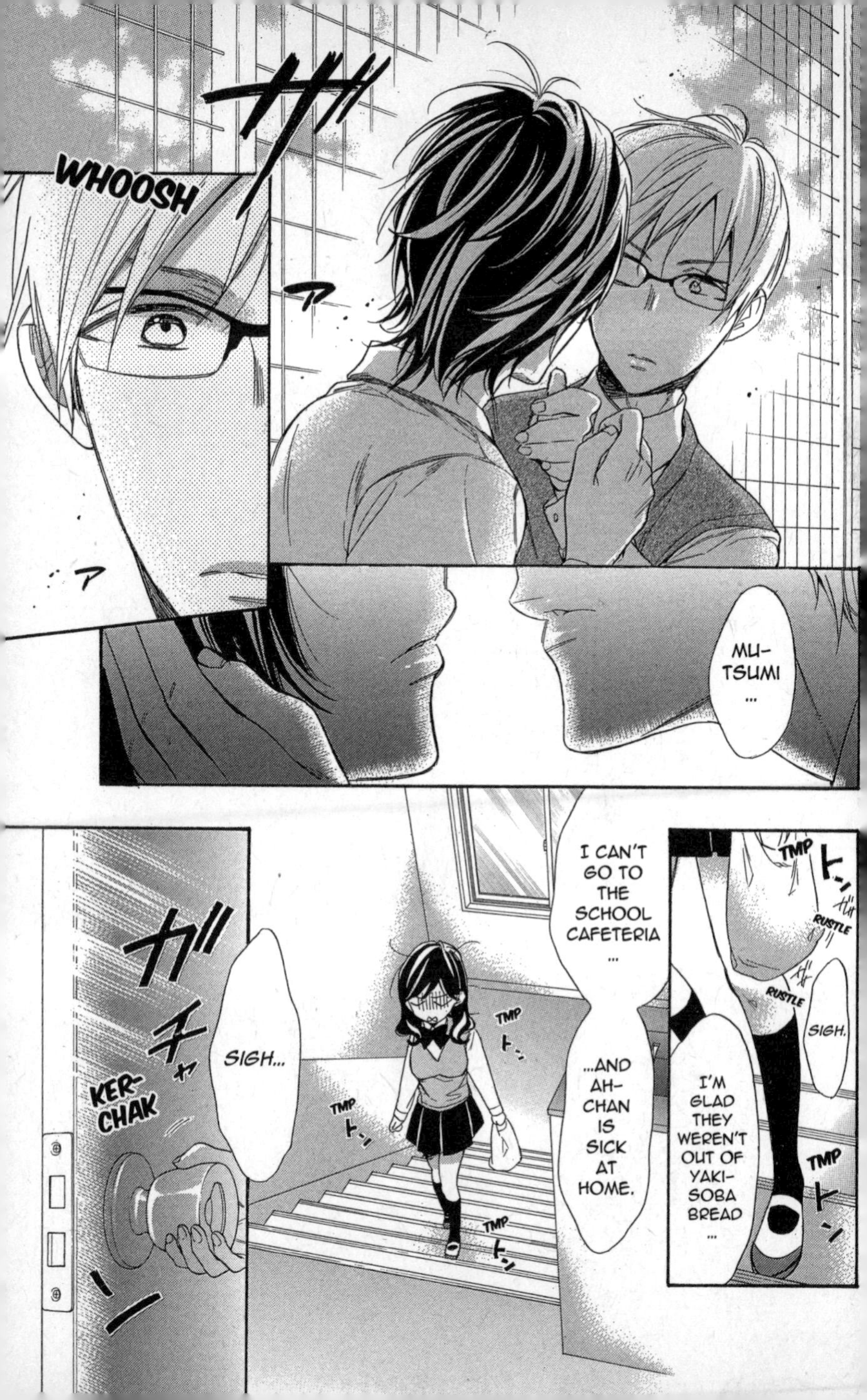
WHOOSH
MU-TSUMI ...
TMP
RUSTLE
RUSTLE
SIGH.
I'M GLAD THEY WEREN'T OUT OF YAKI-SOBA BREAD ...
TMP
I CAN'T GO TO THE SCHOOL CAFETERIA ...
...AND AH-CHAN IS SICK AT HOME.
TMP
TMP
TMP
SIGH...
KER-CHAK

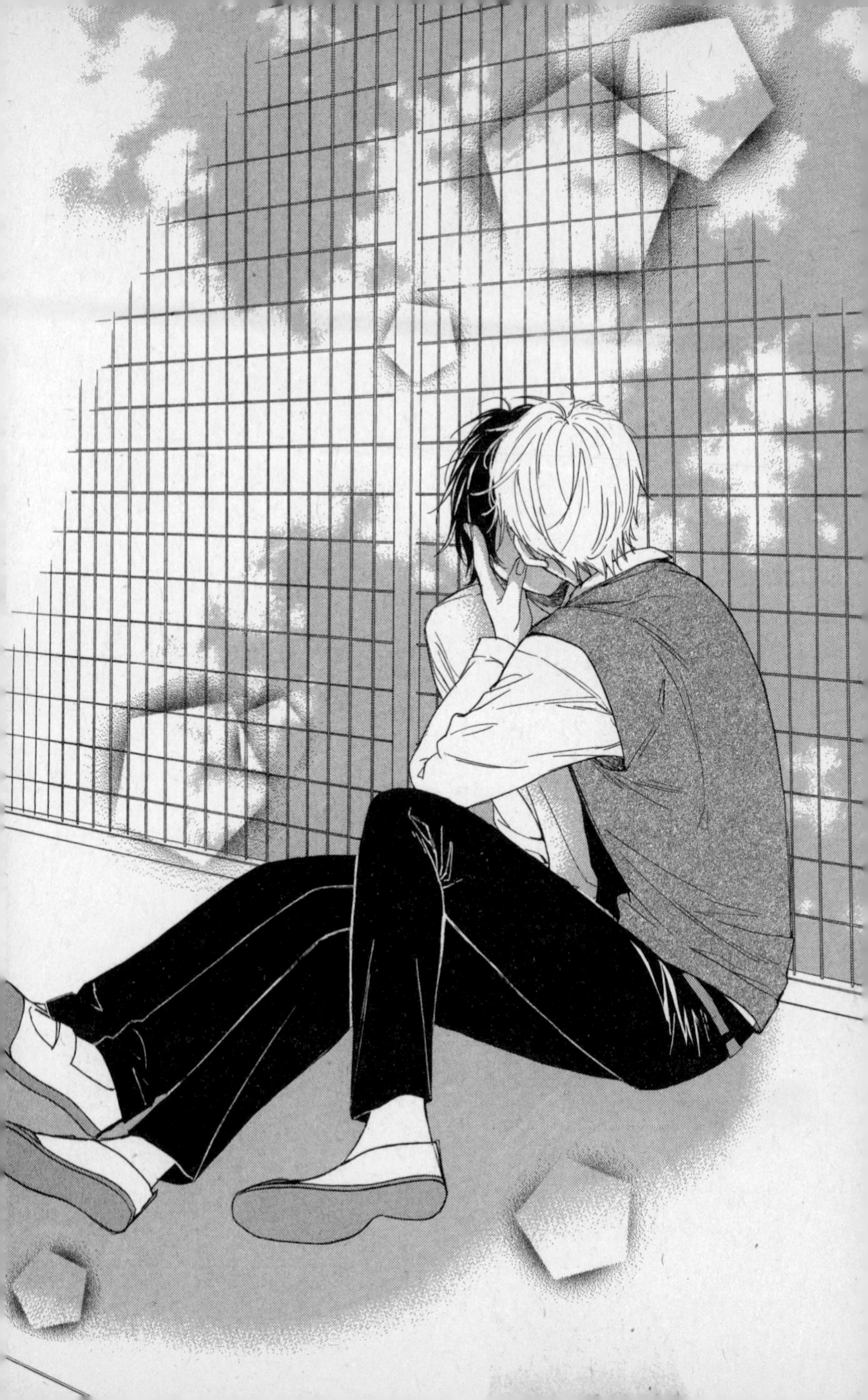

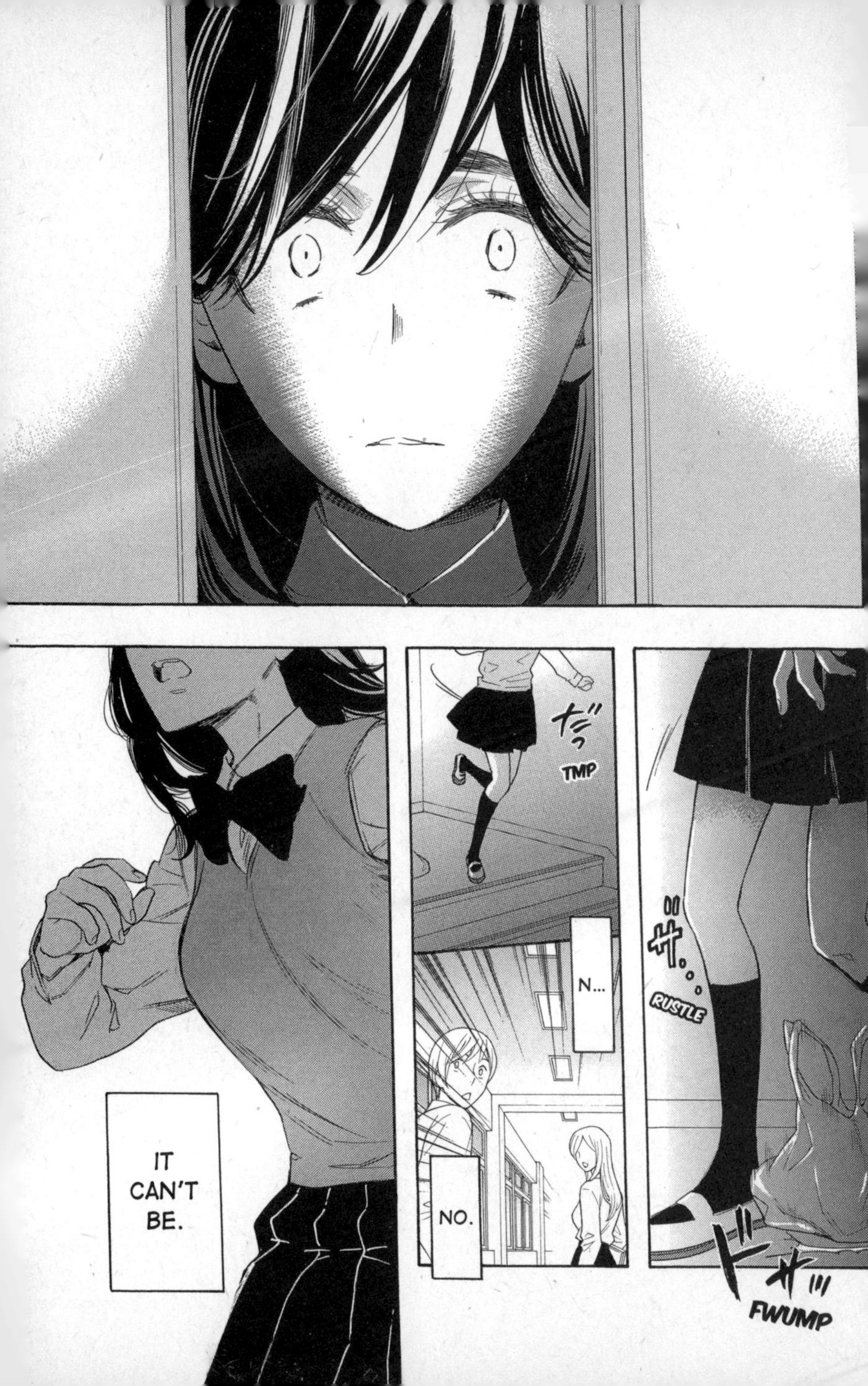
RUSTLE
FWUMP
TMP
N...
NO.
IT CAN'T BE.

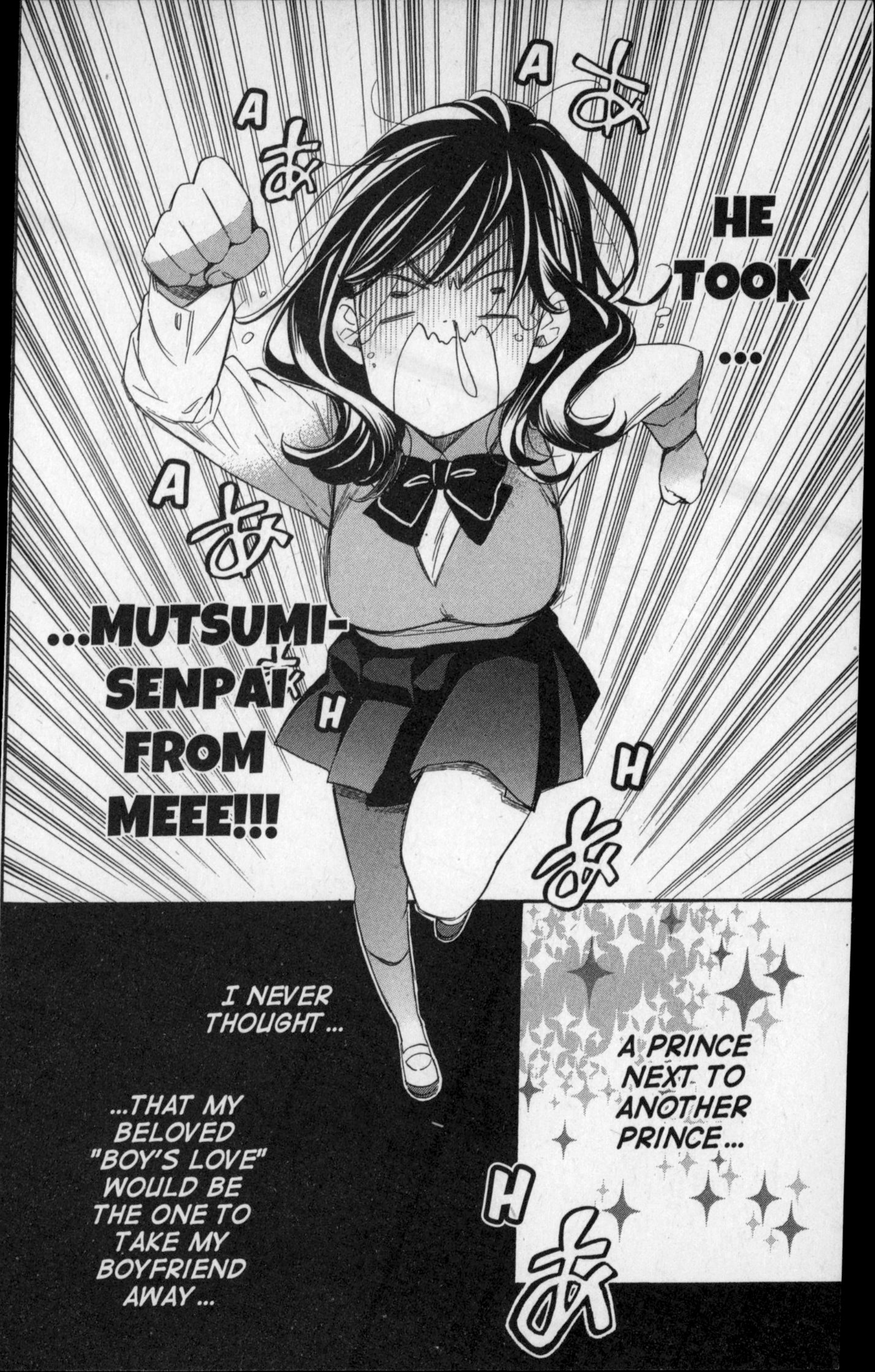
HE TOOK ...
...MUTSUMI-SENPAI FROM MEEE!!!
A あ
A あ
A あ
H あ
H あ
H あ
A PRINCE NEXT TO ANOTHER PRINCE...
I NEVER THOUGHT...
...THAT MY BELOVED "BOY'S LOVE" WOULD BE THE ONE TO TAKE MY BOYFRIEND AWAY...

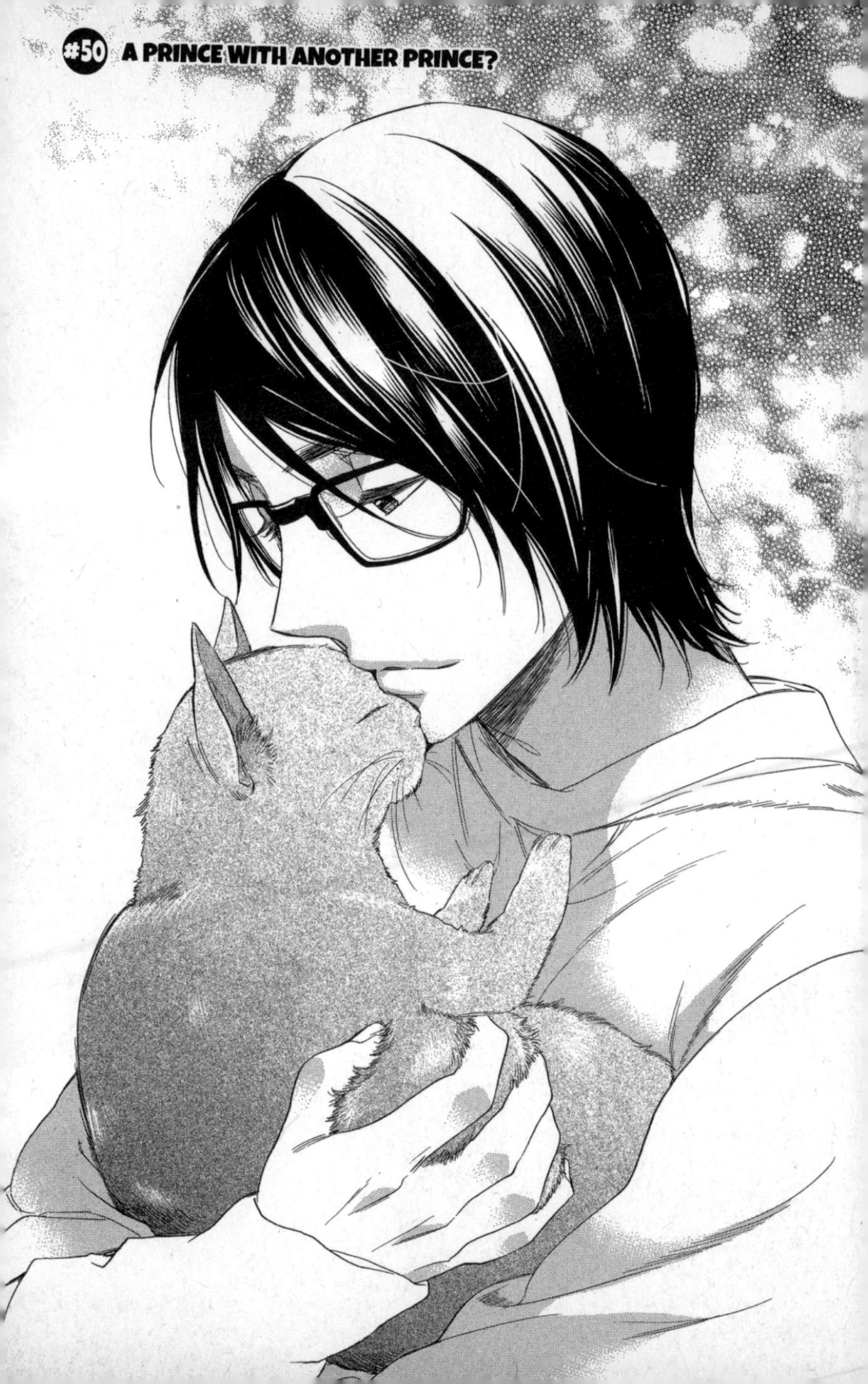
#50 A PRINCE WITH ANOTHER PRINCE?

THOSE TWO REALLY AREN'T GONNA COME, HUH?
CLINK
CLINK
CHATTER
Hey, over here!
CLATTER
CLATTER
CHATTER
CHATTER
Ha ha ha...
CHATTER
CLATTER

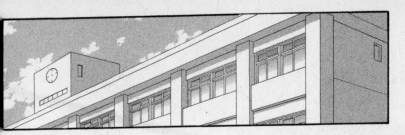

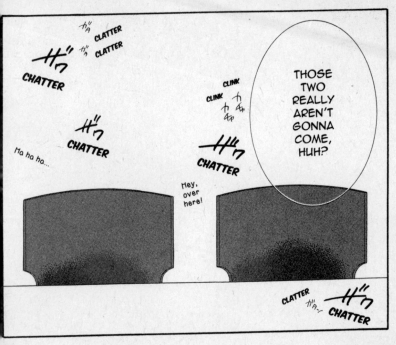

KiSS HiM, NOT ME!

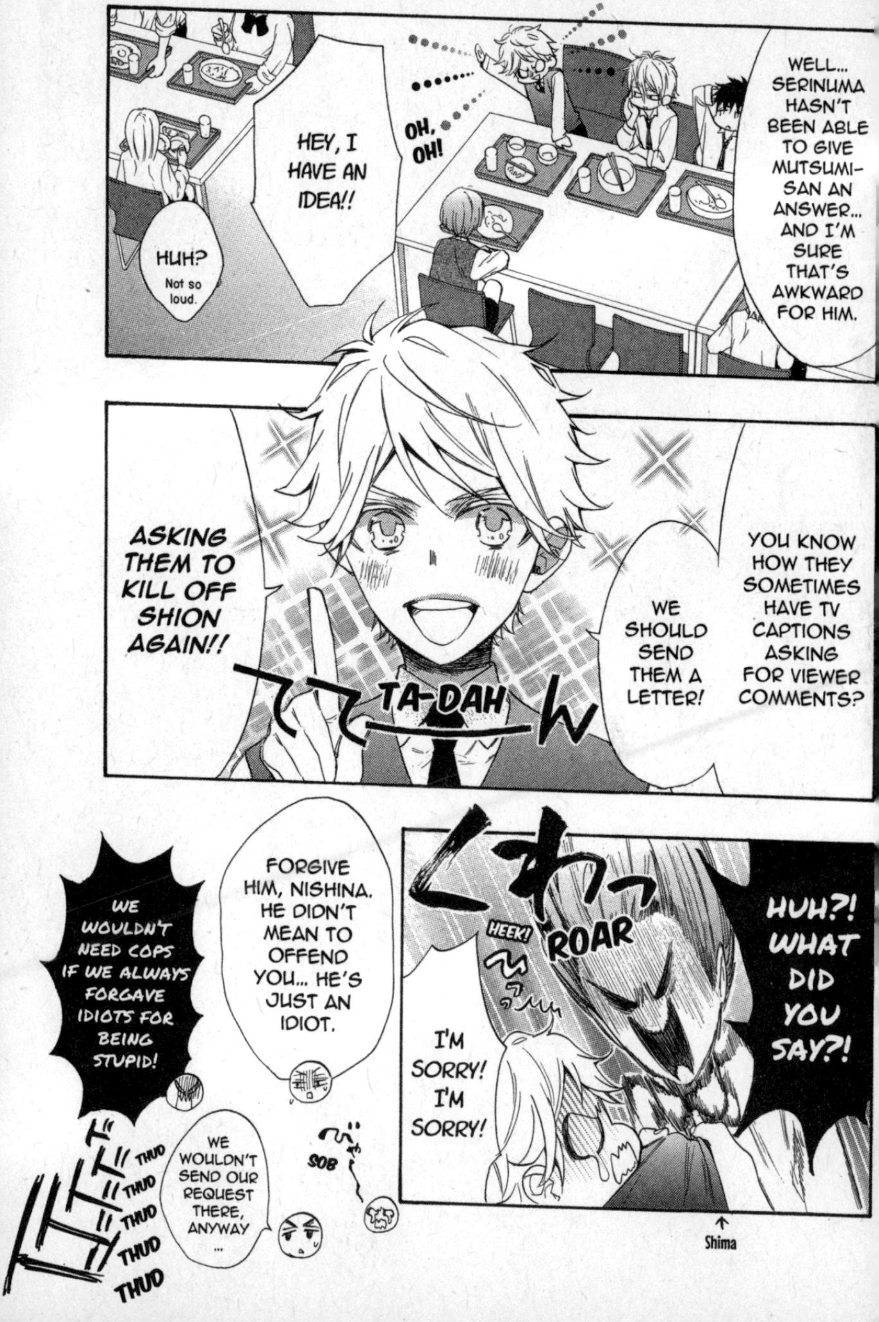
WELL... SERINUMA HASN'T BEEN ABLE TO GIVE MUTSUMI-SAN AN ANSWER... AND I'M SURE THAT'S AWKWARD FOR HIM.
OH, OH!
HEY, I HAVE AN IDEA!!
HUH? Not so loud.
YOU KNOW HOW THEY SOMETIMES HAVE TV CAPTIONS ASKING FOR VIEWER COMMENTS?
WE SHOULD SEND THEM A LETTER!
ASKING THEM TO KILL OFF SHION AGAIN!!
TA-DAH
HUH?! WHAT DID YOU SAY?!
ROAR
HEEK!
I'M SORRY! I'M SORRY!
Shima
FORGIVE HIM, NISHINA. HE DIDN'T MEAN TO OFFEND YOU... HE'S JUST AN IDIOT.
WE WOULDN'T NEED COPS IF WE ALWAYS FORGAVE IDIOTS FOR BEING STUPID!
SOB
WE WOULDN'T SEND OUR REQUEST THERE, ANYWAY ...
THUD
THUD
THUD
THUD
THUD

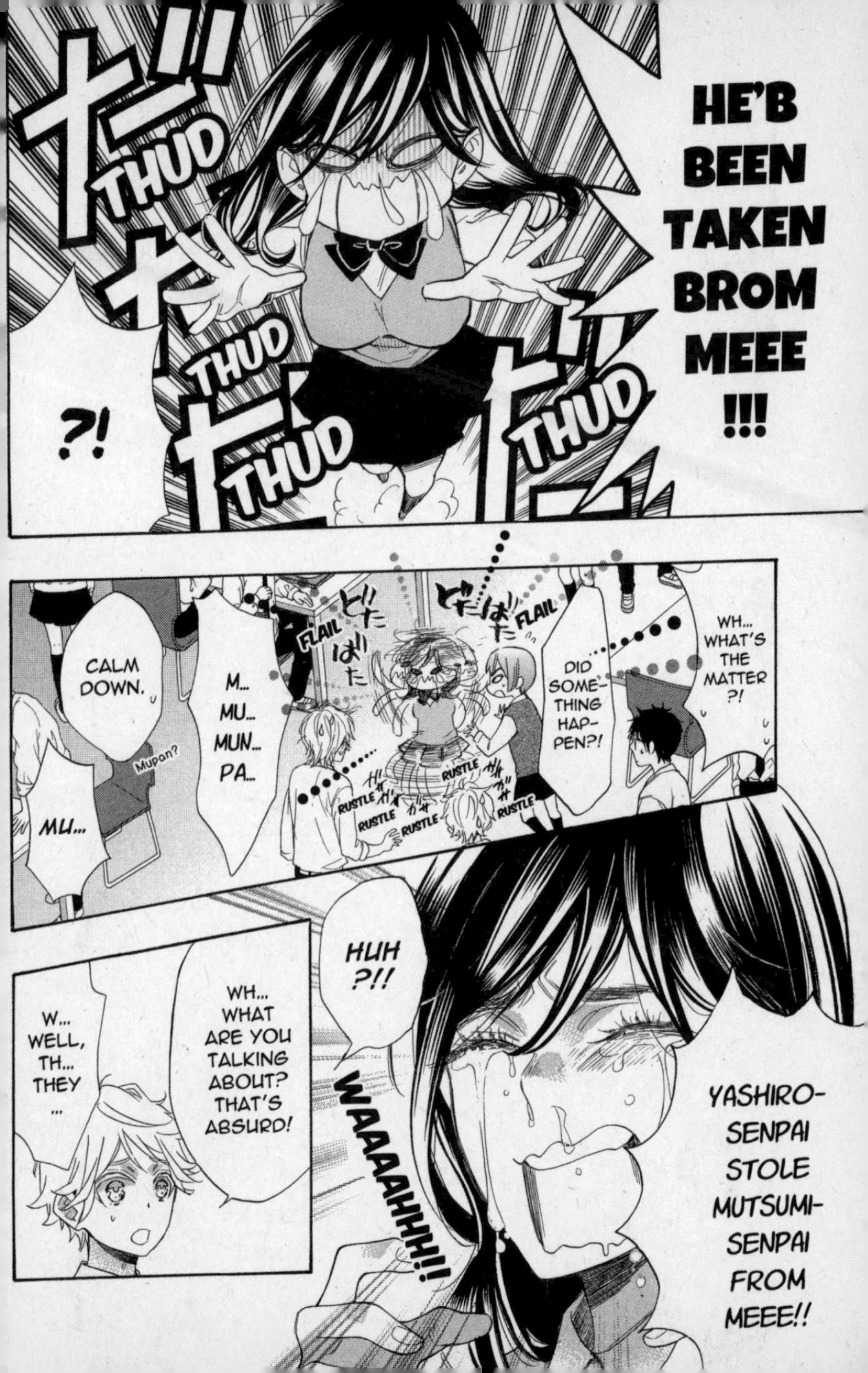
HE'B BEEN TAKEN BROM MEEE!!!
THUD
THUD
THUD
THUD
?!
WH... WHAT'S THE MATTER?!
DID SOME-THING HAP-PEN?!
FLAIL
FLAIL
RUSTLE
RUSTLE
RUSTLE
RUSTLE
RUSTLE
M... MU... MUN... PA...
CALM DOWN.
Mupan?
MU...
YASHIRO-SENPAI STOLE MUTSUMI-SENPAI FROM MEEE!!
WAAAAHHHH!!
HUH?!!
WH... WHAT ARE YOU TALKING ABOUT? THAT'S ABSURD!
W... WELL, TH... THEY ...

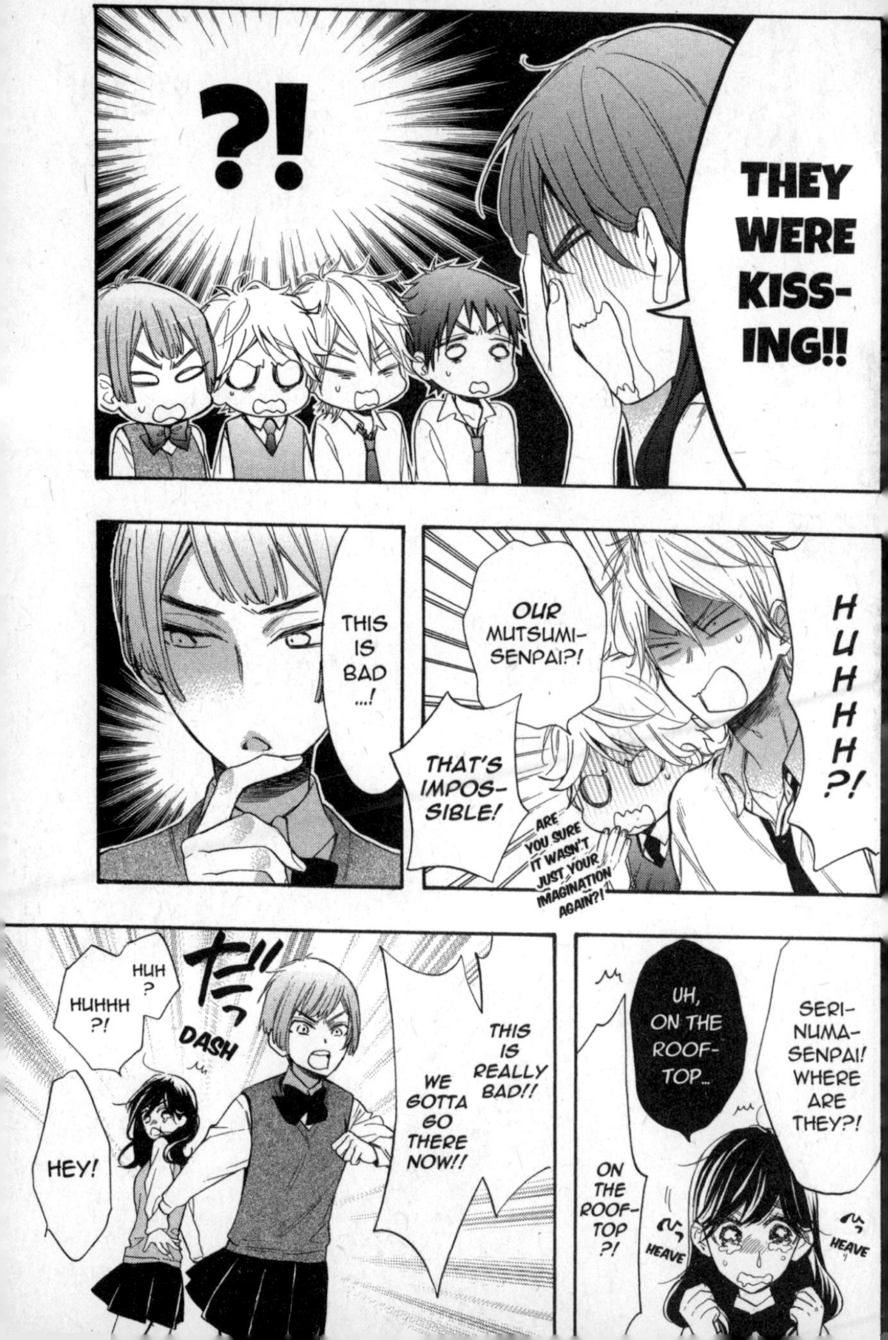
THEY WERE KISS-ING!!
?!
HUHHHH?!
OUR MUTSUMI-SENPAI?!
THAT'S IMPOSSIBLE!
ARE YOU SURE IT WASN'T JUST YOUR IMAGINATION AGAIN?!
THIS IS BAD...!
SERI-NUMA-SENPAI! WHERE ARE THEY?!
UH, ON THE ROOF-TOP...
ON THE ROOF-TOP?!
HEAVE
HEAVE
THIS IS REALLY BAD!!
WE GOTTA GO THERE NOW!!
DASH
HUH?
HUHHH?!
HEY!

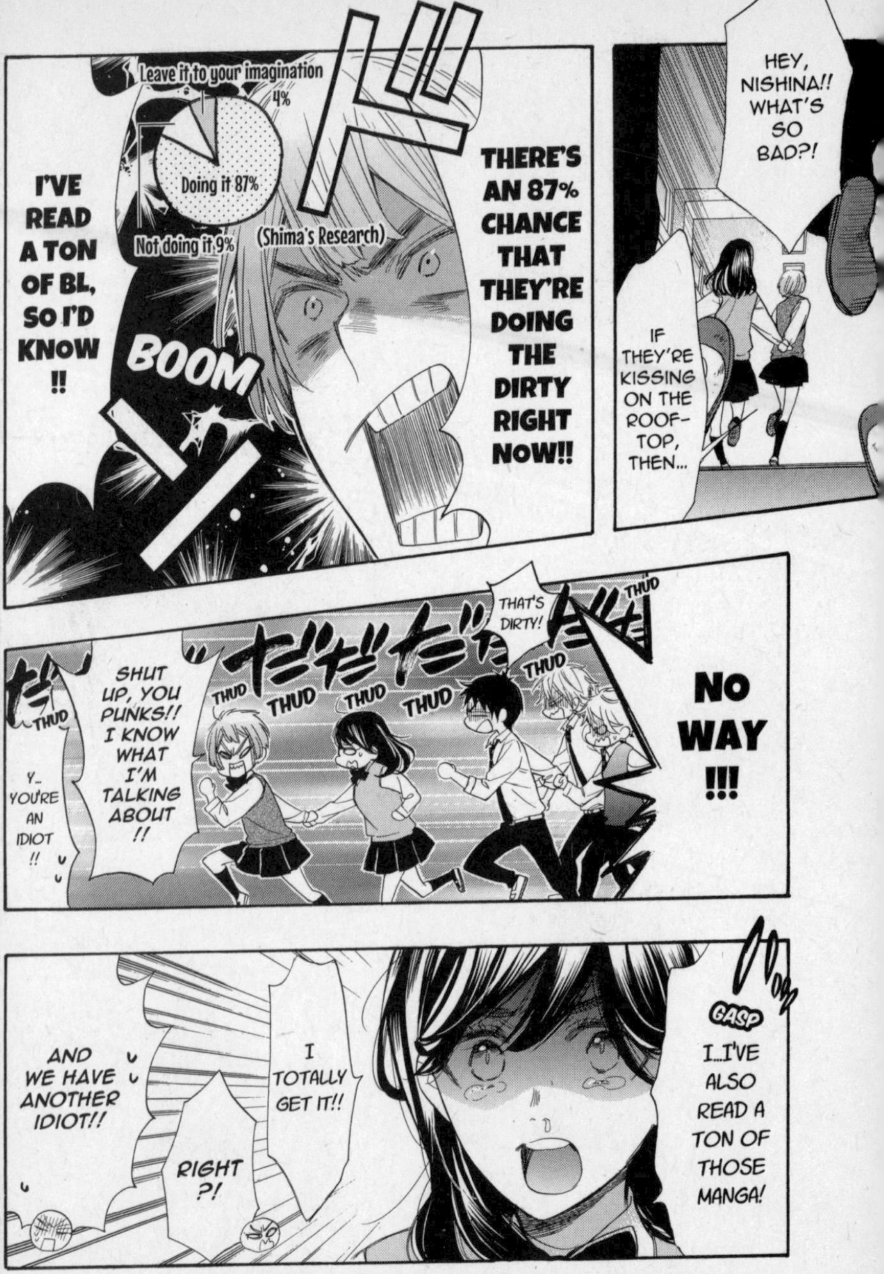
HEY, NISHINA!! WHAT'S SO BAD?!
IF THEY'RE KISSING ON THE ROOF-TOP, THEN...
THERE'S AN 87% CHANCE THAT THEY'RE DOING THE DIRTY RIGHT NOW!!
Leave it to your imagination 4%
Doing it 87%
Not doing it 9%
(Shima's Research)
I'VE READ A TON OF BL, SO I'D KNOW!!
BOOM
NO WAY!!!
THUD
THAT'S DIRTY!
THUD
THUD THUD THUD THUD THUD
SHUT UP, YOU PUNKS!! I KNOW WHAT I'M TALKING ABOUT!!
THUD
Y... YOU'RE AN IDIOT!!
GASP
I...I'VE ALSO READ A TON OF THOSE MANGA!
I TOTALLY GET IT!!
RIGHT?!
AND WE HAVE ANOTHER IDIOT!!

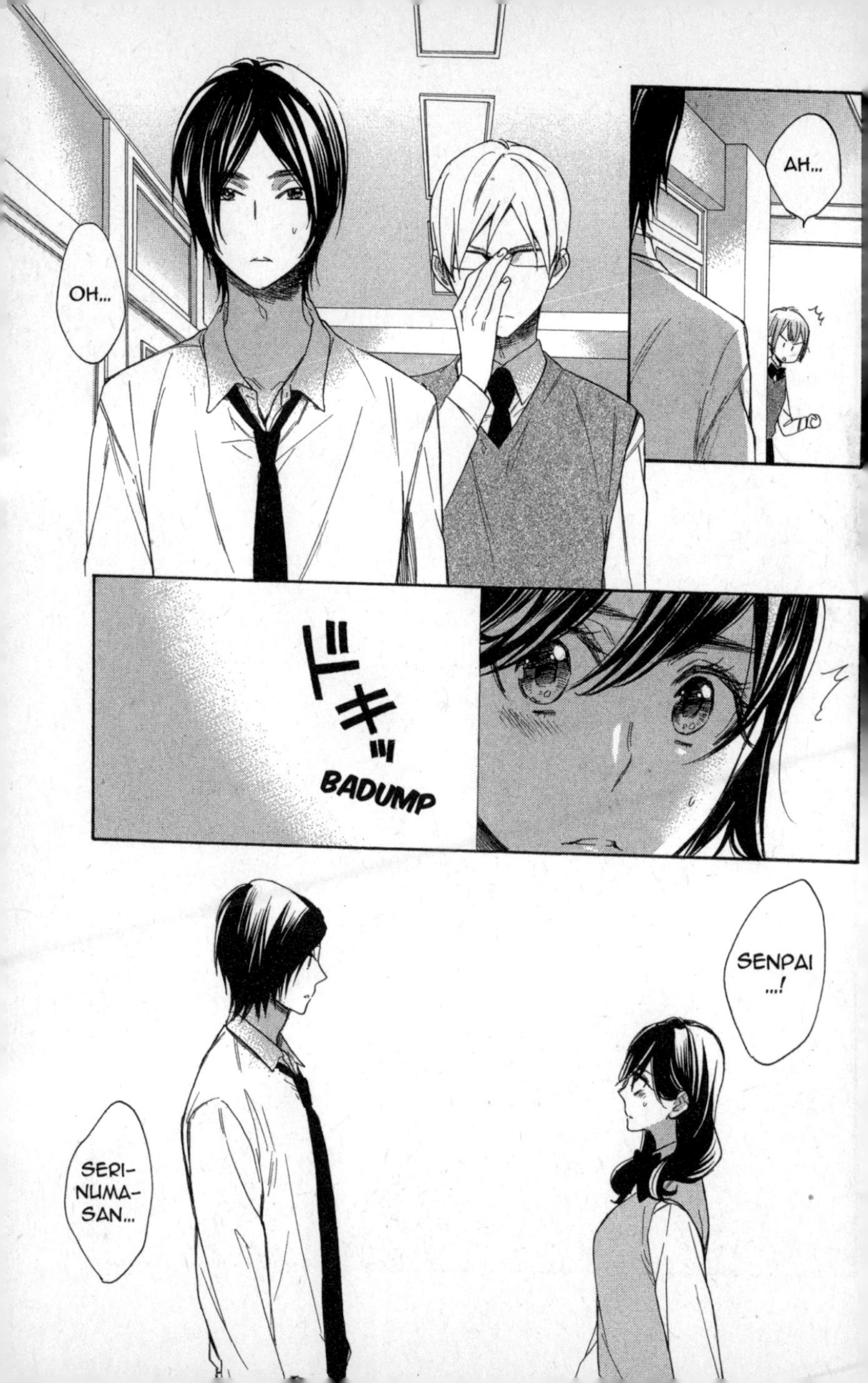
AH...
OH...
ドキッ
BADUMP
SENPAI ...!
SERI-NUMA-SAN...

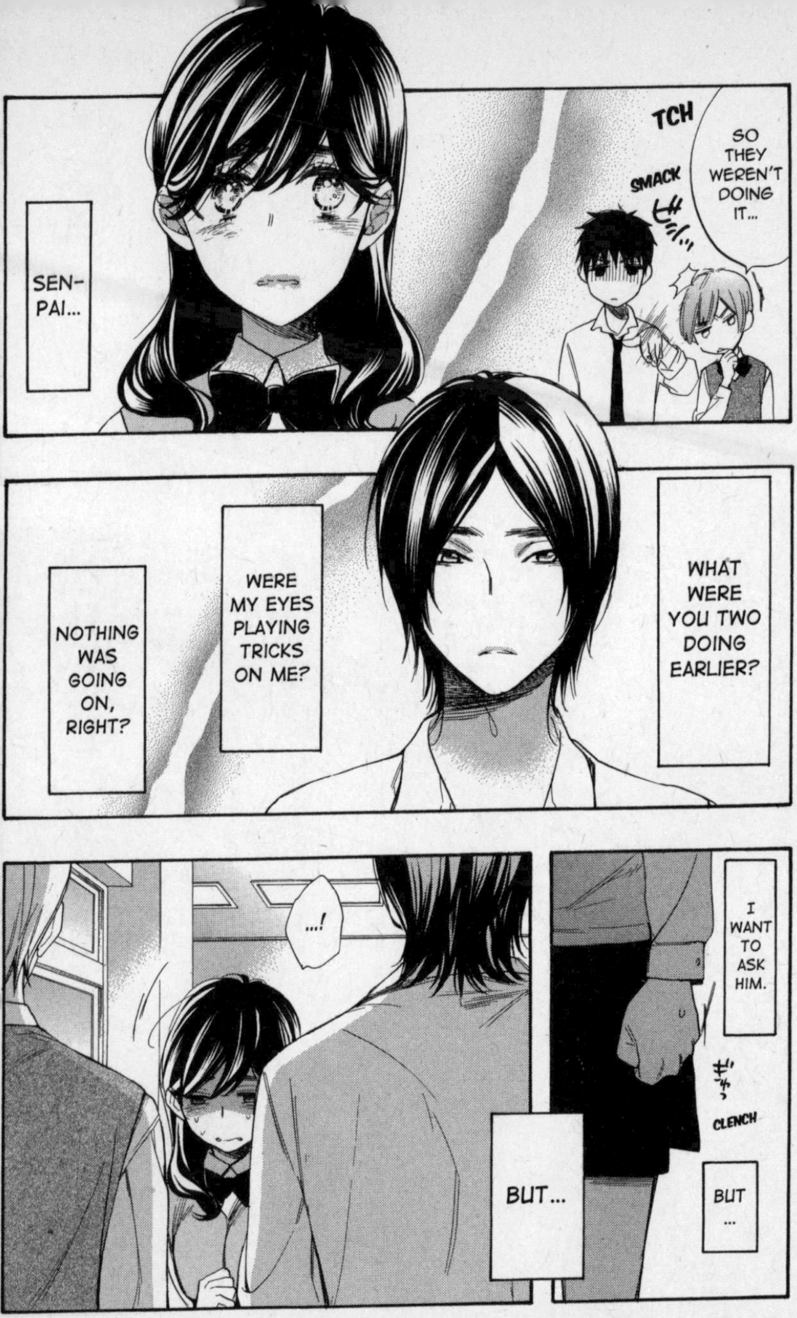
TCH
SO THEY WEREN'T DOING IT...
SMACK
SEN-PAI...
WHAT WERE YOU TWO DOING EARLIER?
WERE MY EYES PLAYING TRICKS ON ME?
NOTHING WAS GOING ON, RIGHT?
I WANT TO ASK HIM.
CLENCH
BUT ...
...!
BUT...

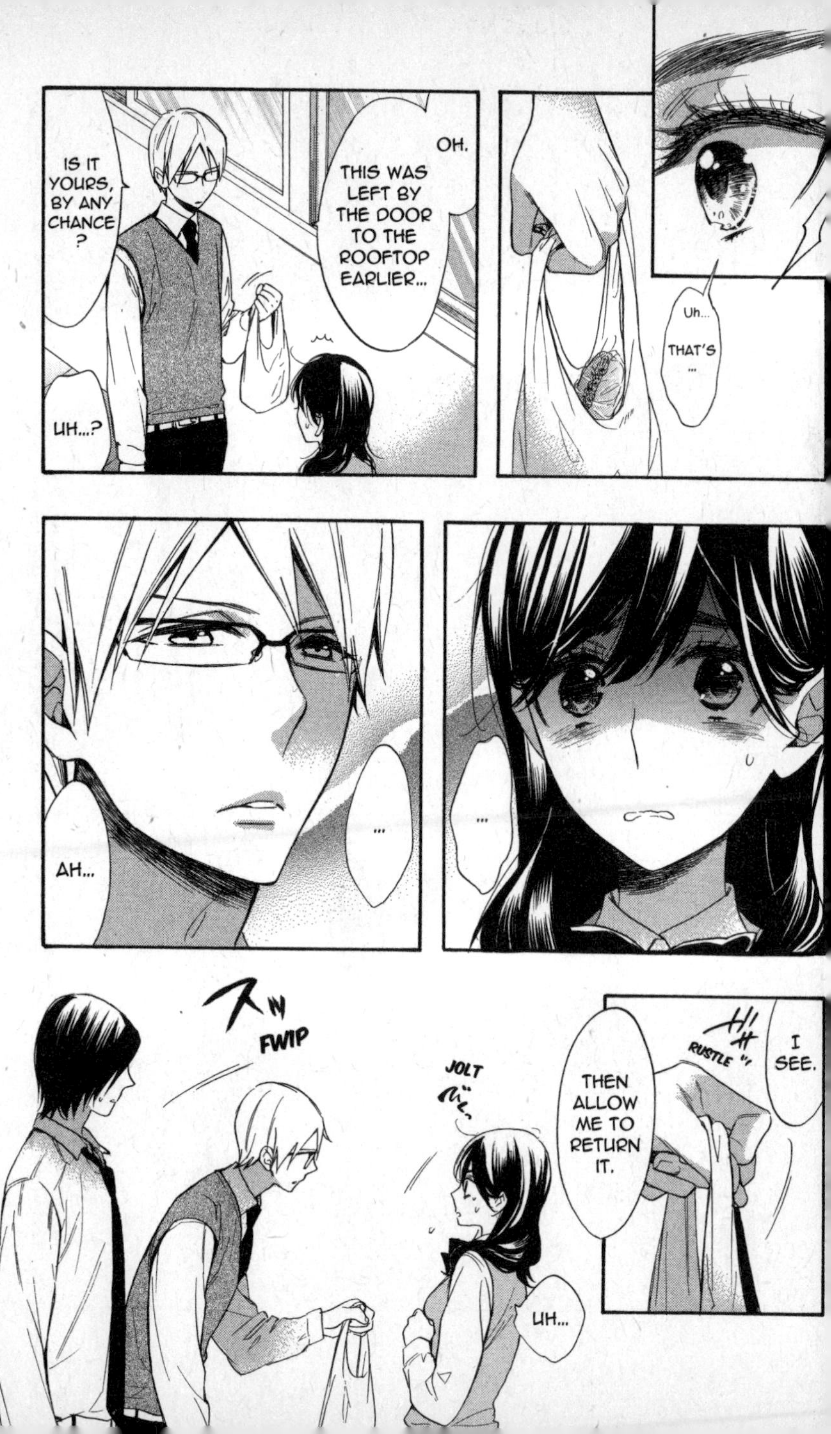
Uh...
THAT'S ...
OH.
THIS WAS LEFT BY THE DOOR TO THE ROOFTOP EARLIER...
IS IT YOURS, BY ANY CHANCE?
UH...?
...
...
AH...
I SEE.
RUSTLE
THEN ALLOW ME TO RETURN IT.
JOLT
FWIP
UH...

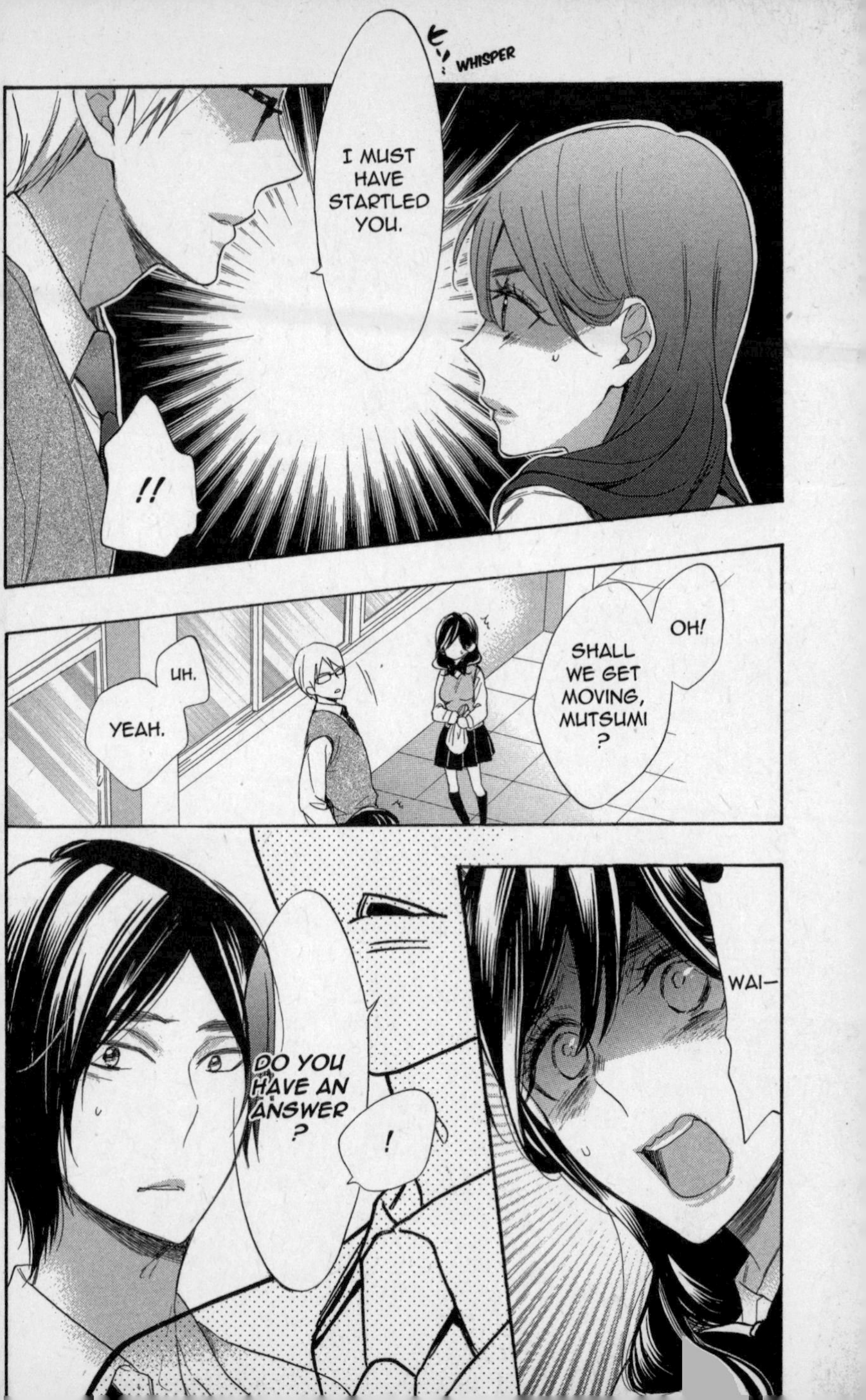
WHISPER
I MUST HAVE STARTLED YOU.
!!
OH!
SHALL WE GET MOVING, MUTSUMI?
UH.
YEAH.
WAI—
DO YOU HAVE AN ANSWER?
!

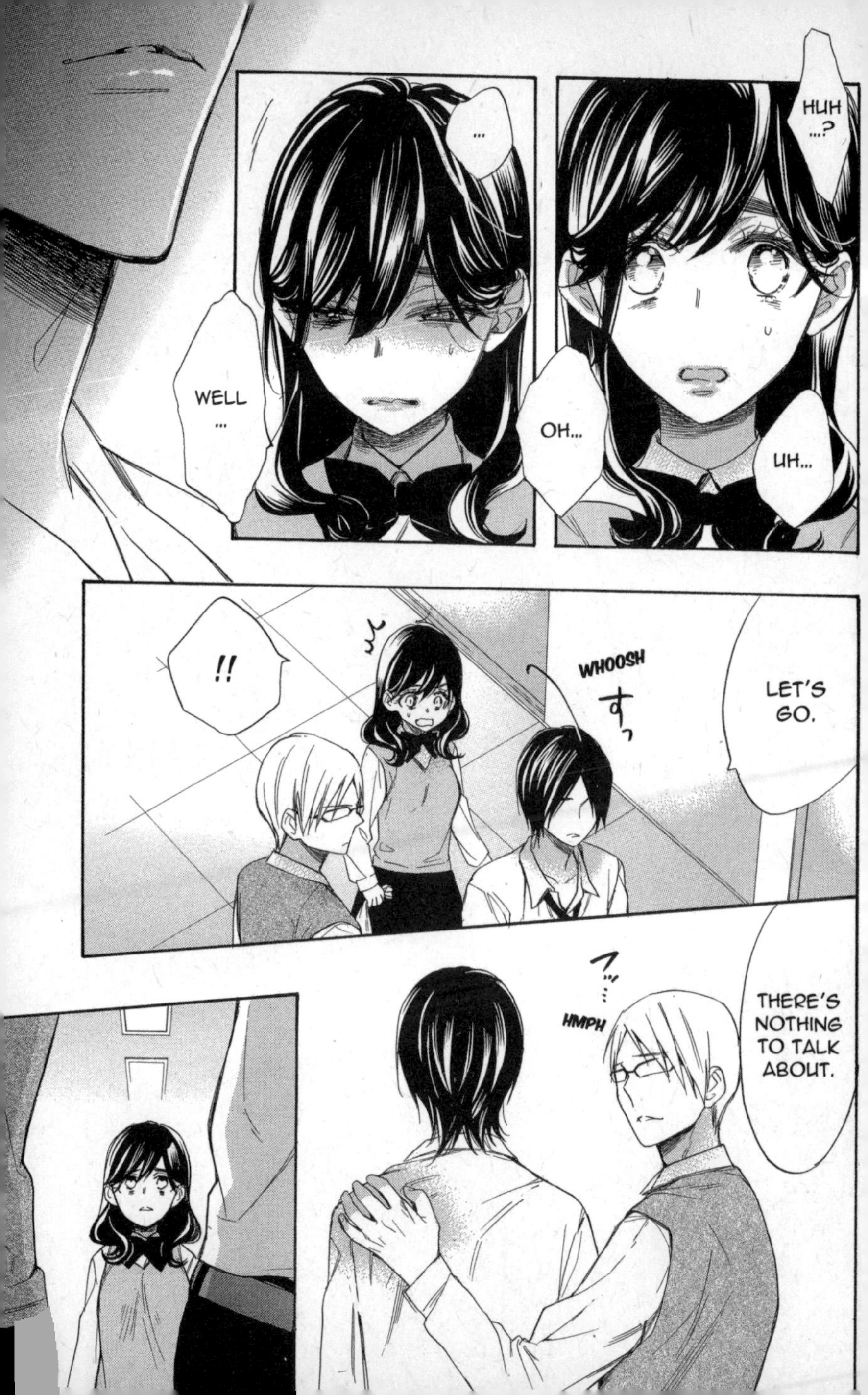
HUH ...?
UH...
OH...
...
WELL ...
LET'S GO.
WHOOSH
!!
THERE'S NOTHING TO TALK ABOUT.
HMPH

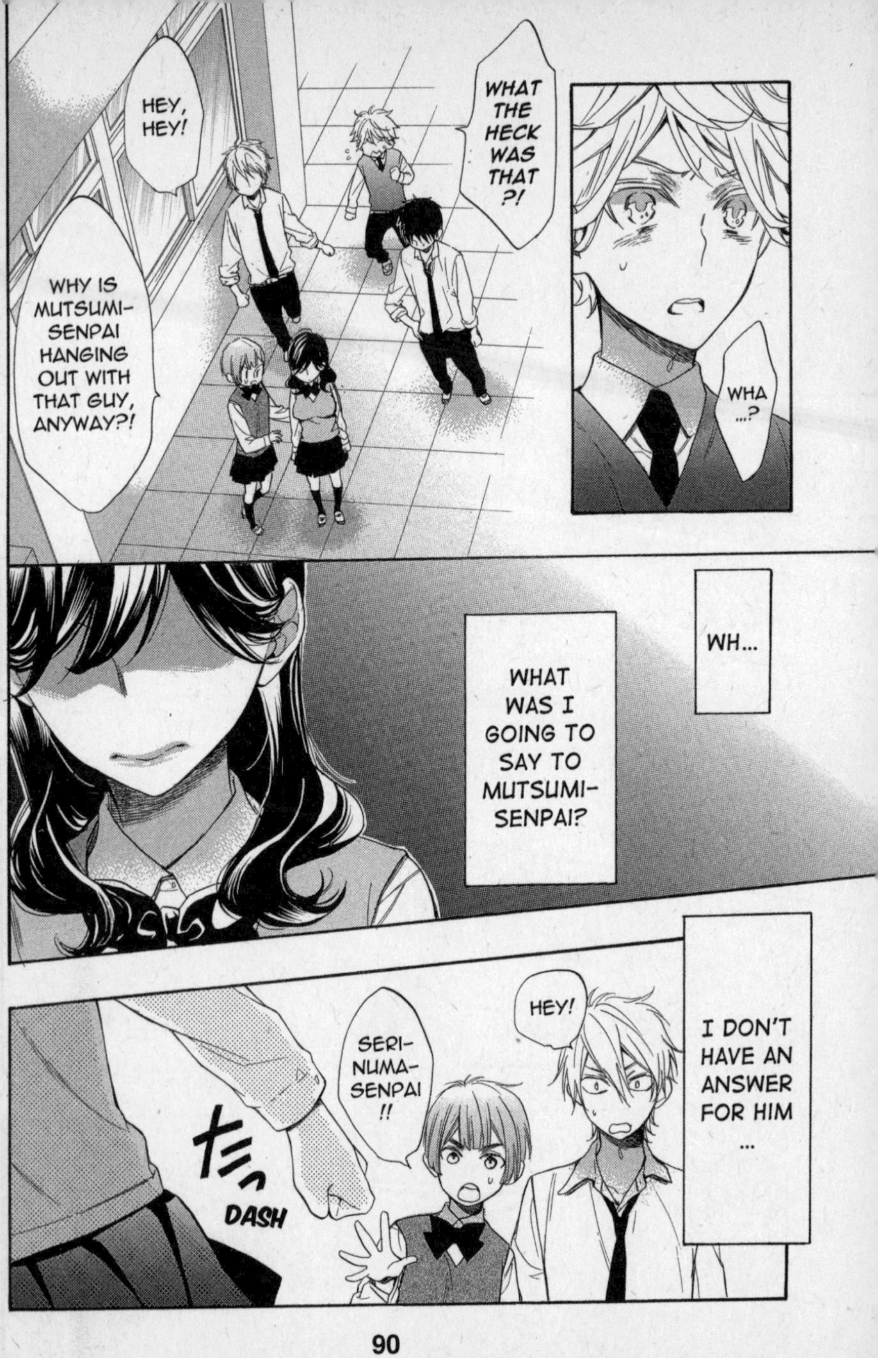
WHA ...?
WHAT THE HECK WAS THAT?!
HEY, HEY!
WHY IS MUTSUMI-SENPAI HANGING OUT WITH THAT GUY, ANYWAY?!
WH...
WHAT WAS I GOING TO SAY TO MUTSUMI-SENPAI?
I DON'T HAVE AN ANSWER FOR HIM ...
HEY!
SERI-NUMA-SENPAI !!
DASH

I HAVE NO RIGHT...

And so...

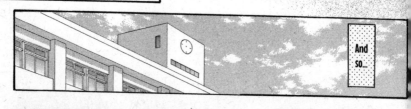

Day 3

WITHER
WITHER
WITHER

Day 2

WITHER

Day 1

BOOM

JOLT

JOLT

UNNN- NNGH!

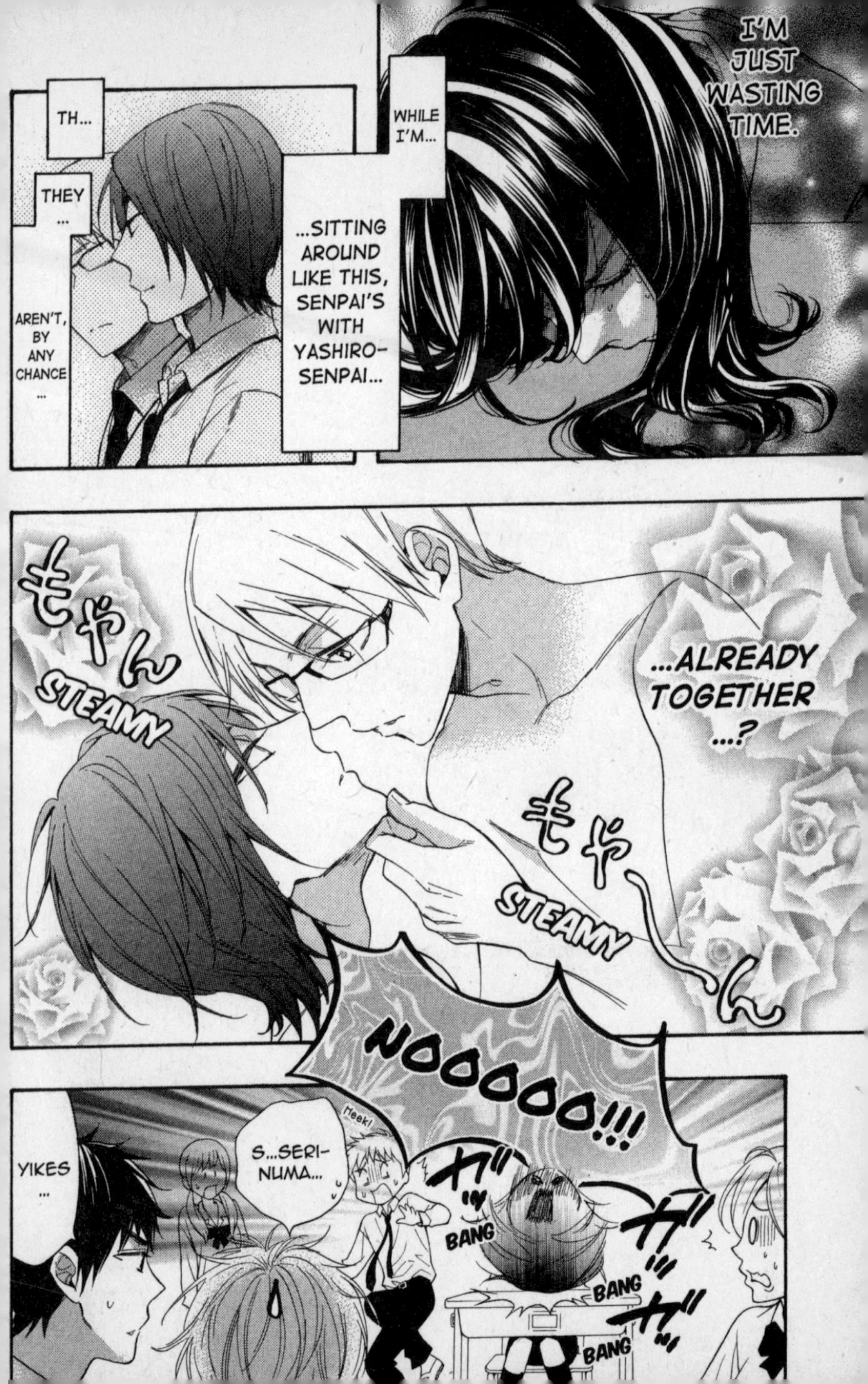
I'M JUST WASTING TIME.
WHILE I'M...
...SITTING AROUND LIKE THIS, SENPAI'S WITH YASHIRO-SENPAI...
TH...
THEY...
AREN'T, BY ANY CHANCE...
...ALREADY TOGETHER...?
もやん
STEAMY
もや～ん
STEAMY
NOOOOOO!!!
BANG
BANG
BANG
Meek!
S...SERI-NUMA...
YIKES...

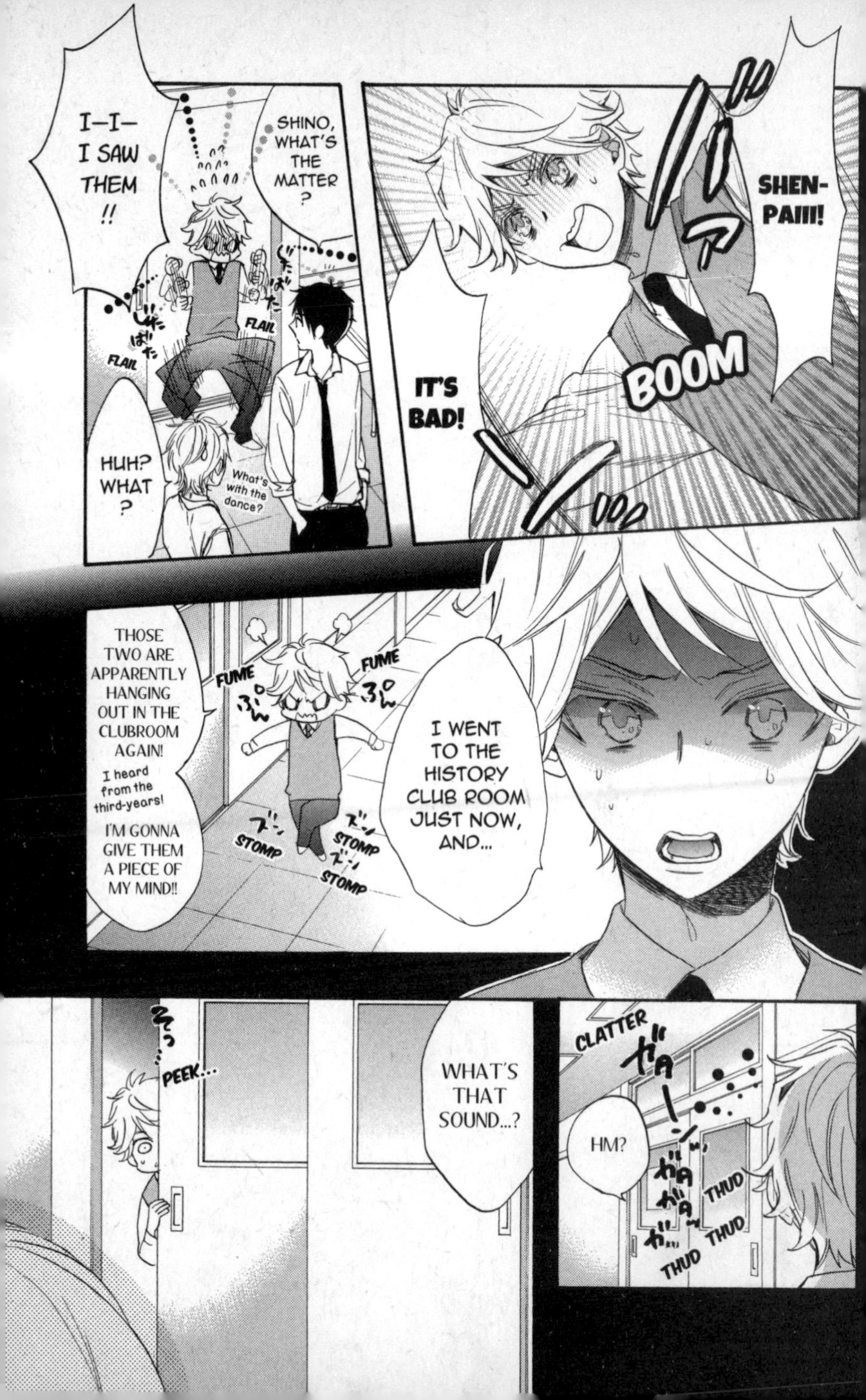
SHEN-PAIII!
BOOM
IT'S BAD!
SHINO, WHAT'S THE MATTER?
I—I— I SAW THEM!!
FLAIL
FLAIL
HUH? WHAT?
What's with the dance?
I WENT TO THE HISTORY CLUB ROOM JUST NOW, AND...
FUME
FUME
THOSE TWO ARE APPARENTLY HANGING OUT IN THE CLUBROOM AGAIN!
I heard from the third-years!
I'M GONNA GIVE THEM A PIECE OF MY MIND!!
STOMP
STOMP
STOMP
CLATTER
HM?
THUD
THUD
THUD
WHAT'S THAT SOUND...?
PEEK...

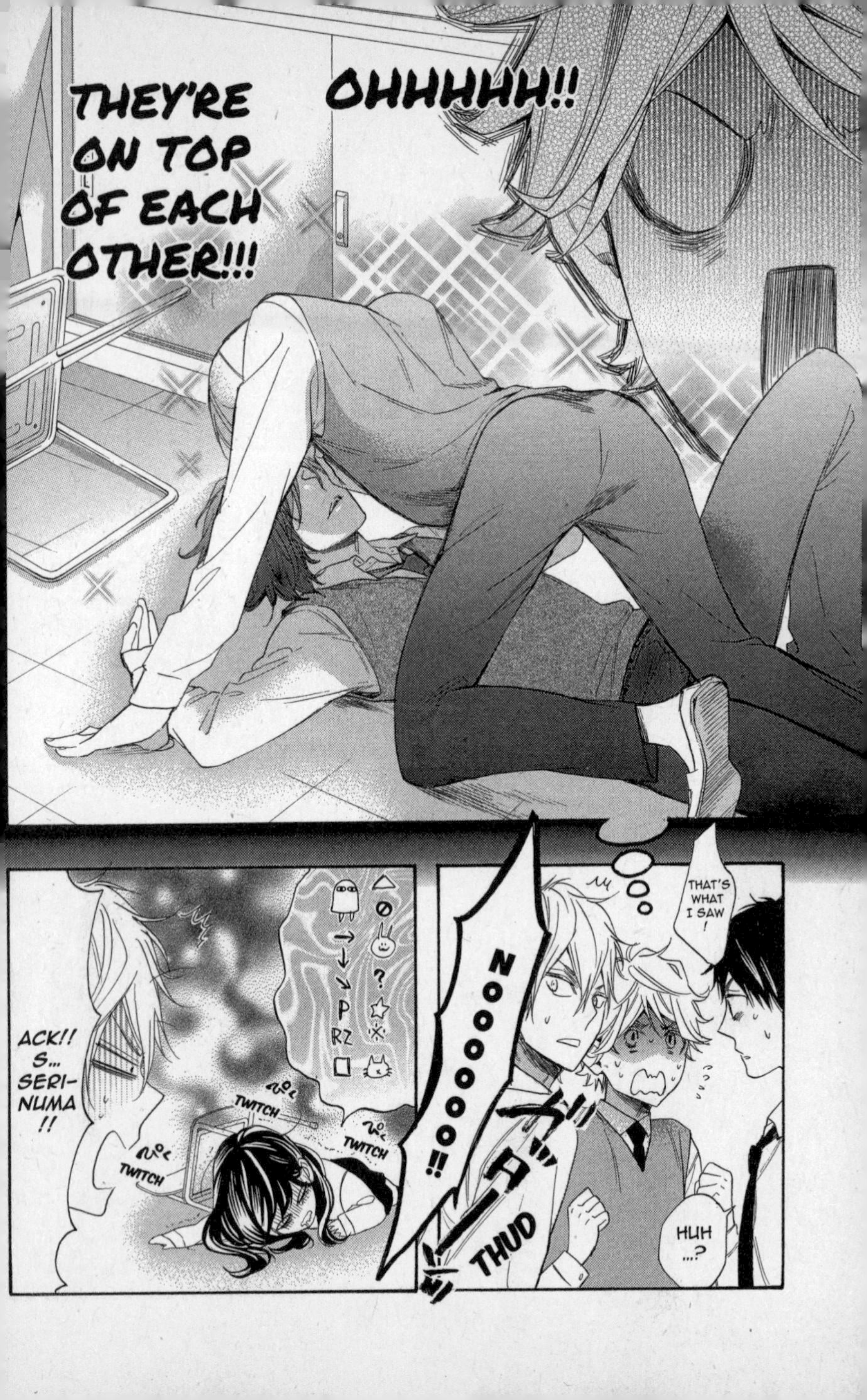
OHHHHHH!!
THEY'RE ON TOP OF EACH OTHER!!!
THAT'S WHAT I SAW!
NOOOOOOOO!!
HUH ...?
THUD
ACK!! S... SERI-NUMA!!
TWITCH
TWITCH
TWITCH

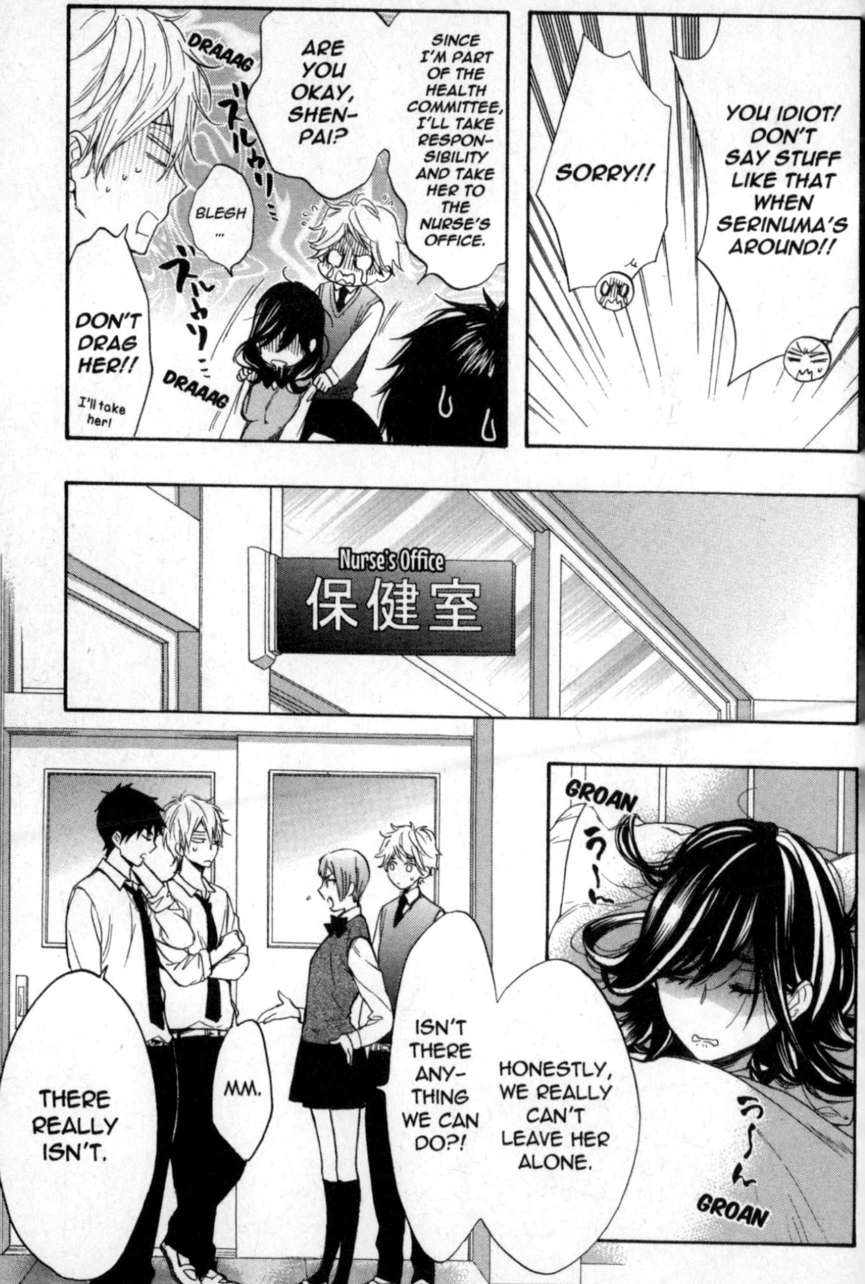
YOU IDIOT! DON'T SAY STUFF LIKE THAT WHEN SERINUMA'S AROUND!!
SORRY!!
SINCE I'M PART OF THE HEALTH COMMITTEE, I'LL TAKE RESPON-SIBILITY AND TAKE HER TO THE NURSE'S OFFICE.
ARE YOU OKAY, SHEN-PAI?
DRAAAG
BLEGH ...
DRAAAG
DON'T DRAG HER!!
I'll take her!
Nurse's Office
保健室
GROAN
GROAN
HONESTLY, WE REALLY CAN'T LEAVE HER ALONE.
ISN'T THERE ANY-THING WE CAN DO?!
MM.
THERE REALLY ISN'T.

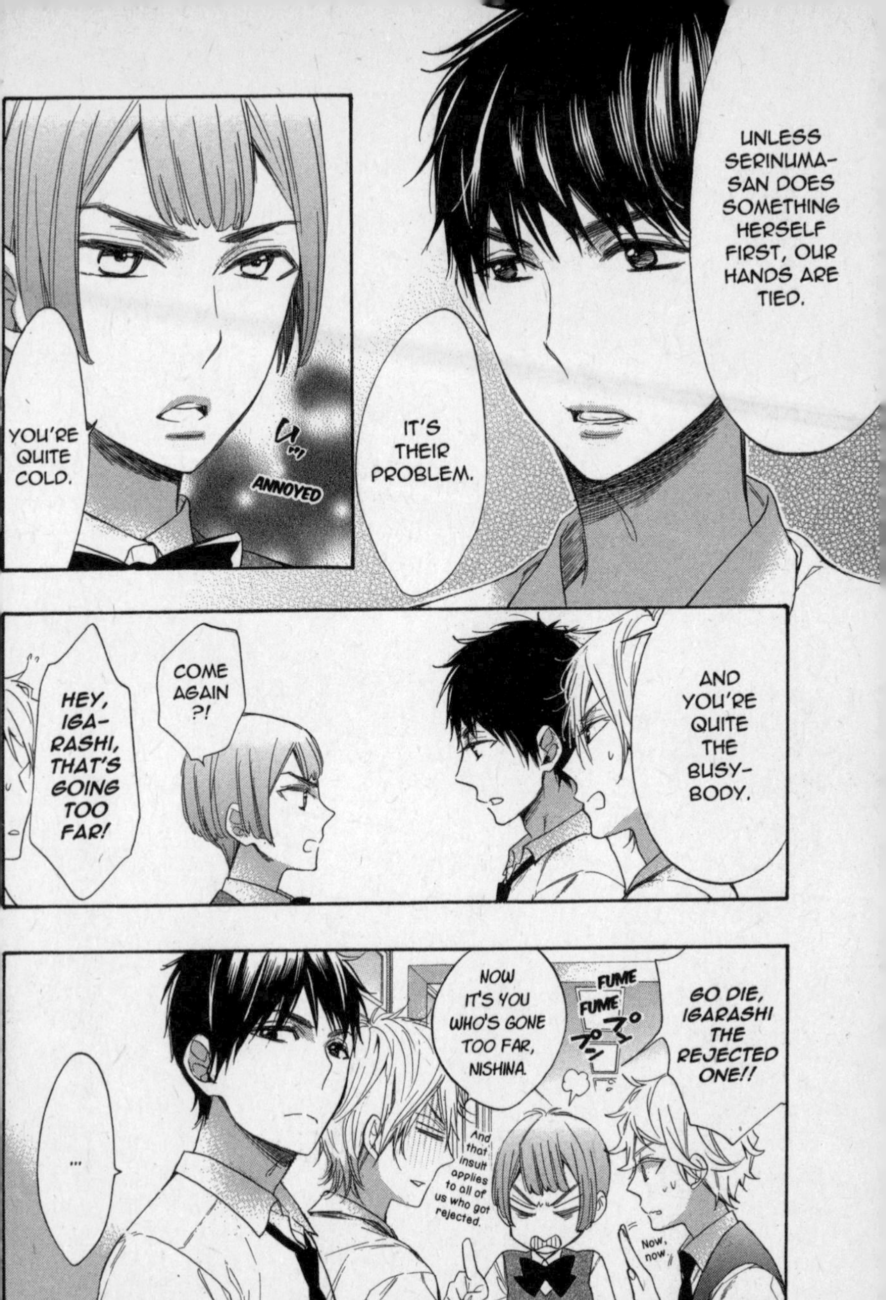
UNLESS SERINUMA-SAN DOES SOMETHING HERSELF FIRST, OUR HANDS ARE TIED.
IT'S THEIR PROBLEM.
ANNOYED
YOU'RE QUITE COLD.
AND YOU'RE QUITE THE BUSY-BODY.
COME AGAIN?!
HEY, IGA-RASHI, THAT'S GOING TOO FAR!
GO DIE, IGARASHI THE REJECTED ONE!!
FUME FUME
NOW IT'S YOU WHO'S GONE TOO FAR, NISHINA.
Now, now.
And that insult applies to all of us who got rejected.
...

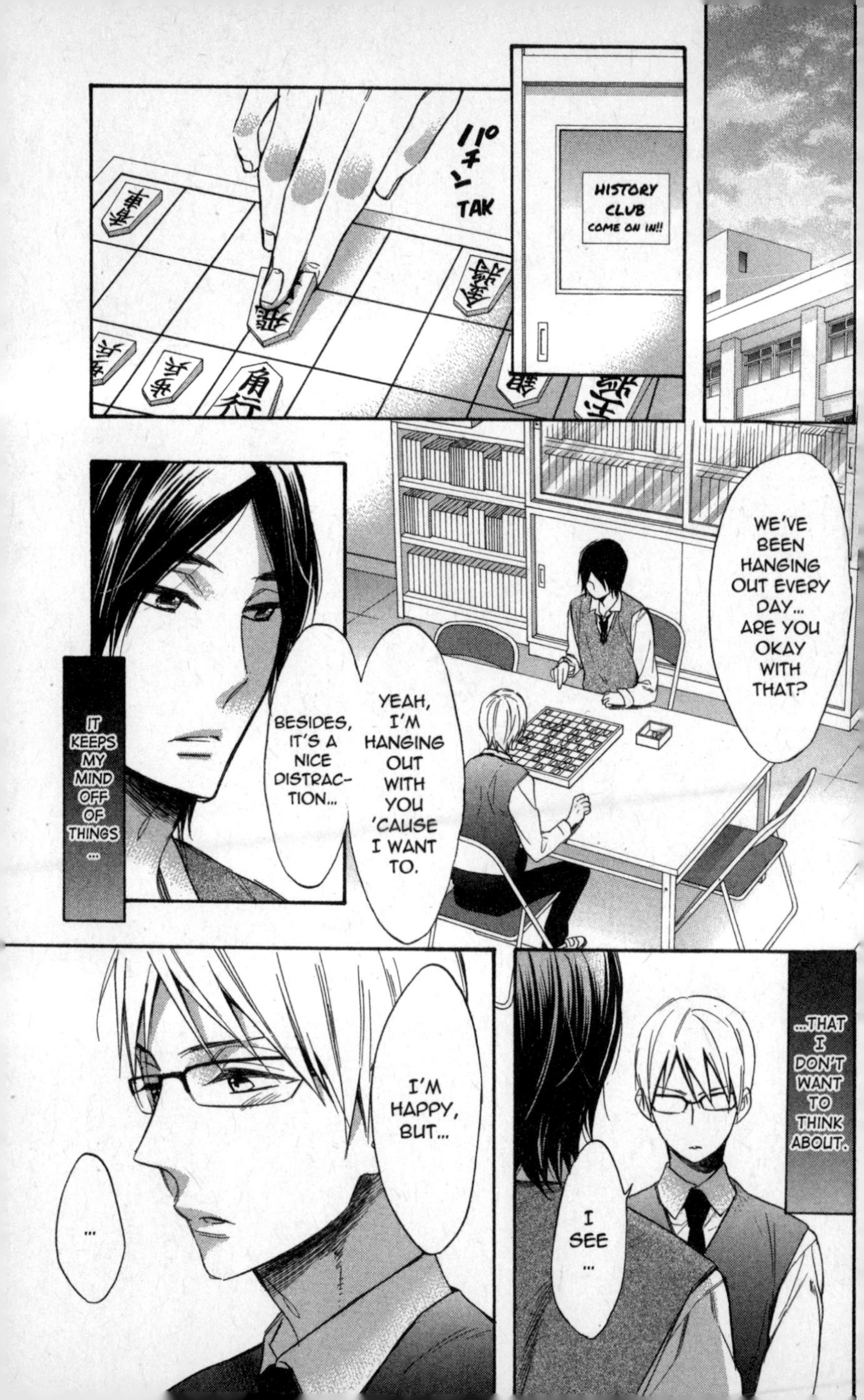
HISTORY CLUB
COME ON IN!!
パチン
TAK
WE'VE BEEN HANGING OUT EVERY DAY... ARE YOU OKAY WITH THAT?
YEAH, I'M HANGING OUT WITH YOU 'CAUSE I WANT TO.
BESIDES, IT'S A NICE DISTRACTION...
IT KEEPS MY MIND OFF OF THINGS...
...THAT I DON'T WANT TO THINK ABOUT.
I SEE...
I'M HAPPY, BUT...
...

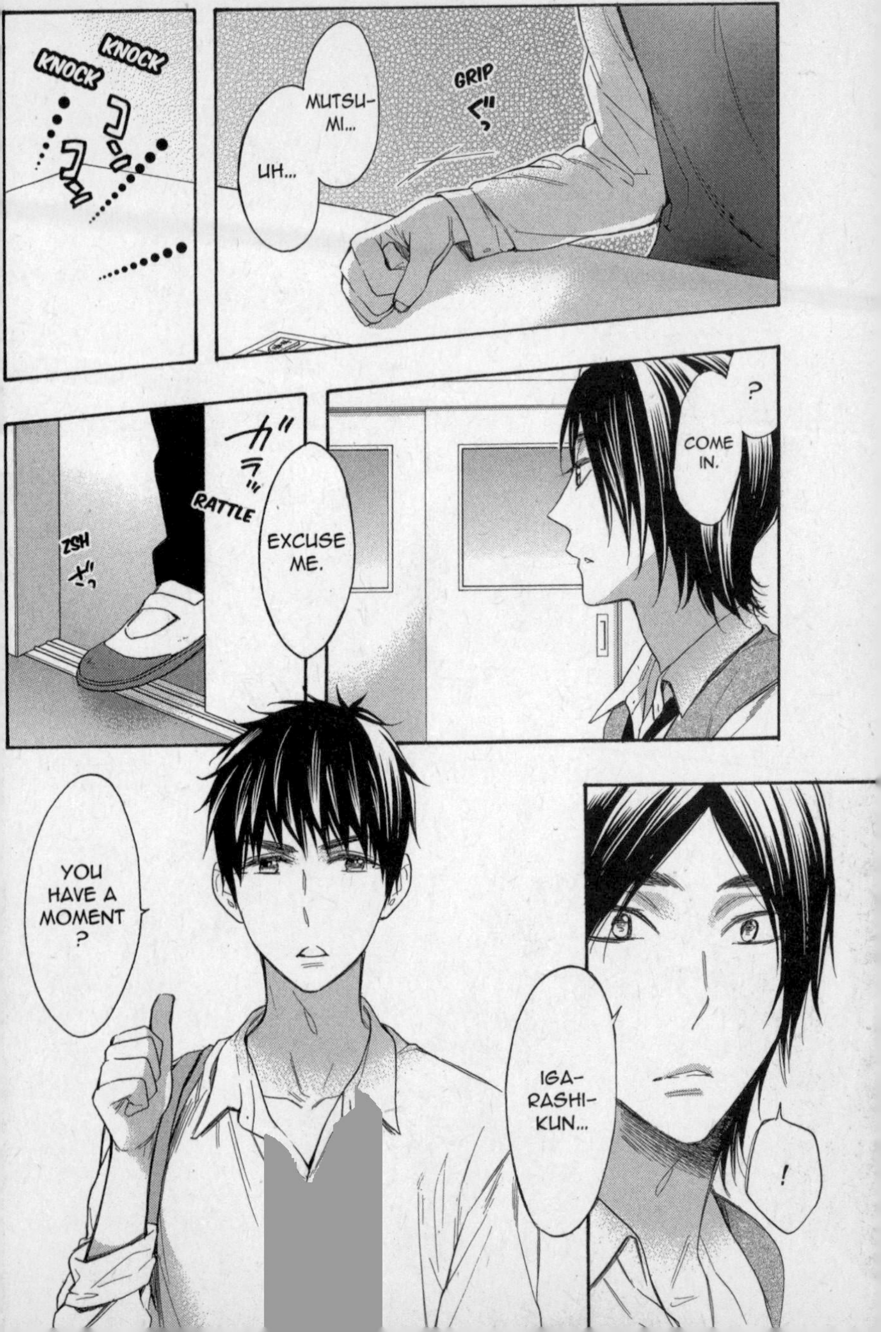
MUTSUMI...
UH...
GRIP
ぐっ
KNOCK
KNOCK
コンコン
?
COME IN.
ガラッ
RATTLE
EXCUSE ME.
ZSH
ざっ
...!
IGARASHI-KUN...
YOU HAVE A MOMENT?

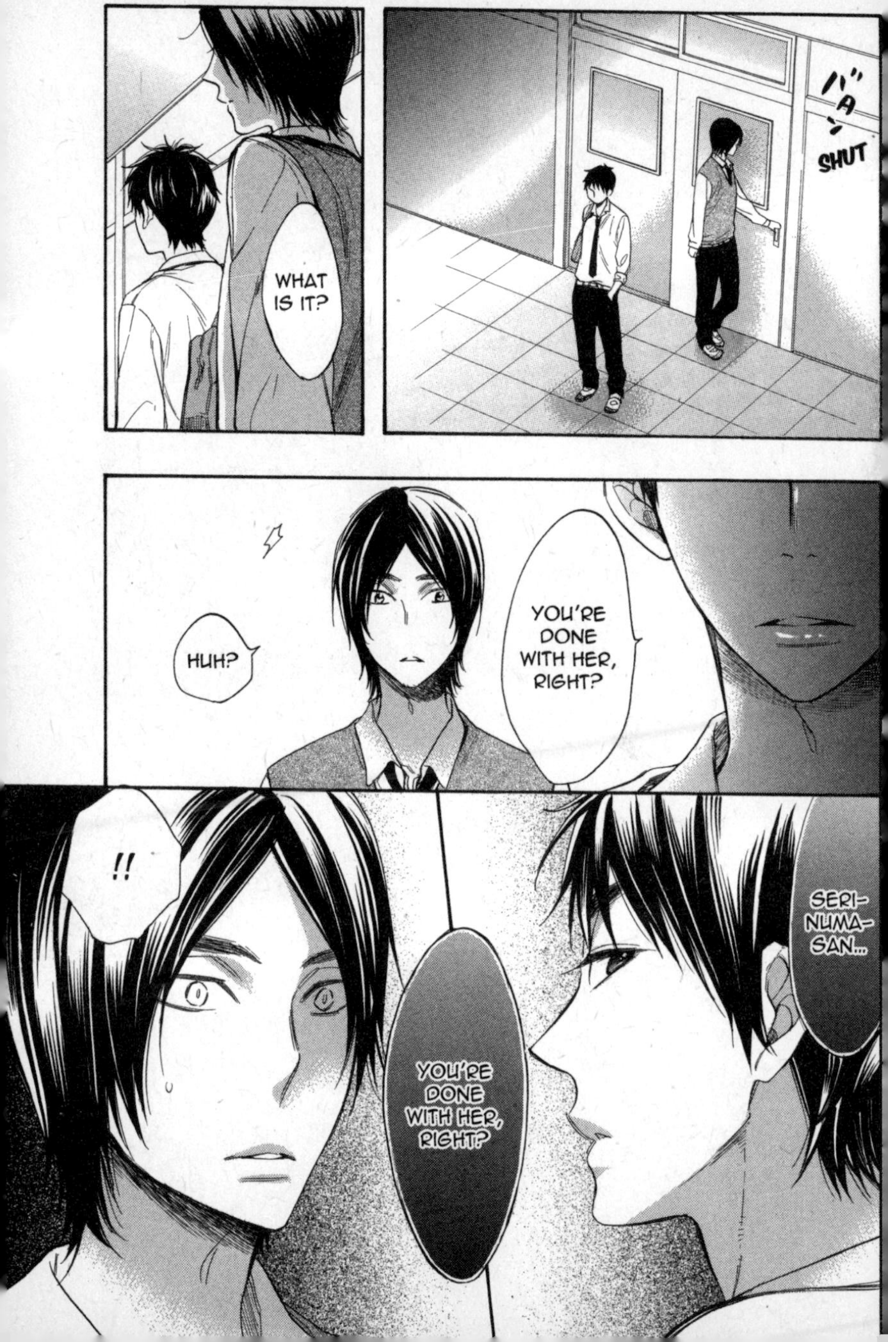

バン
SHUT
WHAT IS IT?
YOU'RE DONE WITH HER, RIGHT?
HUH?
SERI-NUMA-SAN...
YOU'RE DONE WITH HER, RIGHT?
!!

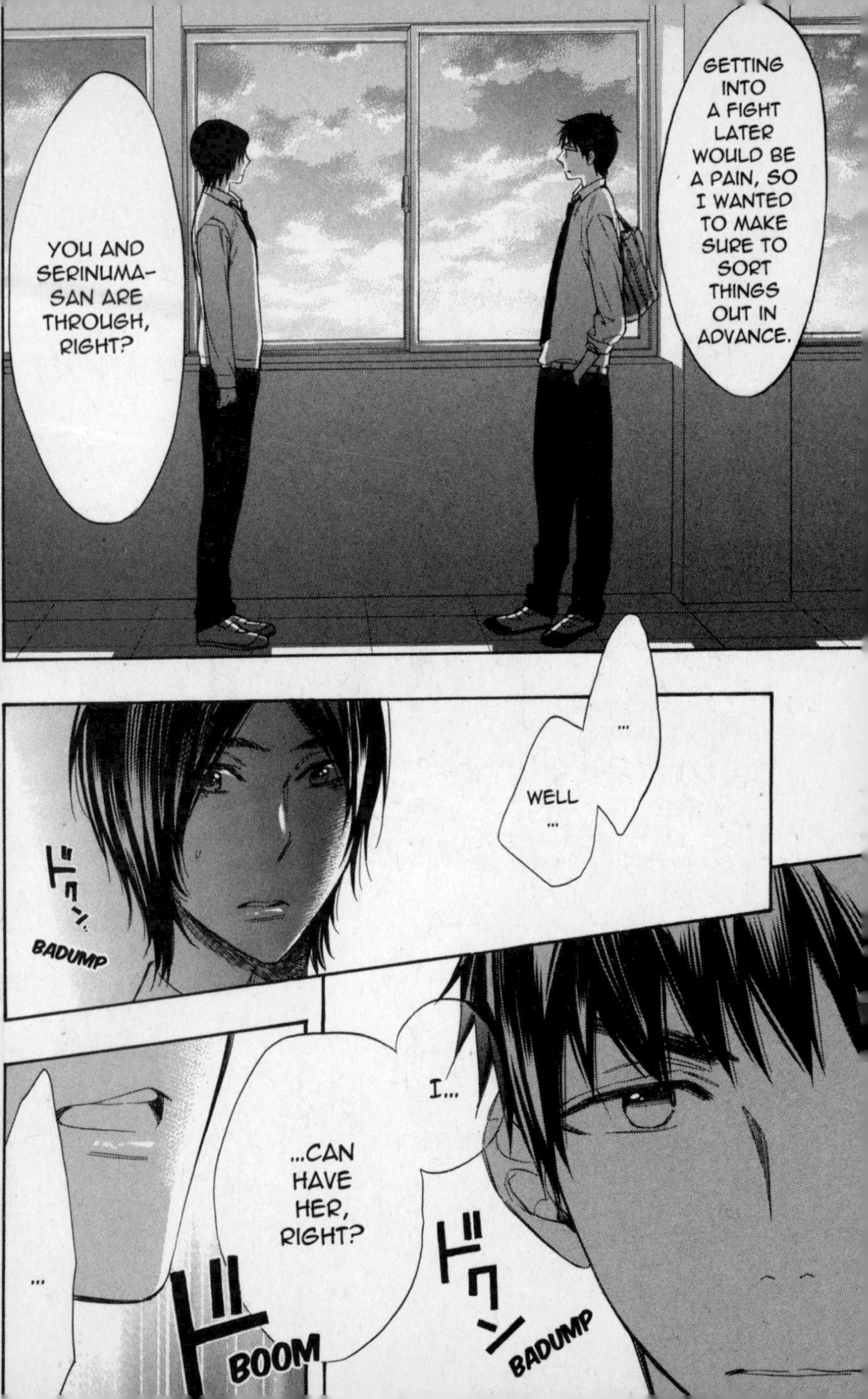
GETTING INTO A FIGHT LATER WOULD BE A PAIN, SO I WANTED TO MAKE SURE TO SORT THINGS OUT IN ADVANCE.
YOU AND SERINUMA-SAN ARE THROUGH, RIGHT?
... WELL ...
BADUMP
I...
...CAN HAVE HER, RIGHT?
BADUMP
...
BOOM

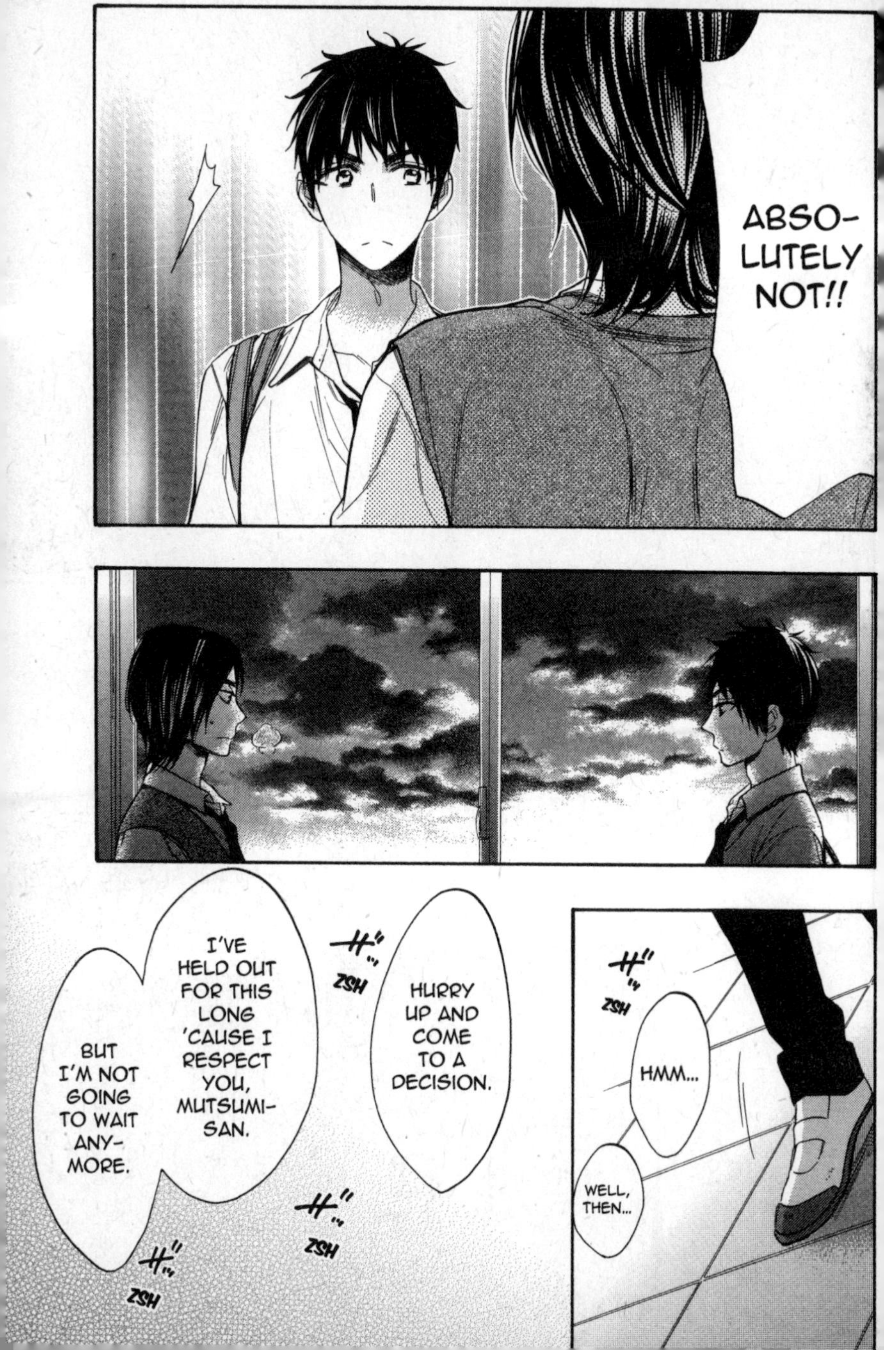
ABSO-LUTELY NOT!!
ZSH
HMM...
WELL, THEN...
ZSH
HURRY UP AND COME TO A DECISION.
I'VE HELD OUT FOR THIS LONG 'CAUSE I RESPECT YOU, MUTSUMI-SAN.
BUT I'M NOT GOING TO WAIT ANY-MORE.
ZSH
ZSH

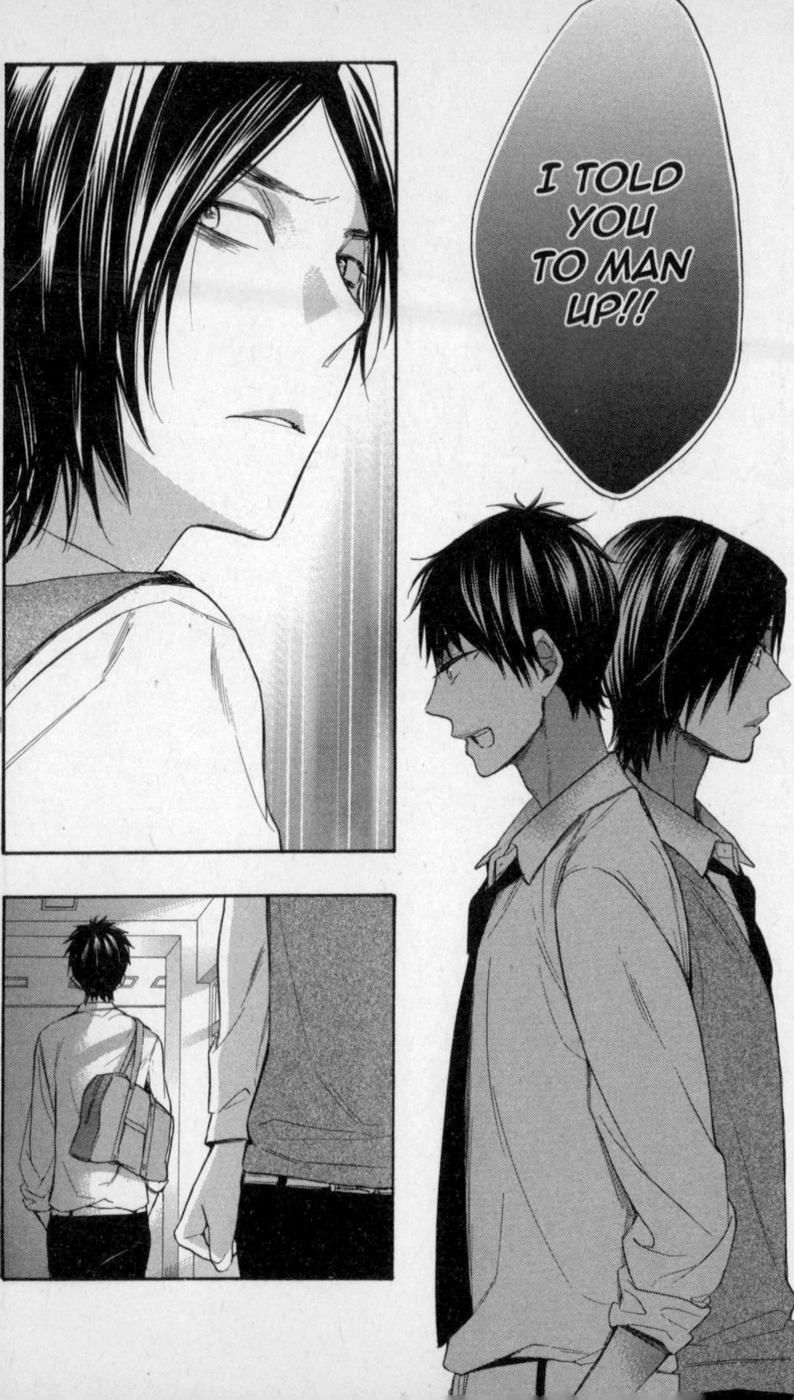
I TOLD YOU TO MAN UP!!

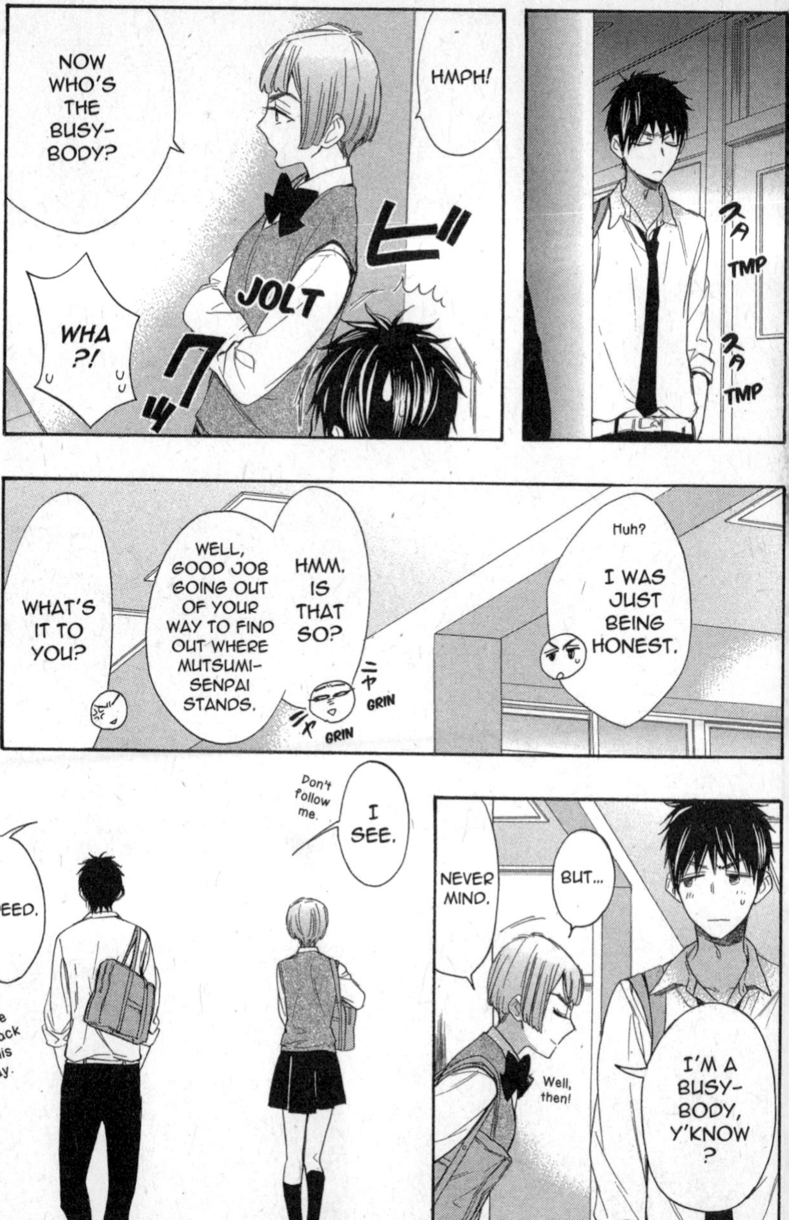
TMP
TMP
HMPH!
NOW WHO'S THE BUSY-BODY?
JOLT
WHA?!
Huh?
I WAS JUST BEING HONEST.
HMM. IS THAT SO?
GRIN
WELL, GOOD JOB GOING OUT OF YOUR WAY TO FIND OUT WHERE MUTSUMI-SENPAI STANDS.
GRIN
WHAT'S IT TO YOU?
I'M A BUSY-BODY, Y'KNOW?
BUT...
NEVER MIND.
Well, then!
I SEE.
Don't follow me.
INDEED.
Huh? But the shoe rack is this way.

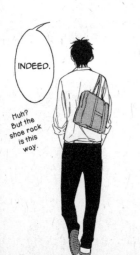

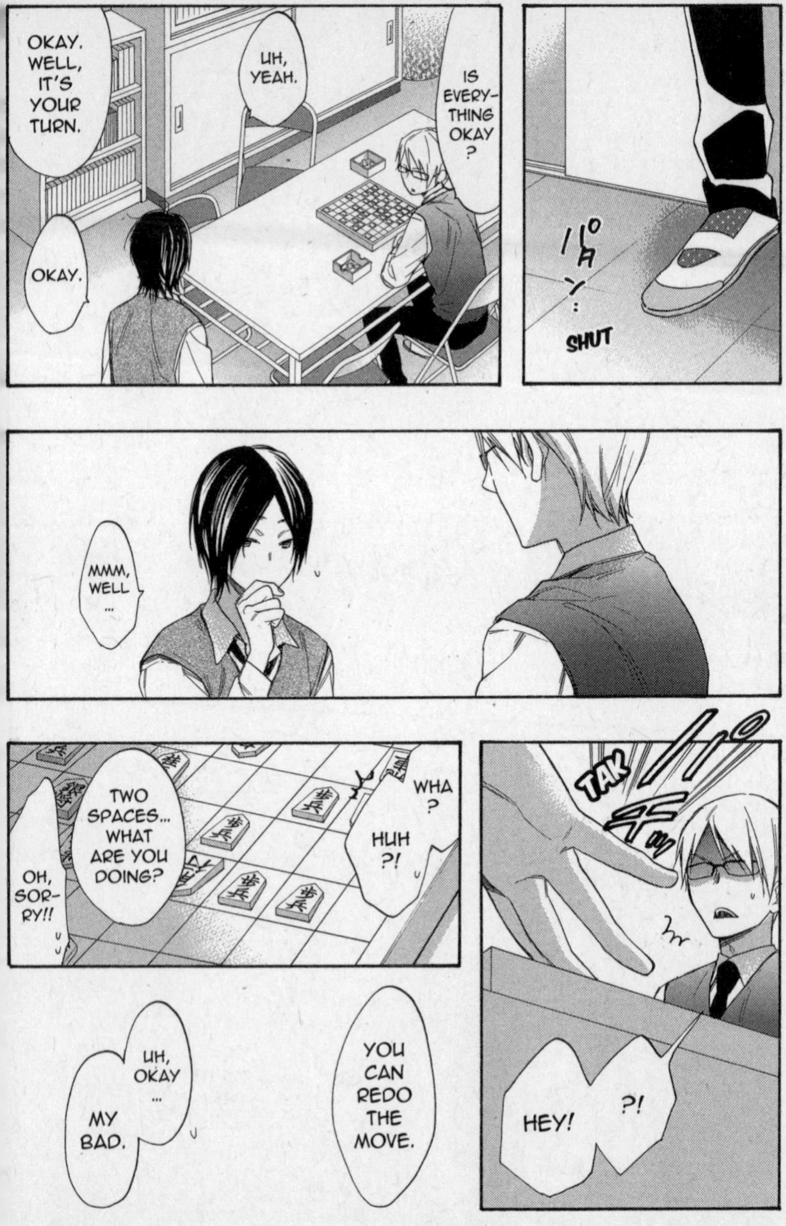
SHUT
IS EVERY-THING OKAY?
UH, YEAH.
OKAY. WELL, IT'S YOUR TURN.
OKAY.
MMM, WELL...
TAK
HEY!
?!
WHA? HUH?!
TWO SPACES... WHAT ARE YOU DOING?
OH, SOR-RY!!
YOU CAN REDO THE MOVE.
UH, OKAY... MY BAD.

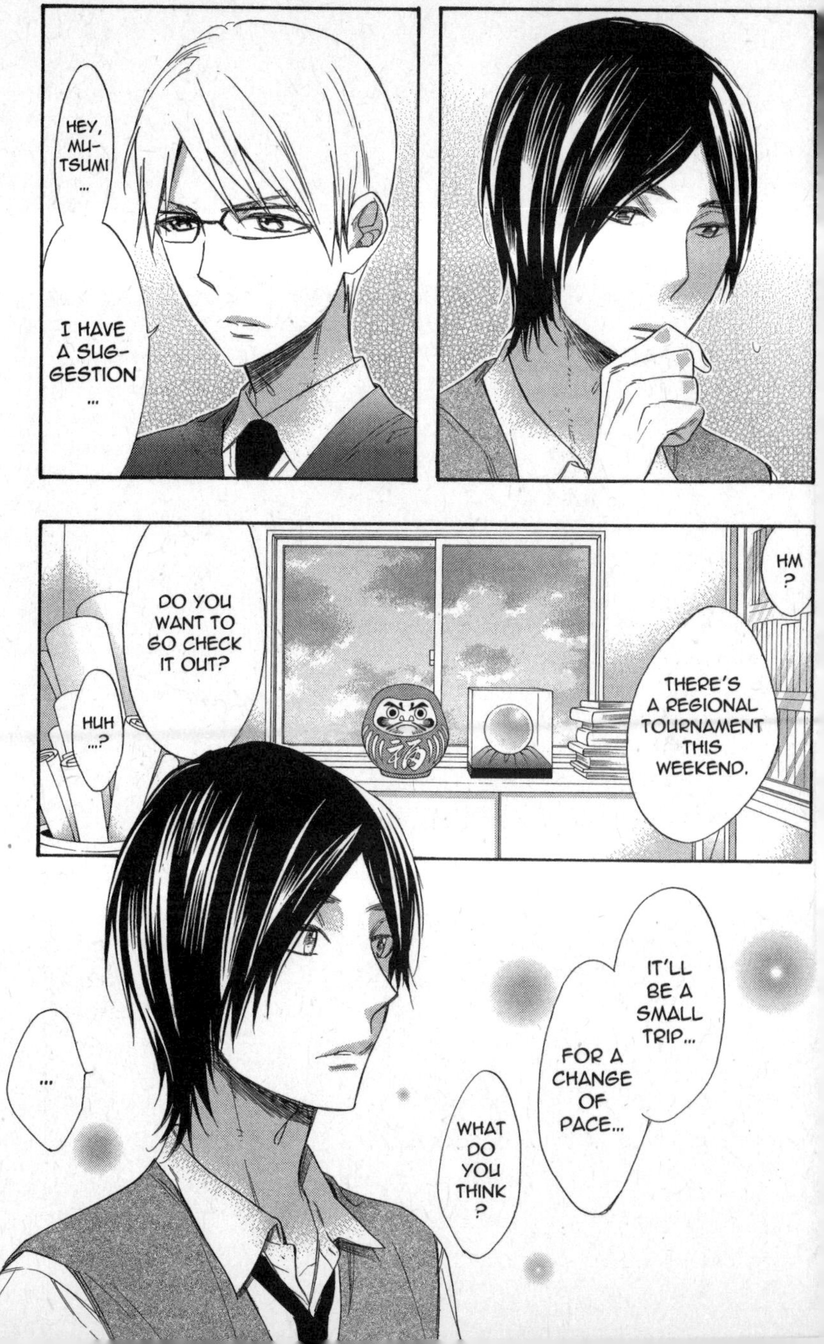
HEY, MU-TSUMI ...
I HAVE A SUG-GESTION ...
HM?
THERE'S A REGIONAL TOURNAMENT THIS WEEKEND.
DO YOU WANT TO GO CHECK IT OUT?
HUH ...?
IT'LL BE A SMALL TRIP...
FOR A CHANGE OF PACE...
WHAT DO YOU THINK?
...

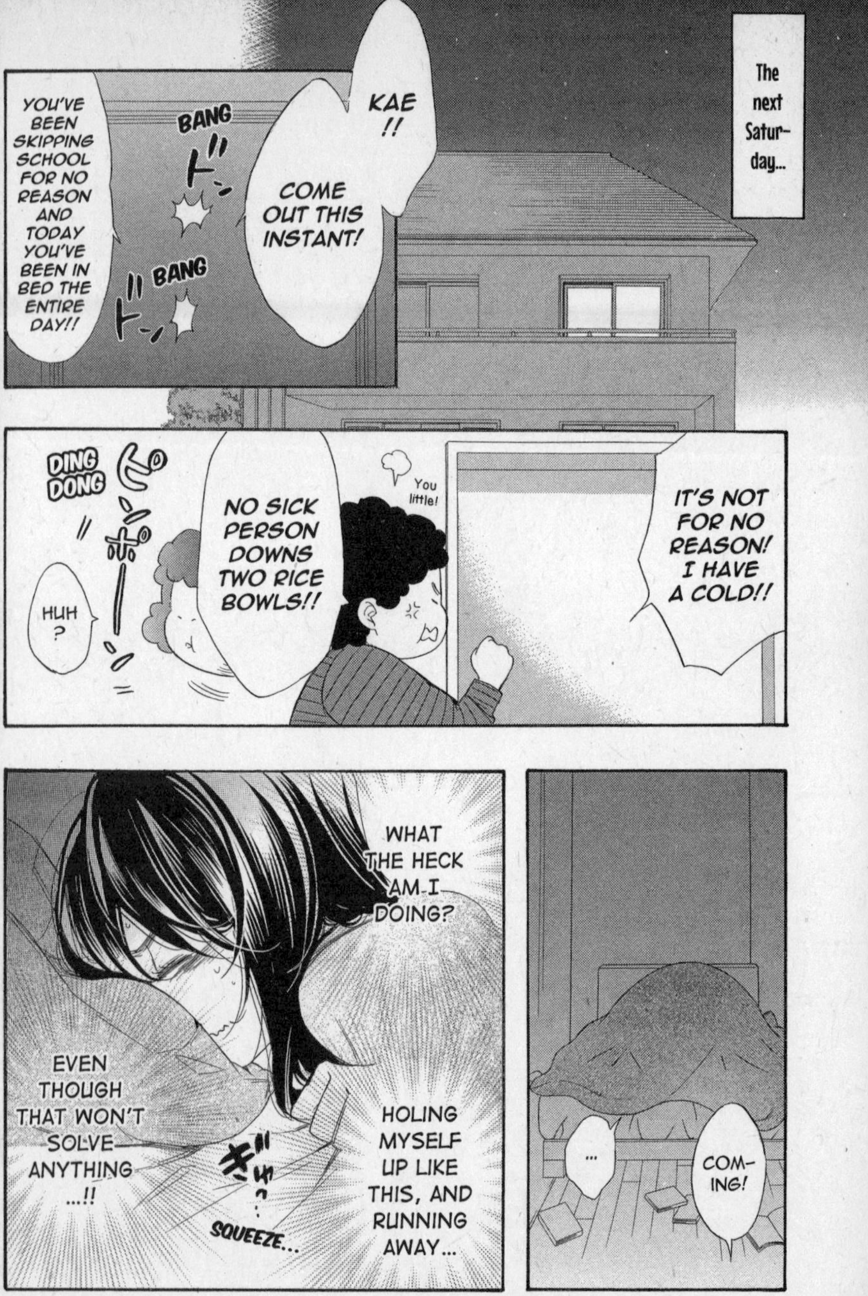
The next Saturday...
KAE!!
COME OUT THIS INSTANT!
BANG
BANG
YOU'VE BEEN SKIPPING SCHOOL FOR NO REASON AND TODAY YOU'VE BEEN IN BED THE ENTIRE DAY!!
IT'S NOT FOR NO REASON! I HAVE A COLD!!
You little!
NO SICK PERSON DOWNS TWO RICE BOWLS!!
DING DONG
HUH?
COMING!
...
WHAT THE HECK AM I DOING?
HOLING MYSELF UP LIKE THIS, AND RUNNING AWAY...
SQUEEZE...
EVEN THOUGH THAT WON'T SOLVE ANYTHING...!!

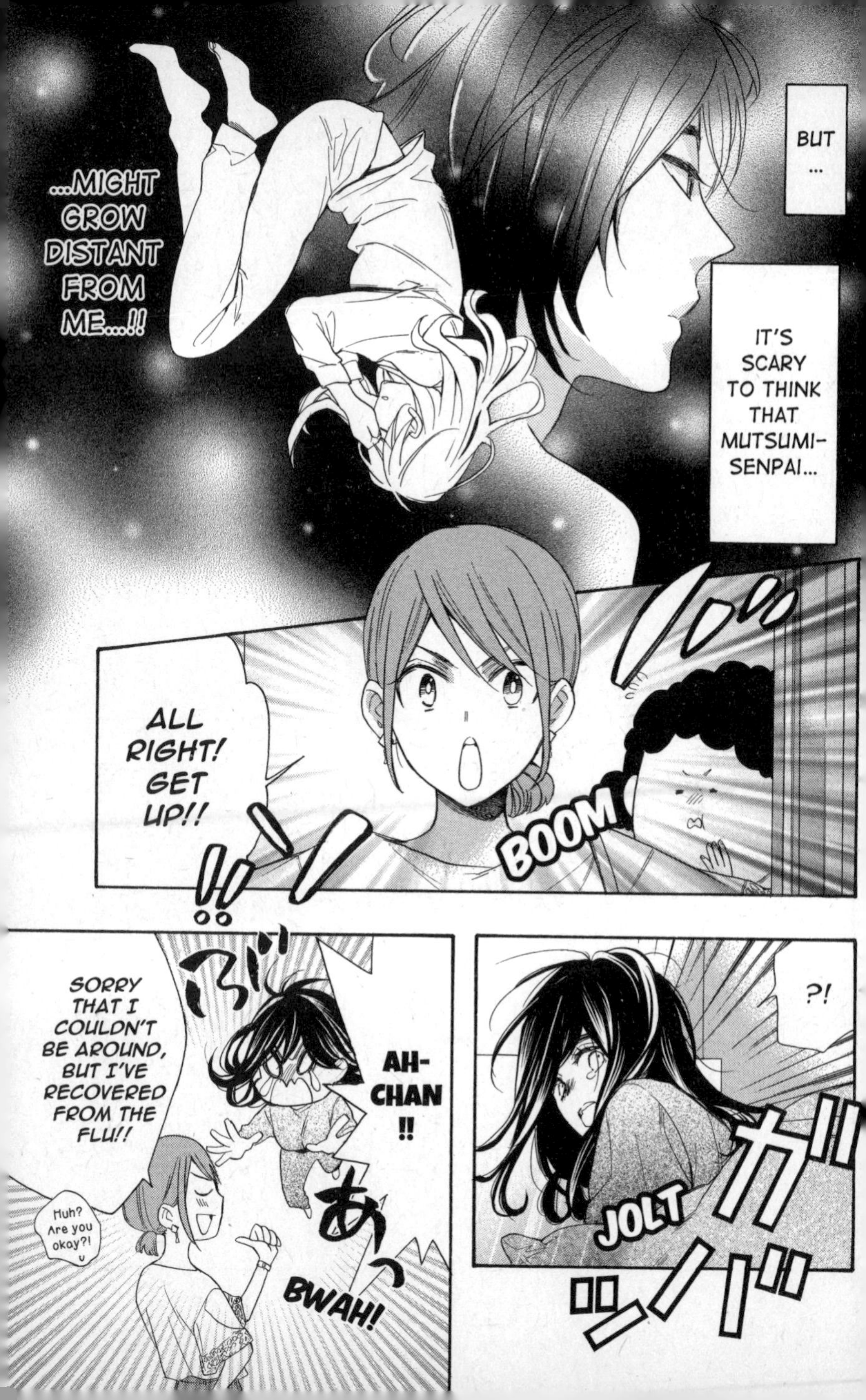
BUT ...
IT'S SCARY TO THINK THAT MUTSUMI-SENPAI...
...MIGHT GROW DISTANT FROM ME...!!
ALL RIGHT! GET UP!!
BOOM
!!
?!
JOLT
AH-CHAN!!
SORRY THAT I COULDN'T BE AROUND, BUT I'VE RECOVERED FROM THE FLU!!
BWAH!
Huh? Are you okay?!

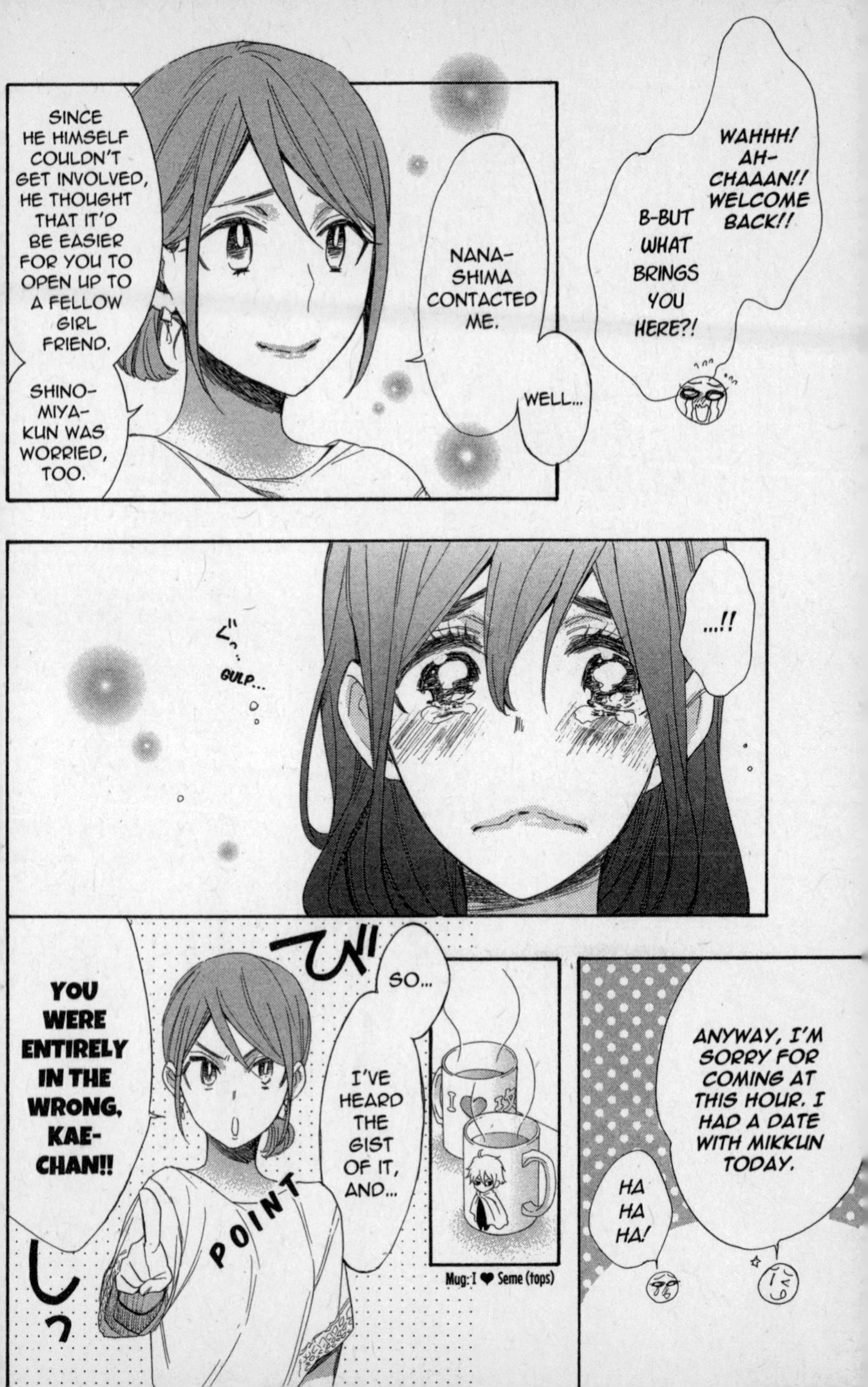
WAHHH! AH-CHAAAN!! WELCOME BACK!!
B-BUT WHAT BRINGS YOU HERE?!
WELL...
NANA-SHIMA CONTACTED ME.
SINCE HE HIMSELF COULDN'T GET INVOLVED, HE THOUGHT THAT IT'D BE EASIER FOR YOU TO OPEN UP TO A FELLOW GIRL FRIEND.
SHINO-MIYA-KUN WAS WORRIED, TOO.
...!!
GULP...
ANYWAY, I'M SORRY FOR COMING AT THIS HOUR. I HAD A DATE WITH MIKKUN TODAY.
HA HA HA!
Mug: I ❤ Seme (tops)
SO...
I'VE HEARD THE GIST OF IT, AND...
YOU WERE ENTIRELY IN THE WRONG, KAE-CHAN!!
POINT

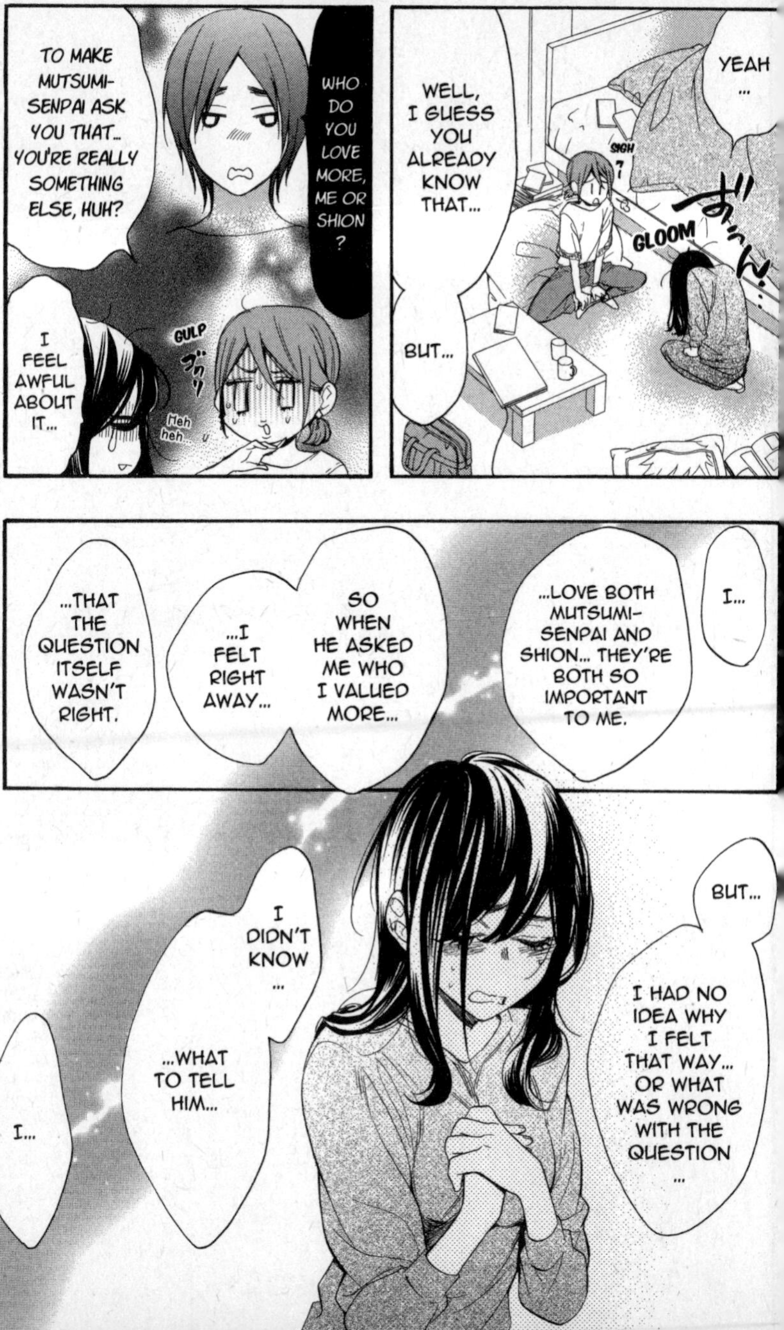
YEAH...
SIGH
GLOOM
WELL, I GUESS YOU ALREADY KNOW THAT...
BUT...
WHO DO YOU LOVE MORE, ME OR SHION?
TO MAKE MUTSUMI-SENPAI ASK YOU THAT... YOU'RE REALLY SOMETHING ELSE, HUH?
GULP
Heh heh...
I FEEL AWFUL ABOUT IT...
I...
...LOVE BOTH MUTSUMI-SENPAI AND SHION... THEY'RE BOTH SO IMPORTANT TO ME.
SO WHEN HE ASKED ME WHO I VALUED MORE...
...I FELT RIGHT AWAY...
...THAT THE QUESTION ITSELF WASN'T RIGHT.
BUT...
I HAD NO IDEA WHY I FELT THAT WAY... OR WHAT WAS WRONG WITH THE QUESTION...
I DIDN'T KNOW...
...WHAT TO TELL HIM...
I...

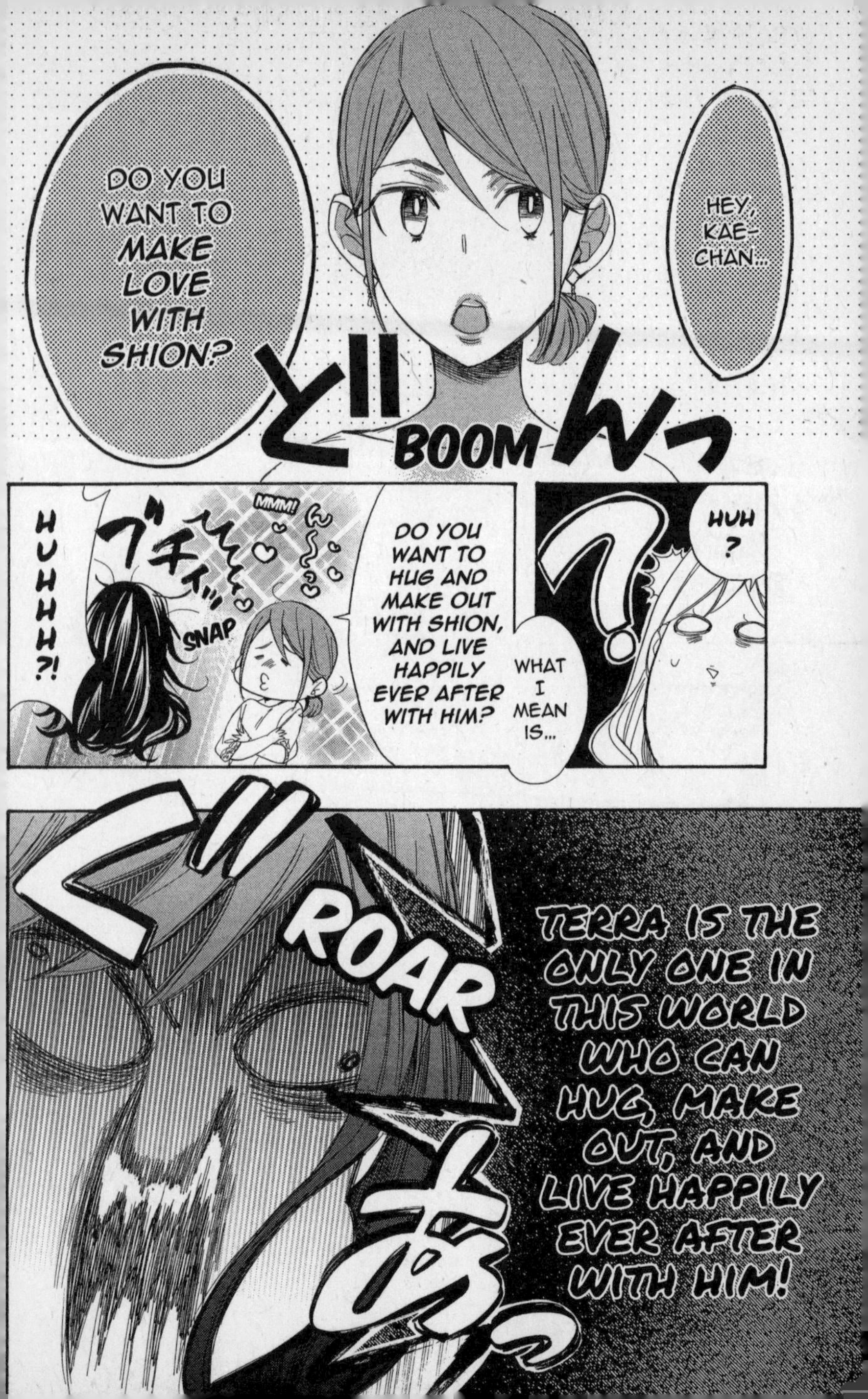
HEY, KAE-CHAN...
DO YOU WANT TO MAKE LOVE WITH SHION?
BOOM
HUH?
WHAT I MEAN IS...
DO YOU WANT TO HUG AND MAKE OUT WITH SHION, AND LIVE HAPPILY EVER AFTER WITH HIM?
MMM!
SNAP
HUHHHH?!
ROAR
TERRA IS THE ONLY ONE IN THIS WORLD WHO CAN HUG, MAKE OUT, AND LIVE HAPPILY EVER AFTER WITH HIM!

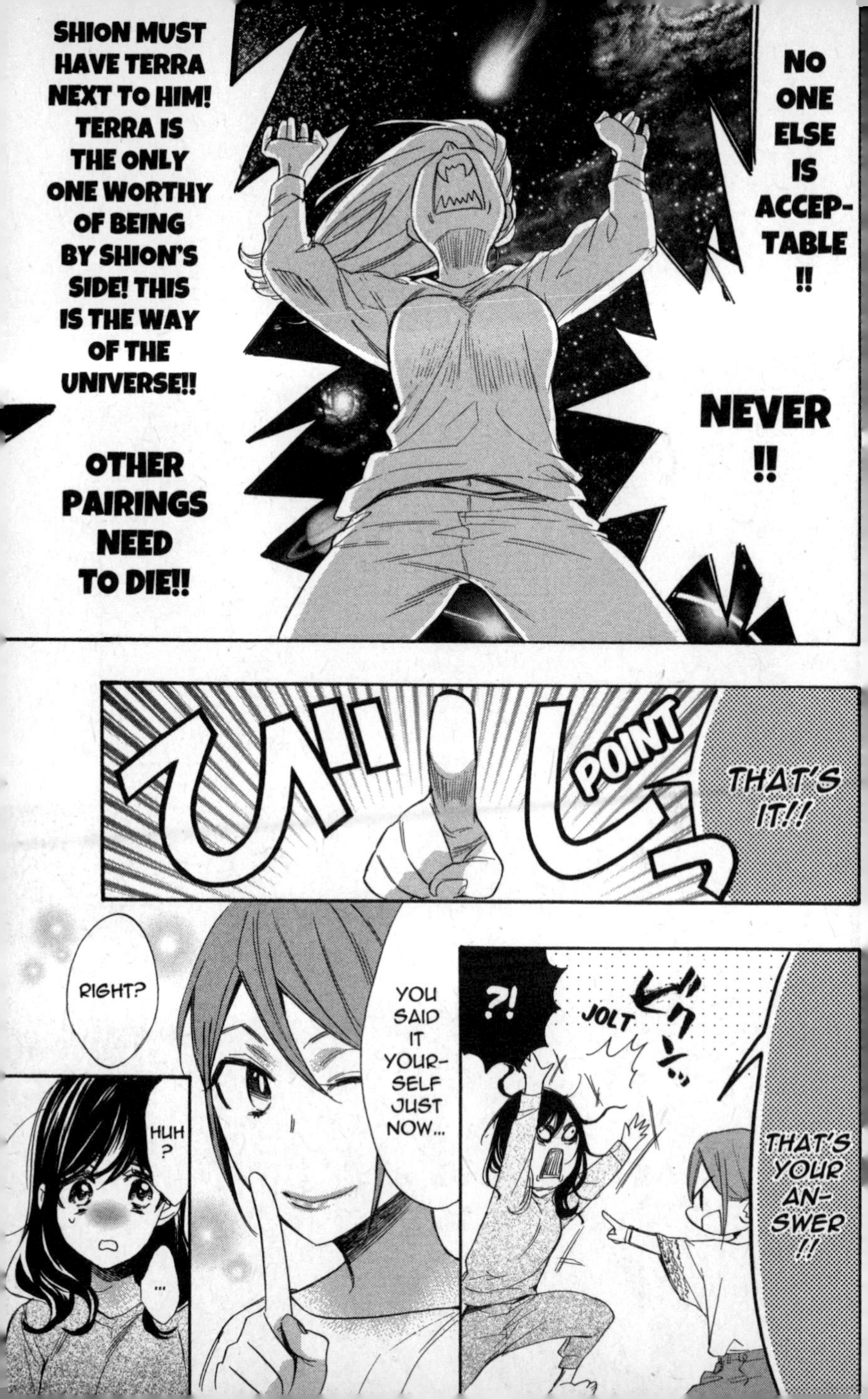
NO ONE ELSE IS ACCEPTABLE!!
SHION MUST HAVE TERRA NEXT TO HIM! TERRA IS THE ONLY ONE WORTHY OF BEING BY SHION'S SIDE! THIS IS THE WAY OF THE UNIVERSE!!
NEVER!!
OTHER PAIRINGS NEED TO DIE!!
THAT'S IT!!
POINT
びしっ
THAT'S YOUR AN-SWER!!
?!
JOLT
ビクン…
YOU SAID IT YOUR-SELF JUST NOW...
RIGHT?
HUH?
...

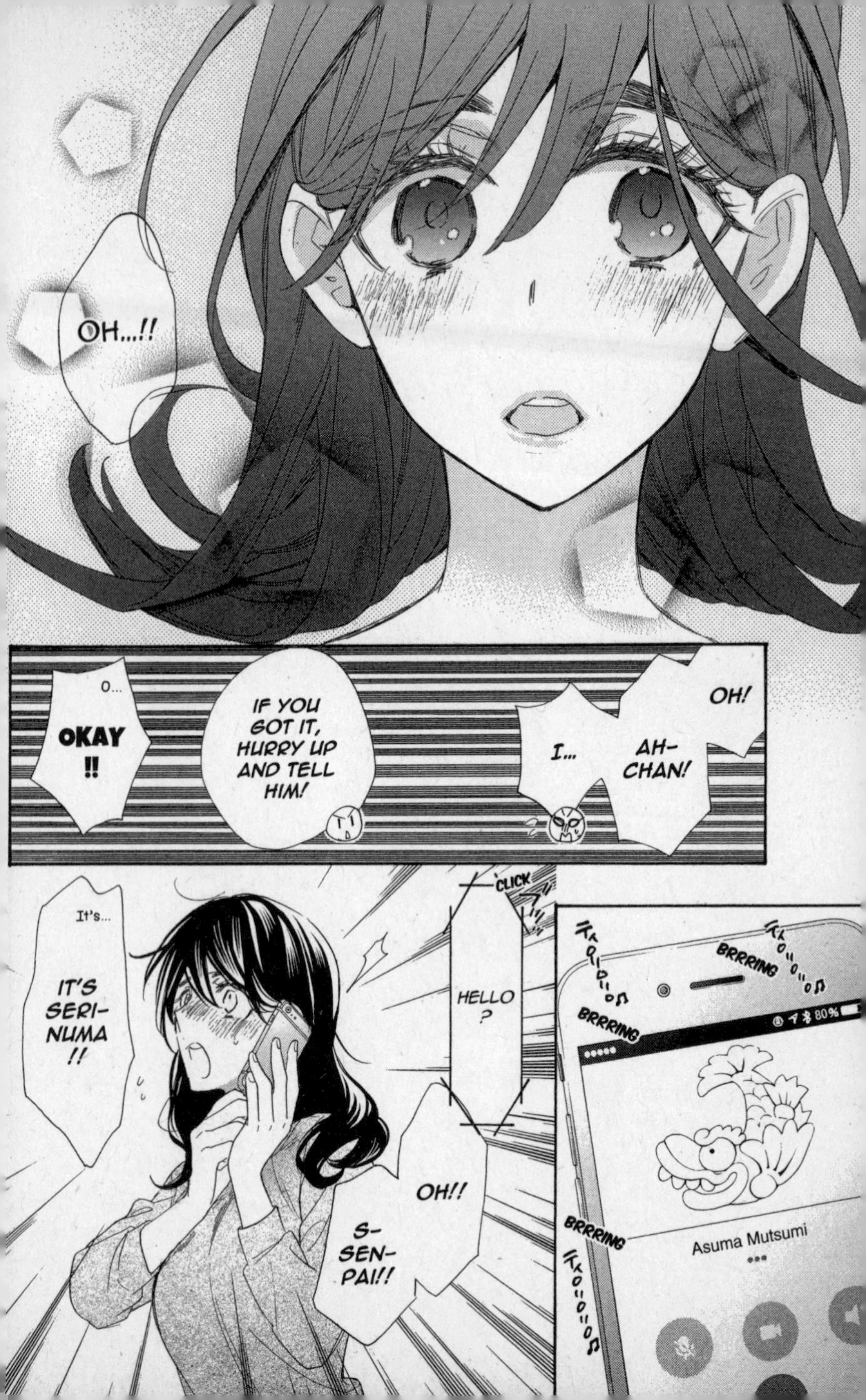
OH...!!
OH! AH-CHAN!
I...
IF YOU GOT IT, HURRY UP AND TELL HIM!
O... OKAY!!
BRRRING
BRRRING
BRRRING
Asuma Mutsumi
CLICK
HELLO?
OH!! S-SEN-PAI!!
It's... IT'S SERI-NUMA!!

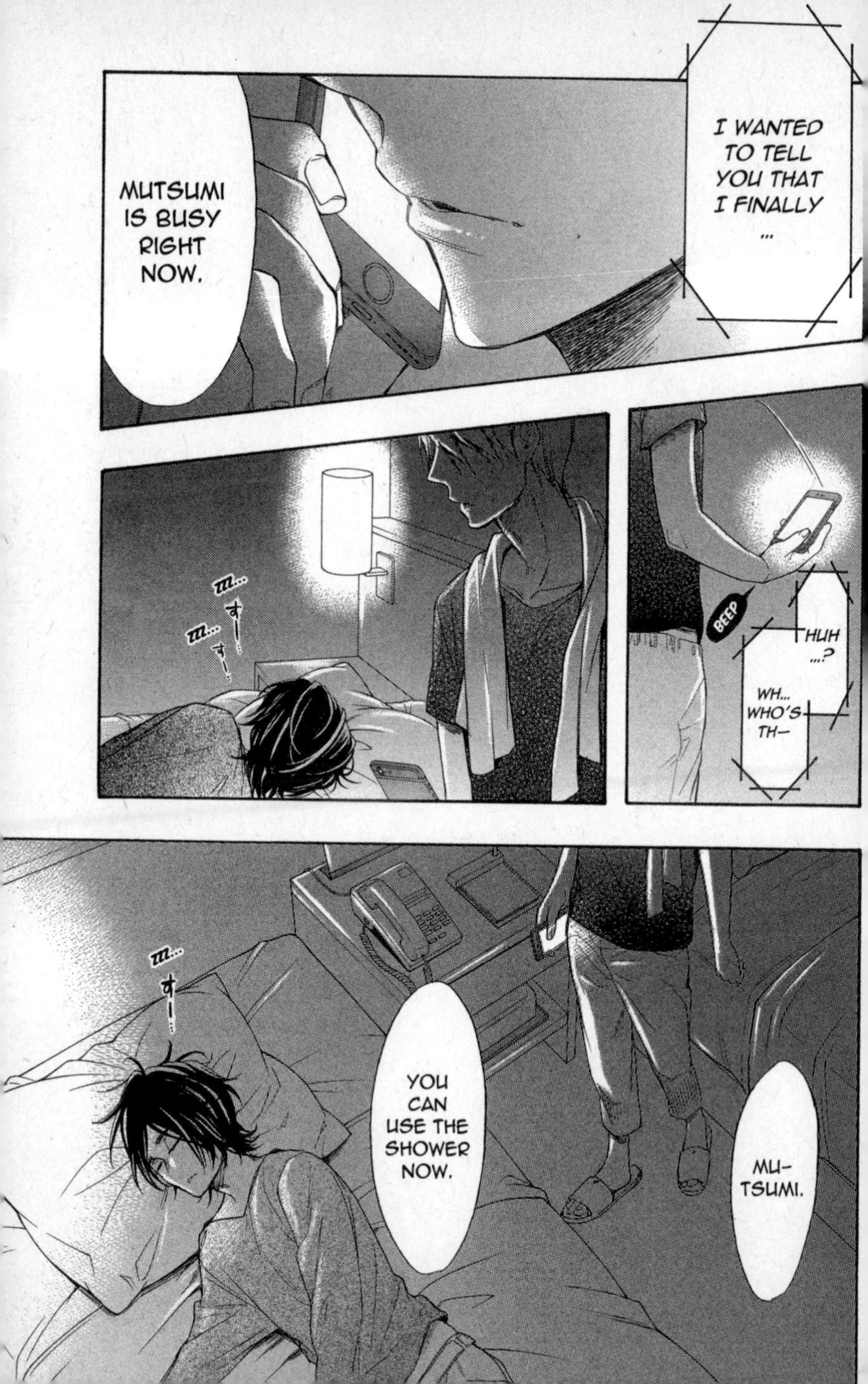
I WANTED TO TELL YOU THAT I FINALLY ...
MUTSUMI IS BUSY RIGHT NOW.
BEEP
HUH ...?
WH... WHO'S TH—
zzz...
すー...
zzz...
すー...
MU-TSUMI.
YOU CAN USE THE SHOWER NOW.
zzz...
すー...

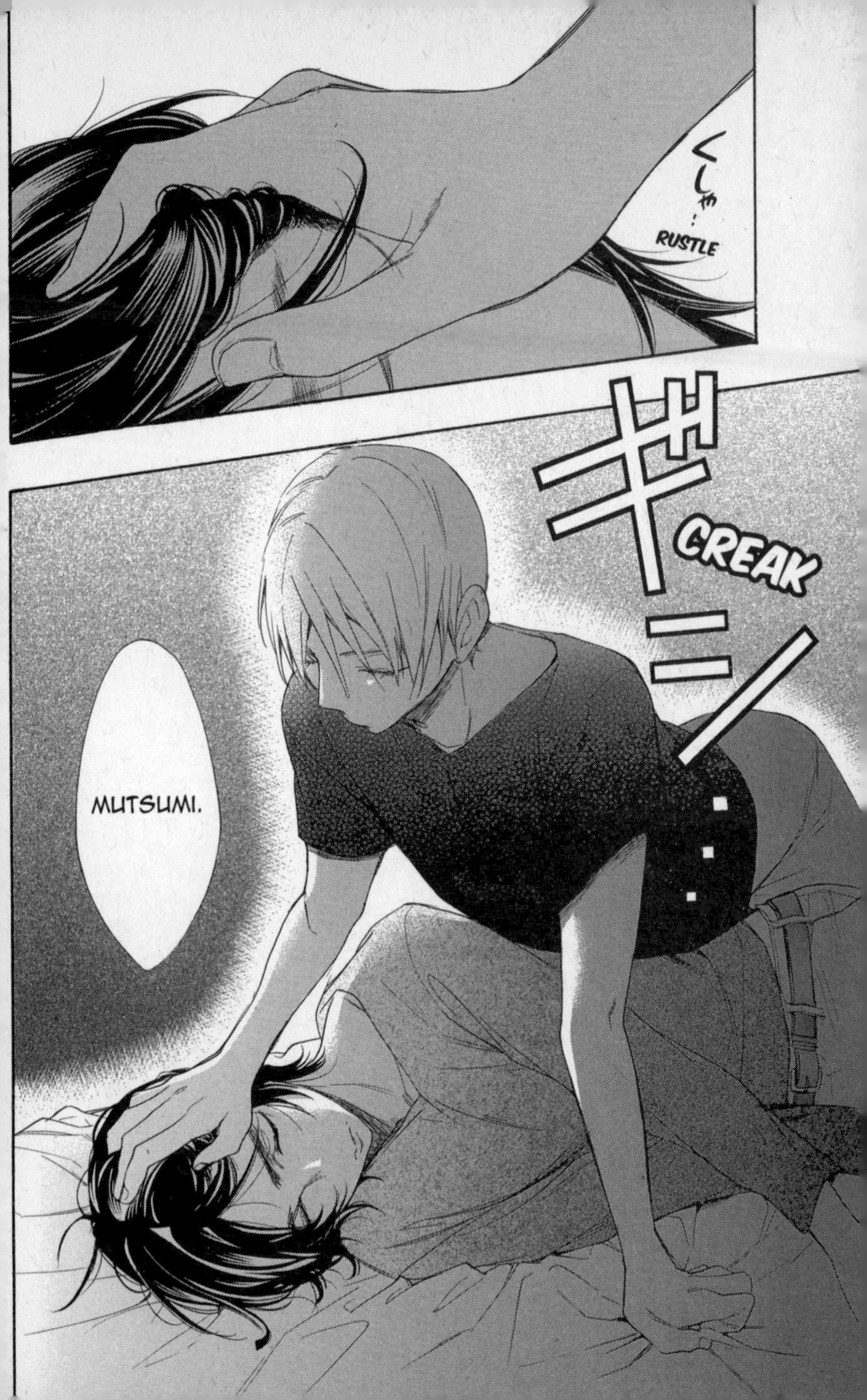
くしゃ…
RUSTLE
CREAK
MUTSUMI.

#51 THE FIGHTING PRINCESS

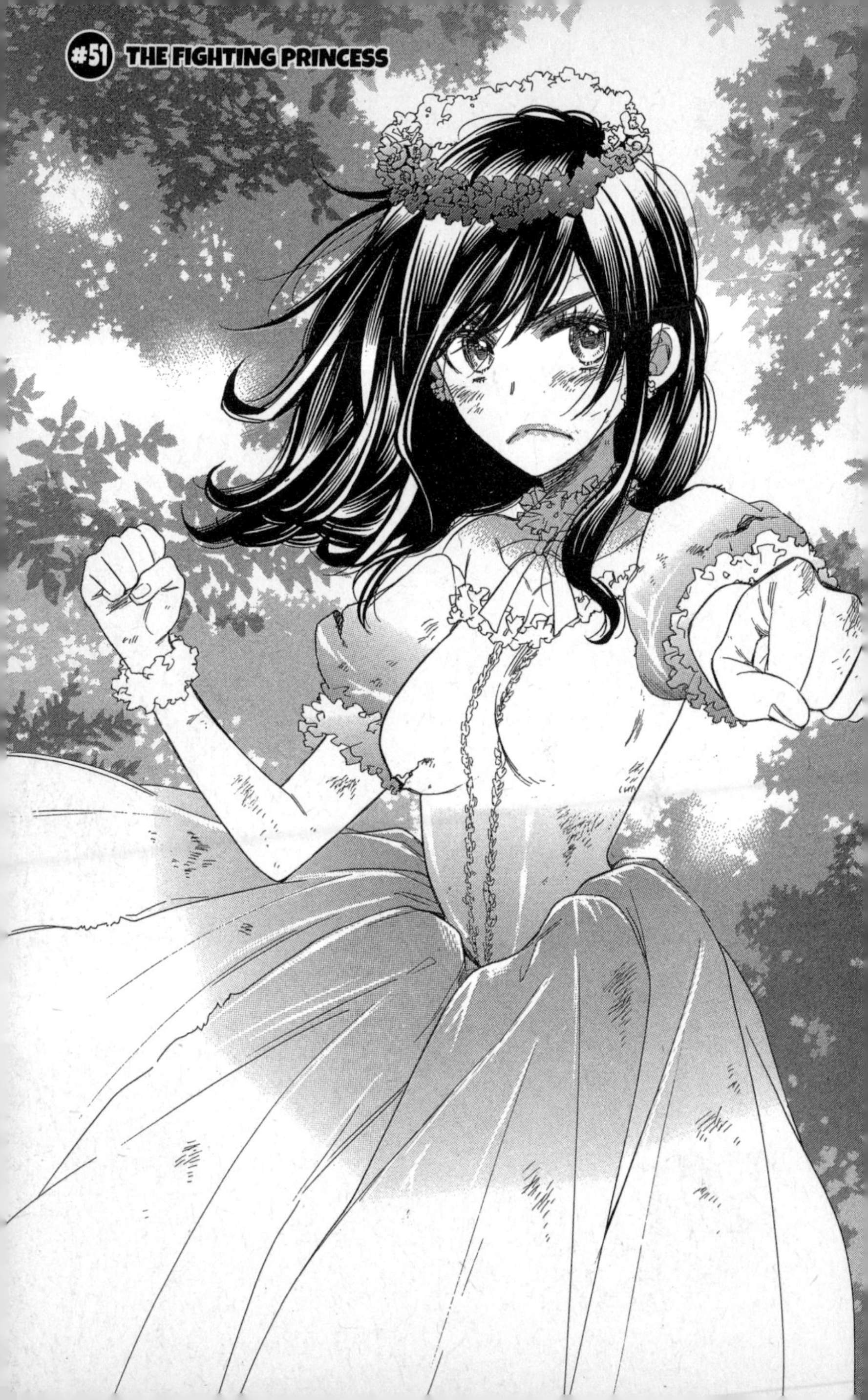

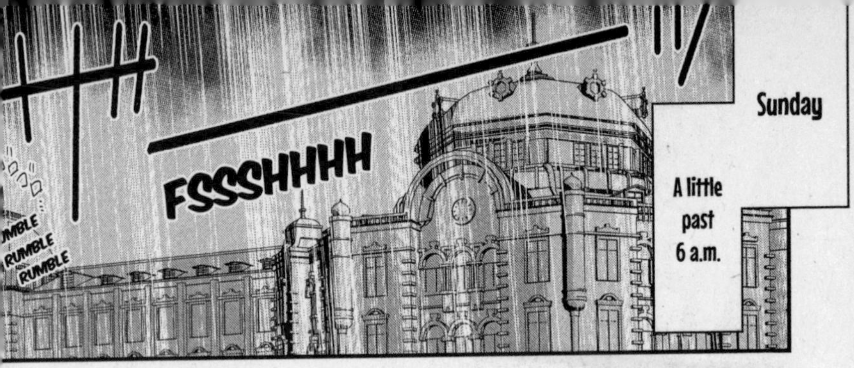
Sunday
A little past 6 a.m.
FSSSHHHH
UMBLE
RUMBLE
RUMBLE
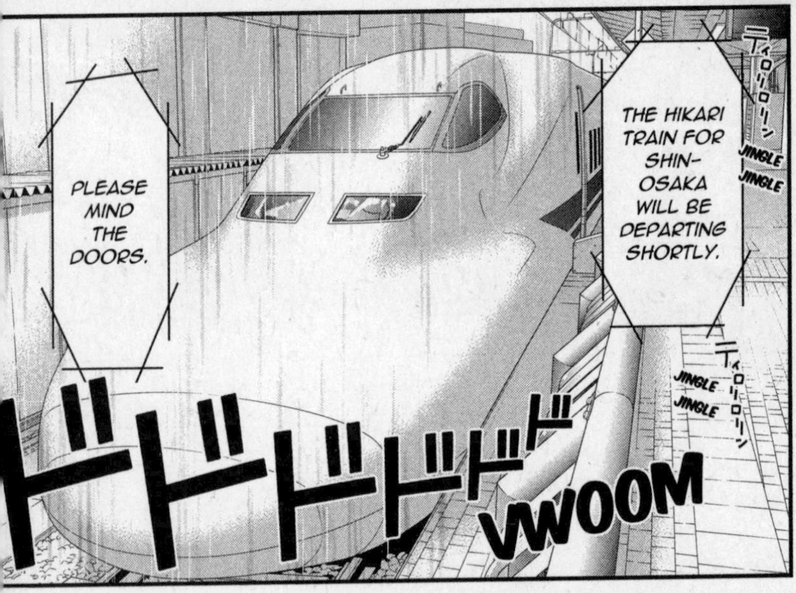
THE HIKARI TRAIN FOR SHIN-OSAKA WILL BE DEPARTING SHORTLY.
JINGLE
JINGLE
JINGLE
JINGLE
PLEASE MIND THE DOORS.
ドドドドド
VWOOM

KiSS HiM, NOT ME!

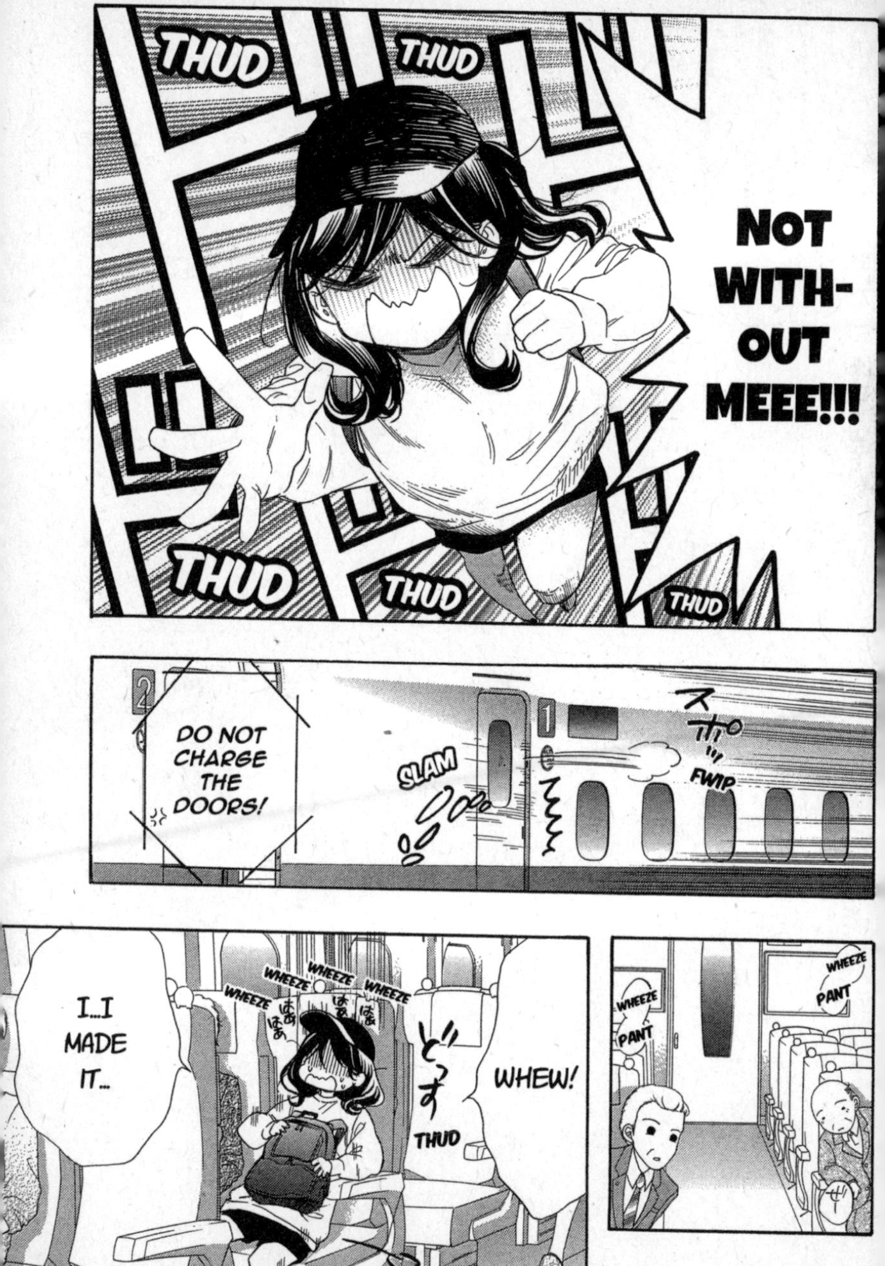
THUD
THUD
NOT WITH-OUT MEEE!!!
THUD
THUD
THUD
SLAM
FWIP
DO NOT CHARGE THE DOORS!
WHEEZE
PANT
WHEEZE
PANT
WHEW!
THUD
WHEEZE
WHEEZE
WHEEZE
WHEEZE
I...I MADE IT...

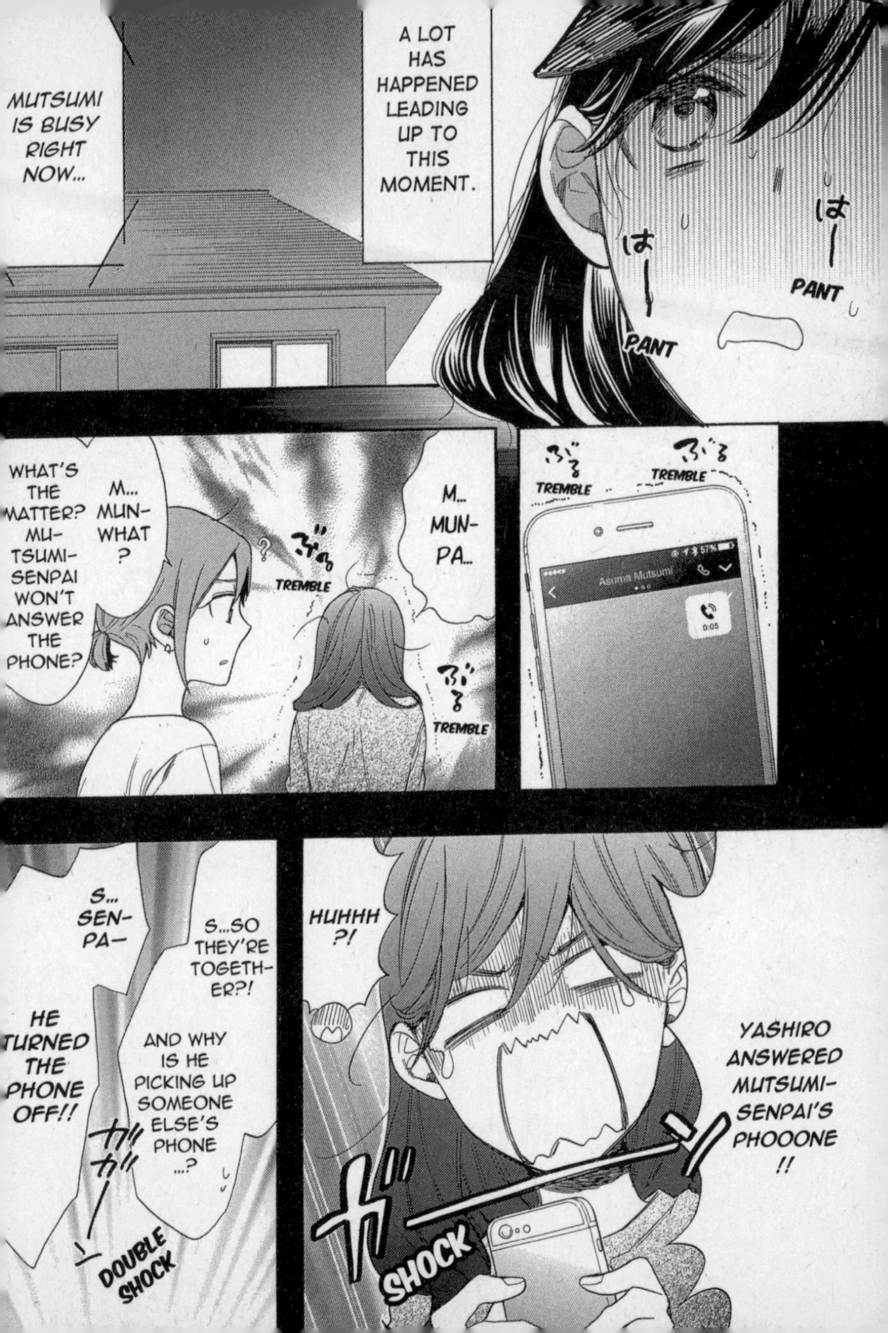
はー
PANT
はー
PANT
A LOT HAS HAPPENED LEADING UP TO THIS MOMENT.
MUTSUMI IS BUSY RIGHT NOW...
ぶる
TREMBLE
ぶる
TREMBLE
Asuma Mutsumi
0:05
M... MUN-PA...
ぶる
TREMBLE
WHAT'S THE MATTER? MUTSUMI-SENPAI WON'T ANSWER THE PHONE?
M... MUN-WHAT?
ぶる
TREMBLE
YASHIRO ANSWERED MUTSUMI-SENPAI'S PHOOONE!!
HUHHH?!
ガーン
SHOCK
S...SO THEY'RE TOGETHER?!
S... SEN-PA—
AND WHY IS HE PICKING UP SOMEONE ELSE'S PHONE...?
HE TURNED THE PHONE OFF!!
ガガーン
DOUBLE SHOCK

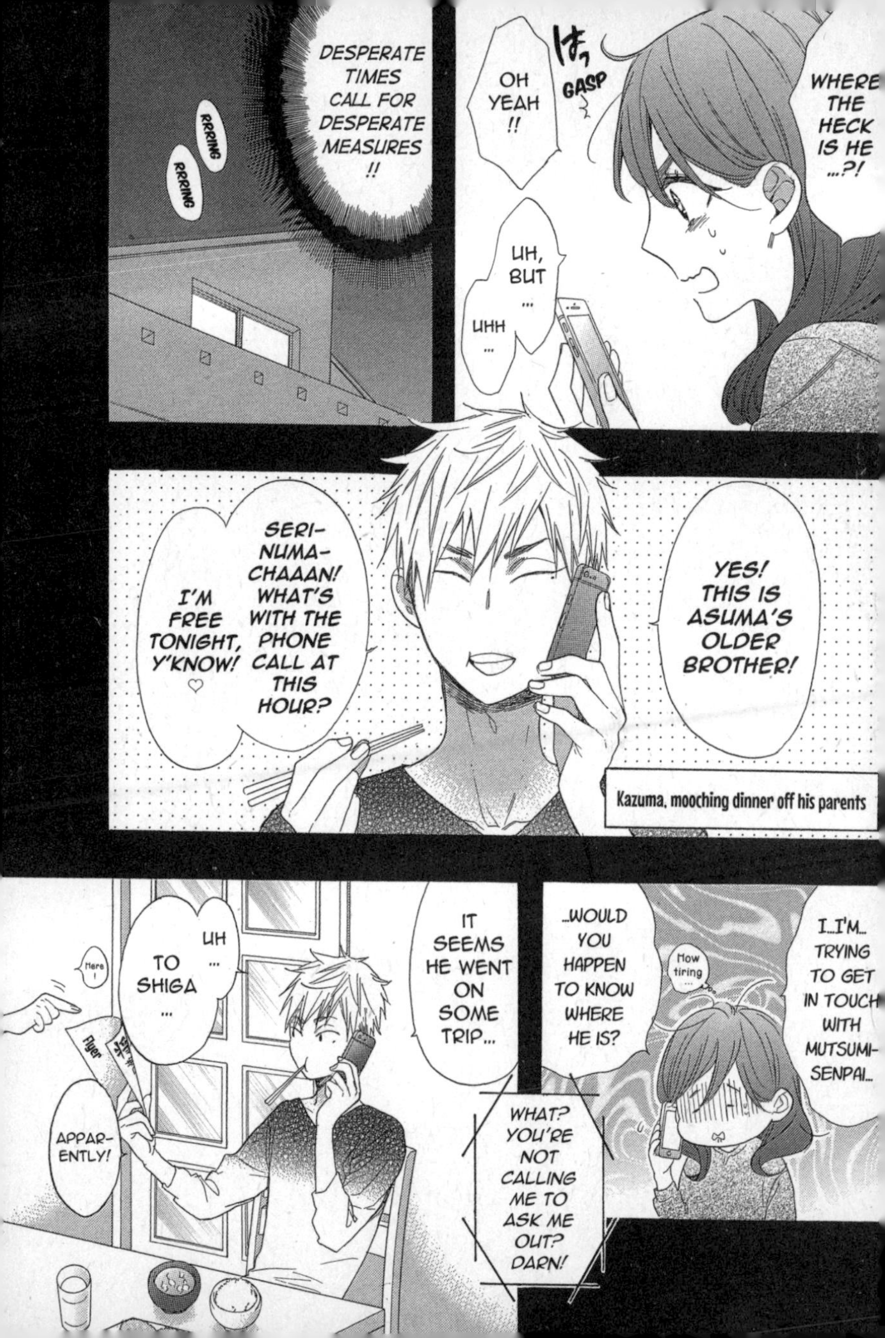
WHERE THE HECK IS HE ...?!
GASP
OH YEAH !!
UH, BUT ...
UHH ...
DESPERATE TIMES CALL FOR DESPERATE MEASURES !!
RRRING
RRRING
YES! THIS IS ASUMA'S OLDER BROTHER!
SERI-NUMA-CHAAAN! WHAT'S WITH THE PHONE CALL AT THIS HOUR?
I'M FREE TONIGHT, Y'KNOW! ♡
Kazuma, mooching dinner off his parents
I..I'M... TRYING TO GET IN TOUCH WITH MUTSUMI-SENPAI...
How tiring ...
...WOULD YOU HAPPEN TO KNOW WHERE HE IS?
WHAT? YOU'RE NOT CALLING ME TO ASK ME OUT? DARN!
IT SEEMS HE WENT ON SOME TRIP...
UH ... TO SHIGA ...
Here !
Flyer
APPAR-ENTLY!

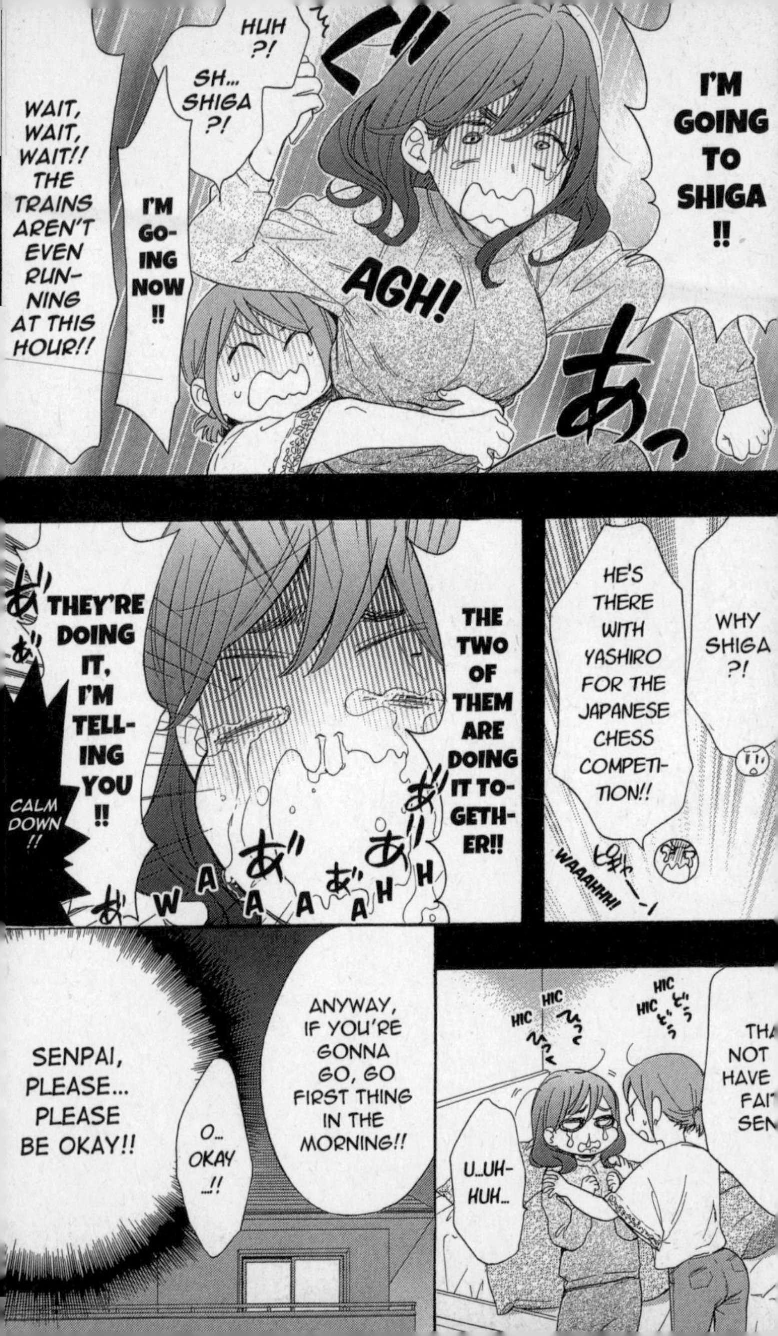
I'M GOING TO SHIGA!!
ぐ
HUH?!
SH... SHIGA?!
I'M GO-ING NOW!!
WAIT, WAIT, WAIT!! THE TRAINS AREN'T EVEN RUN-NING AT THIS HOUR!!
AGH!
あっ
WHY SHIGA?!
HE'S THERE WITH YASHIRO FOR THE JAPANESE CHESS COMPETI-TION!!
WAAAHHH!
THE TWO OF THEM ARE DOING IT TO-GETH-ER!!
THEY'RE DOING IT, I'M TELL-ING YOU!!
CALM DOWN!!
WAAAAAH
THA
NOT
HAVE
FAI
SEN
HIC
HIC
HIC
HIC
U...UH-HUH...
ANYWAY, IF YOU'RE GONNA GO, GO FIRST THING IN THE MORNING!!
O... OKAY...!!
SENPAI, PLEASE... PLEASE BE OKAY!!

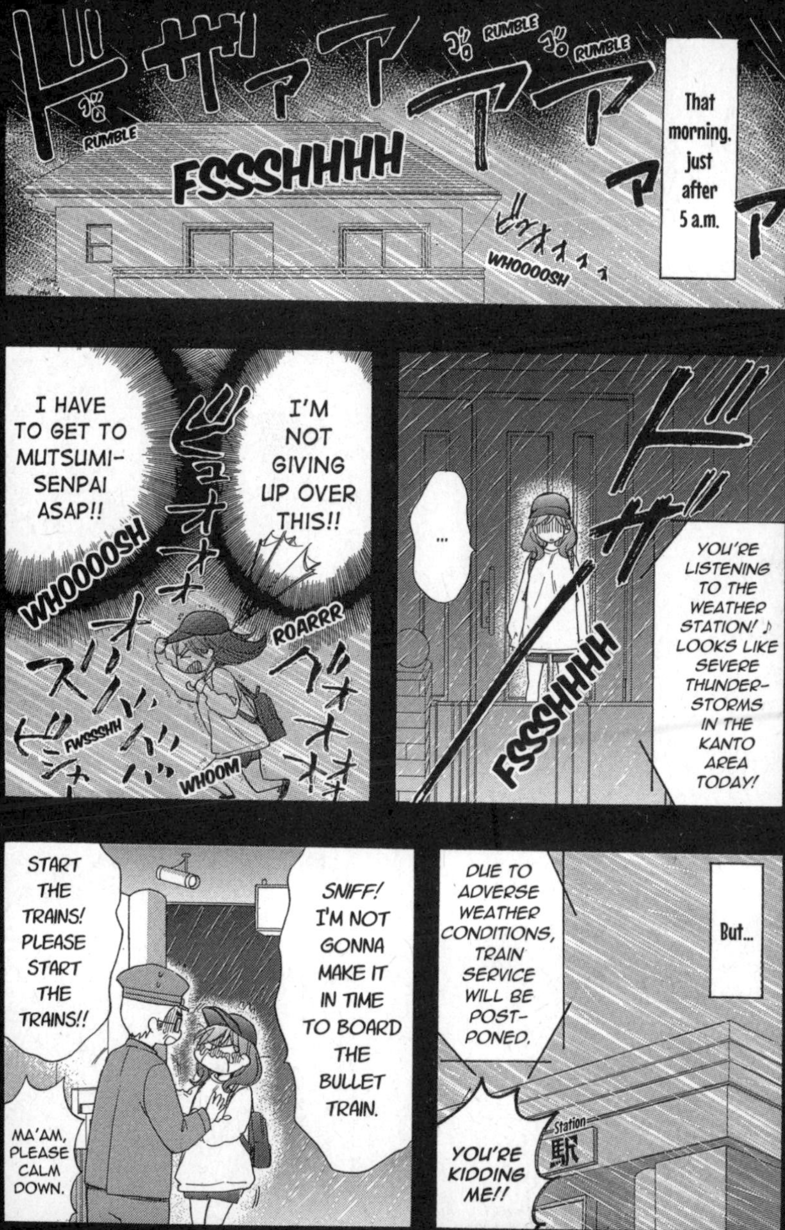
That morning. just after 5 a.m.
RUMBLE
RUMBLE
RUMBLE
FSSSHHHH
WHOOOOSH
YOU'RE LISTENING TO THE WEATHER STATION! ♪ LOOKS LIKE SEVERE THUNDER-STORMS IN THE KANTO AREA TODAY!
...
FSSSHHHH
I'M NOT GIVING UP OVER THIS!!
I HAVE TO GET TO MUTSUMI-SENPAI ASAP!!
WHOOOOSH
ROARRR
FWSSSHH
WHOOM
But...
DUE TO ADVERSE WEATHER CONDITIONS, TRAIN SERVICE WILL BE POST-PONED.
Station
駅
YOU'RE KIDDING ME!!
SNIFF! I'M NOT GONNA MAKE IT IN TIME TO BOARD THE BULLET TRAIN.
START THE TRAINS! PLEASE START THE TRAINS!!
MA'AM, PLEASE CALM DOWN.

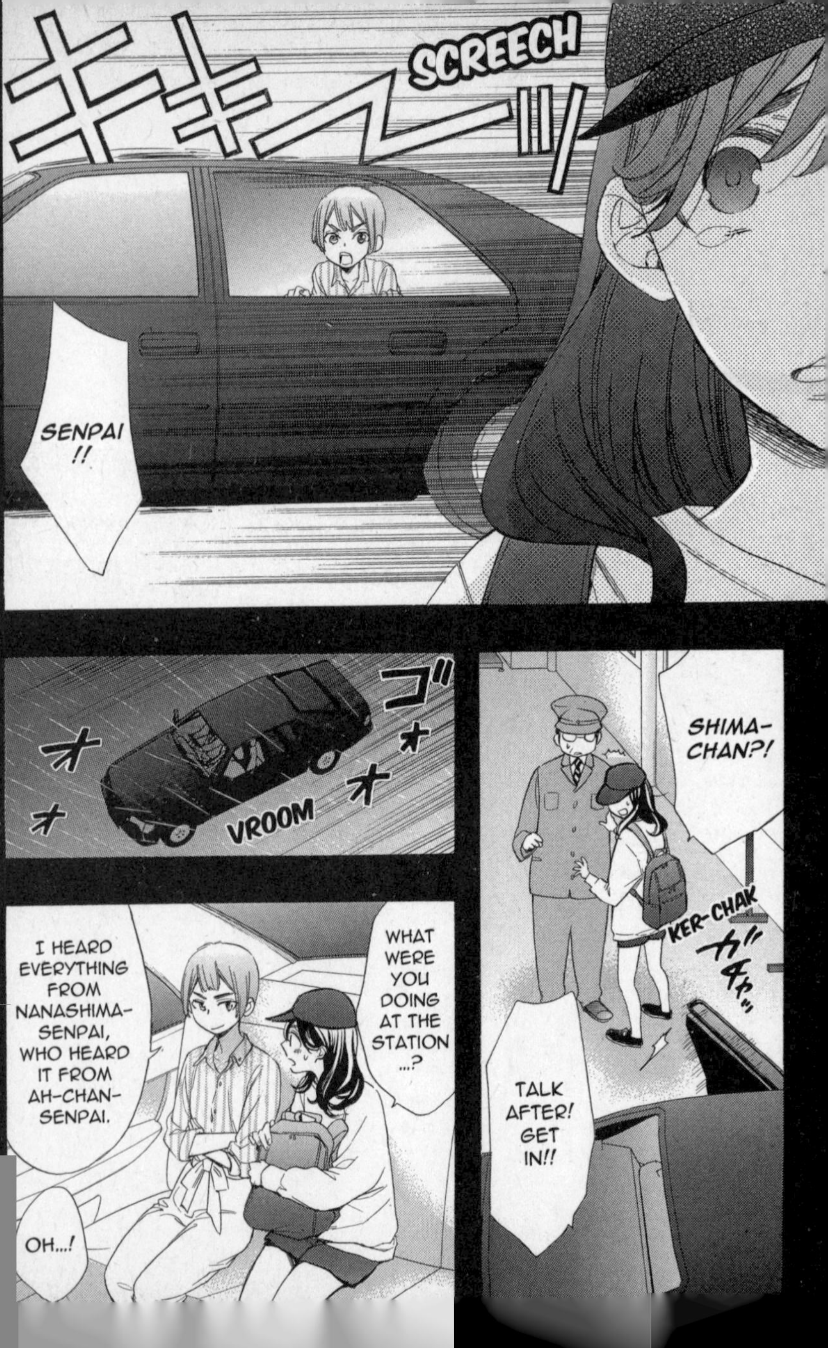
SCREECH
SENPAI!!
SHIMA-CHAN?!
KER-CHAK
TALK AFTER! GET IN!!
VROOM
WHAT WERE YOU DOING AT THE STATION...?
I HEARD EVERYTHING FROM NANASHIMA-SENPAI, WHO HEARD IT FROM AH-CHAN-SENPAI.
OH...!

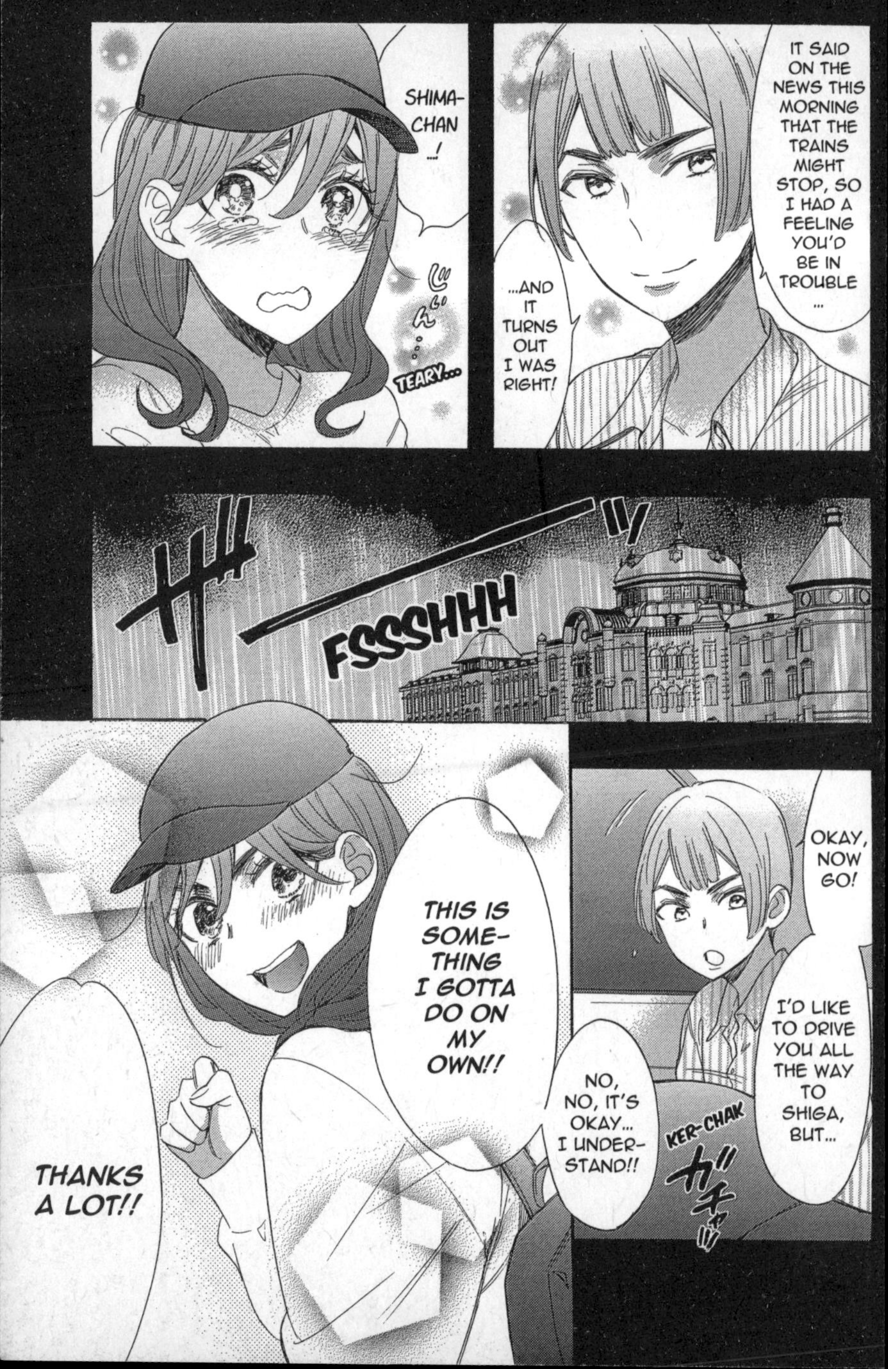
IT SAID ON THE NEWS THIS MORNING THAT THE TRAINS MIGHT STOP, SO I HAD A FEELING YOU'D BE IN TROUBLE ...
...AND IT TURNS OUT I WAS RIGHT!
SHIMA-CHAN ...!
TEARY...
FSSSHHH
OKAY, NOW GO!
I'D LIKE TO DRIVE YOU ALL THE WAY TO SHIGA, BUT...
NO, NO, IT'S OKAY... I UNDERSTAND!!
KER-CHAK
ガチャ!!
THIS IS SOMETHING I GOTTA DO ON MY OWN!!
THANKS A LOT!!

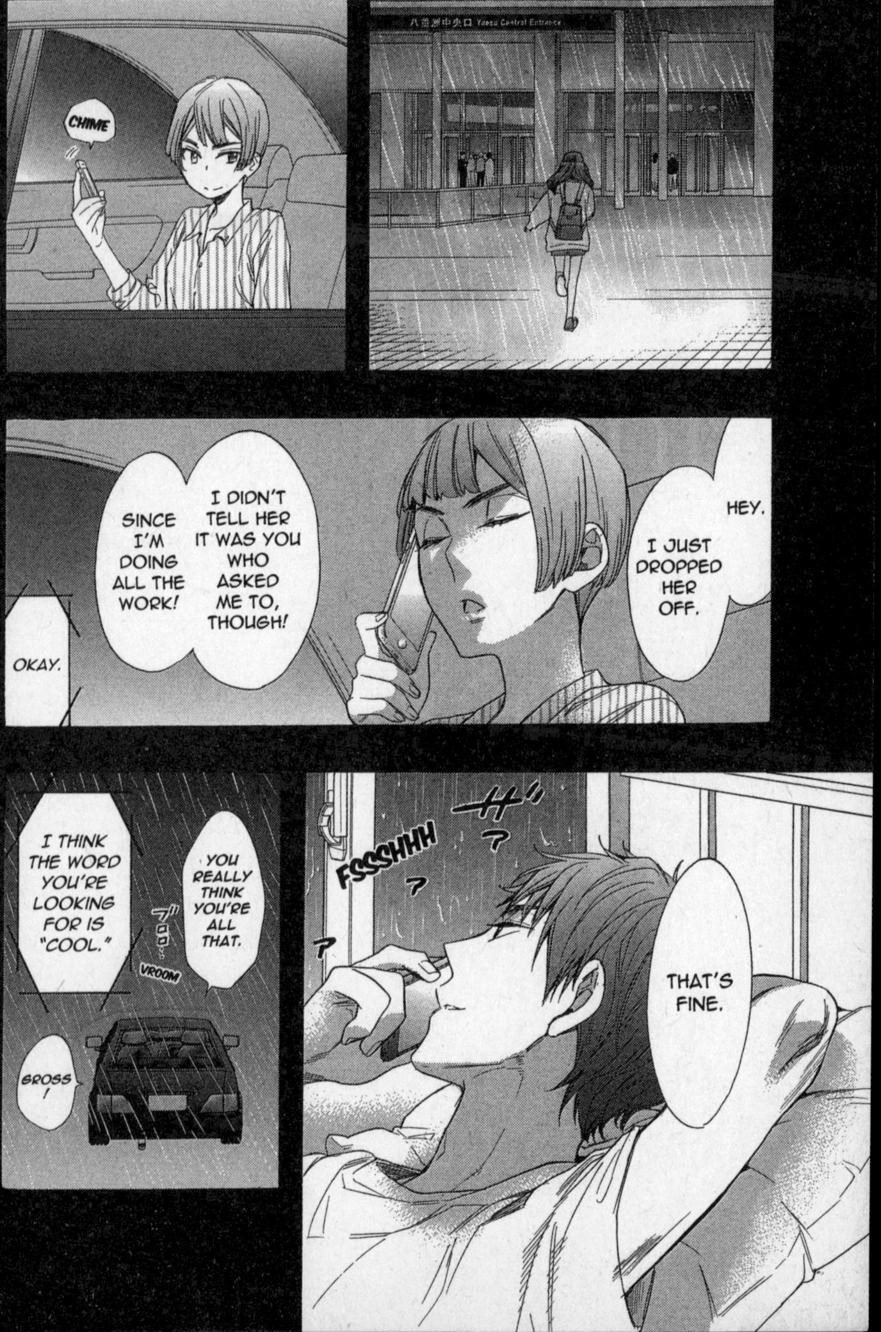
八重洲中央口 Yaesu Central Entrance
CHIME
HEY.
I JUST DROPPED HER OFF.
I DIDN'T TELL HER IT WAS YOU WHO ASKED ME TO, THOUGH!
SINCE I'M DOING ALL THE WORK!
OKAY.
FSSSHHH
THAT'S FINE.
YOU REALLY THINK YOU'RE ALL THAT.
I THINK THE WORD YOU'RE LOOKING FOR IS "COOL."
VROOM
GROSS!

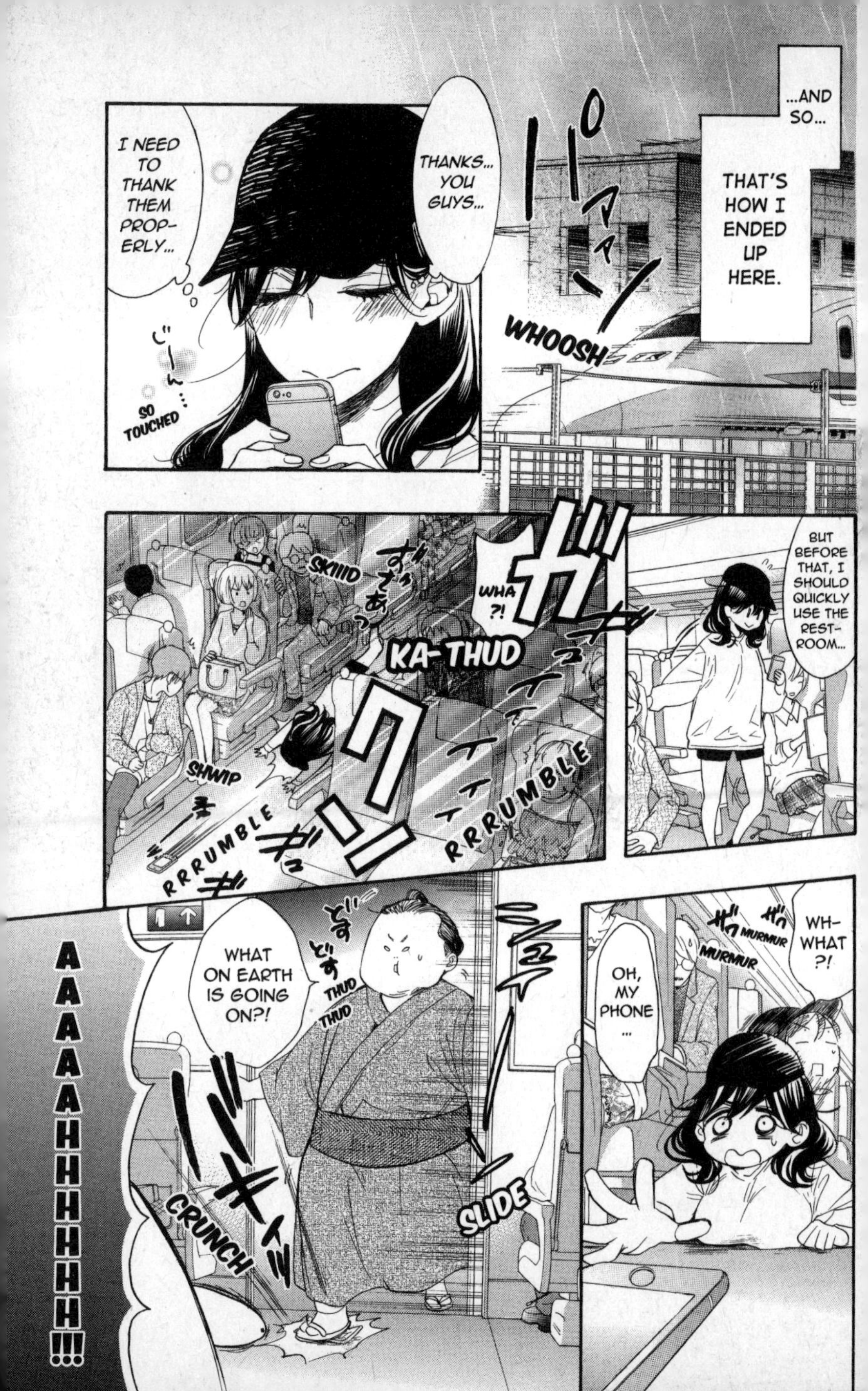
...AND SO...
THAT'S HOW I ENDED UP HERE.
WHOOSH
THANKS... YOU GUYS...
I NEED TO THANK THEM PROPERLY...
SO TOUCHED
BUT BEFORE THAT, I SHOULD QUICKLY USE THE RESTROOM...
WHA?!
SKIIID
KA-THUD
RRRUMBLE
SHWIP
RRRUMBLE
WH-WHAT?!
MURMUR
MURMUR
OH, MY PHONE...
WHAT ON EARTH IS GOING ON?!
THUD
THUD
SLIDE
CRUNCH
AAAAAAHHHHHHHH!!!

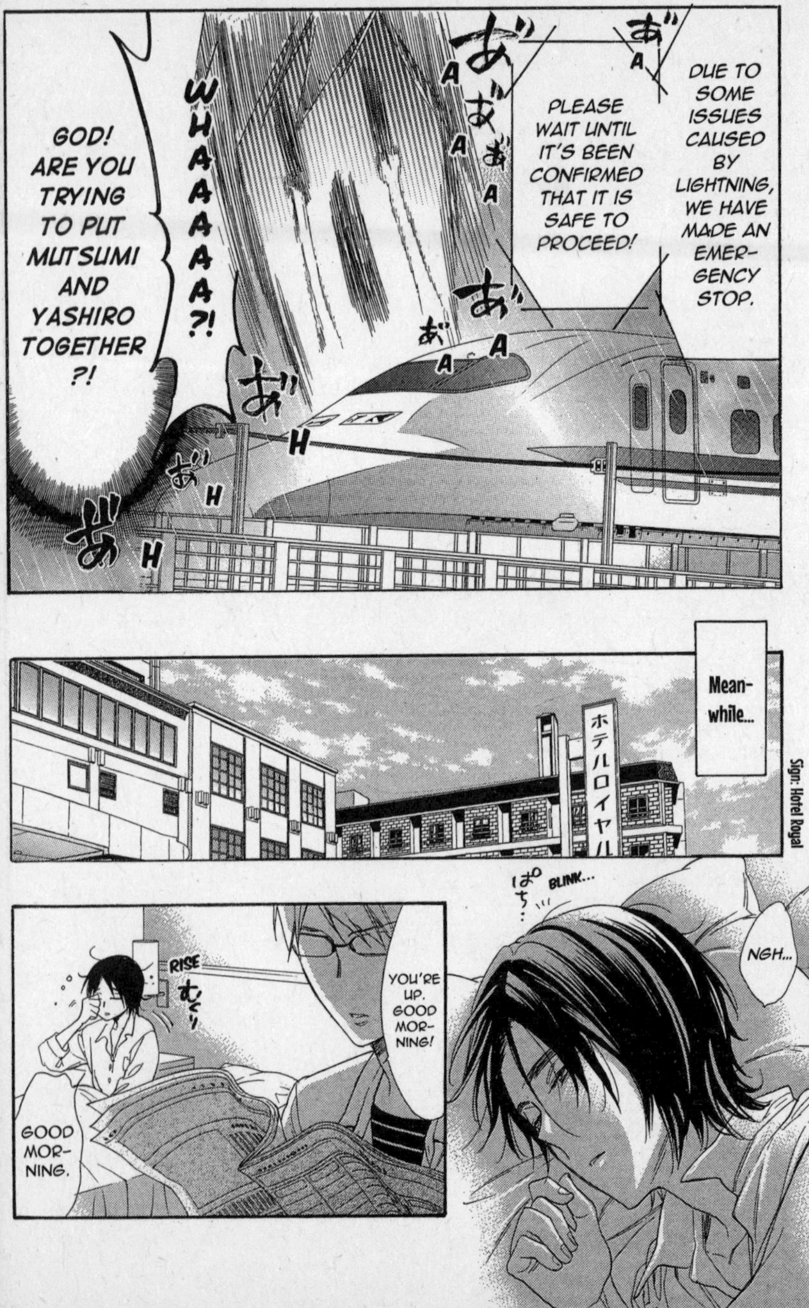
DUE TO SOME ISSUES CAUSED BY LIGHTNING, WE HAVE MADE AN EMERGENCY STOP.
PLEASE WAIT UNTIL IT'S BEEN CONFIRMED THAT IT IS SAFE TO PROCEED!
WHAAAAAAA?!
GOD! ARE YOU TRYING TO PUT MUTSUMI AND YASHIRO TOGETHER?!
Meanwhile...
ホテルロイヤル
Sign: Hotel Royal
ぱち BLINK...
NGH...
RISE むくり
YOU'RE UP. GOOD MORNING!
GOOD MORNING.

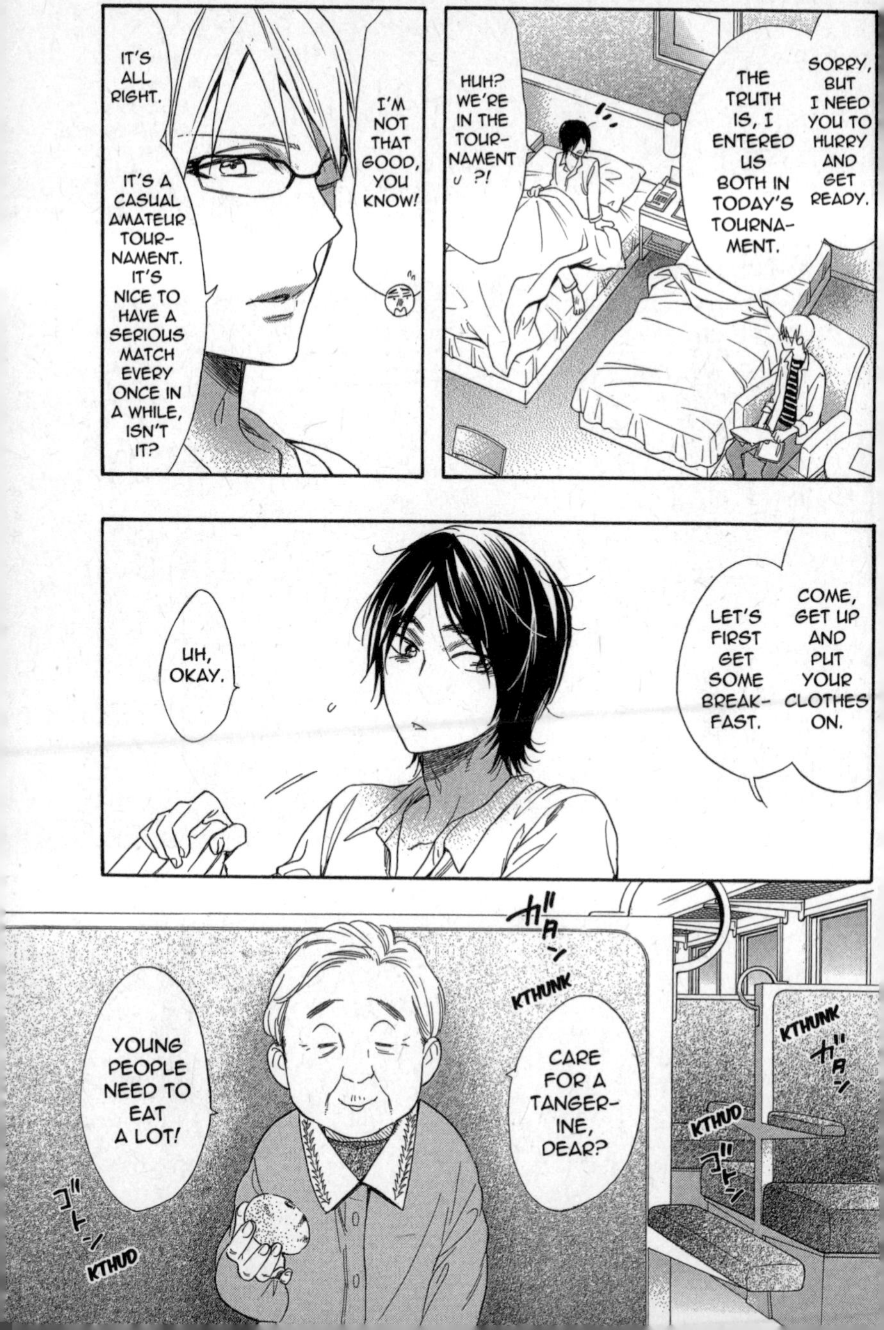
SORRY, BUT I NEED YOU TO HURRY AND GET READY.
THE TRUTH IS, I ENTERED US BOTH IN TODAY'S TOURNAMENT.
HUH? WE'RE IN THE TOURNAMENT?!
I'M NOT THAT GOOD, YOU KNOW!
IT'S ALL RIGHT.
IT'S A CASUAL AMATEUR TOURNAMENT. IT'S NICE TO HAVE A SERIOUS MATCH EVERY ONCE IN A WHILE, ISN'T IT?
COME, GET UP AND PUT YOUR CLOTHES ON.
LET'S FIRST GET SOME BREAKFAST.
UH, OKAY.
KTHUNK
KTHUD
KTHUNK
CARE FOR A TANGERINE, DEAR?
YOUNG PEOPLE NEED TO EAT A LOT!
KTHUD

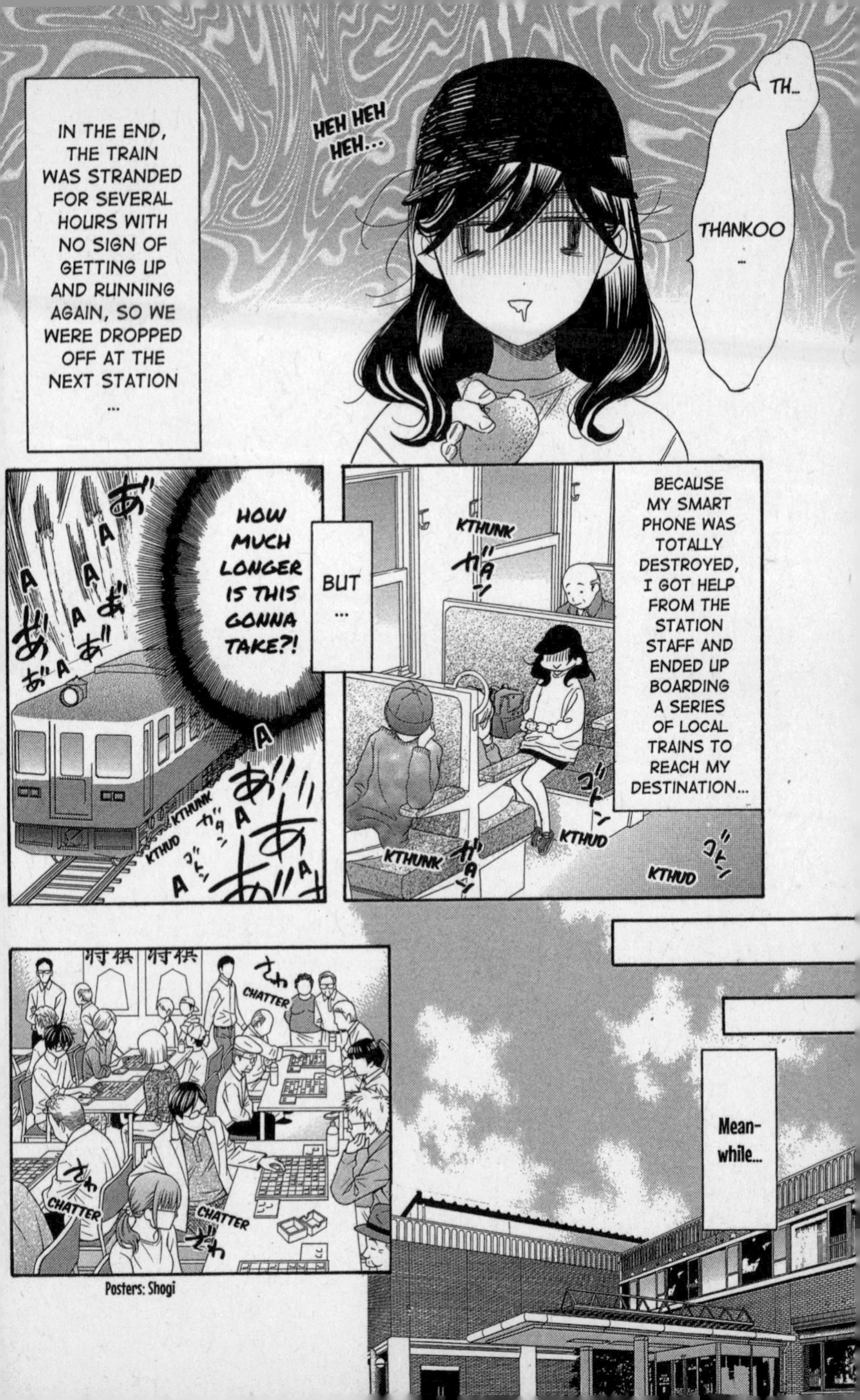
TH... THANKOO ...
HEH HEH HEH...
IN THE END, THE TRAIN WAS STRANDED FOR SEVERAL HOURS WITH NO SIGN OF GETTING UP AND RUNNING AGAIN, SO WE WERE DROPPED OFF AT THE NEXT STATION ...
BECAUSE MY SMART PHONE WAS TOTALLY DESTROYED, I GOT HELP FROM THE STATION STAFF AND ENDED UP BOARDING A SERIES OF LOCAL TRAINS TO REACH MY DESTINATION...
KTHUNK ガタ
KTHUD ゴト
KTHUNK ガタ
KTHUD ゴト
BUT ...
HOW MUCH LONGER IS THIS GONNA TAKE?!
あ A
KTHUNK ガタ
KTHUD ゴト
Mean-while...
将棋 将棋
CHATTER ざわ
CHATTER ざわ
CHATTER ざわ
Posters: Shogi

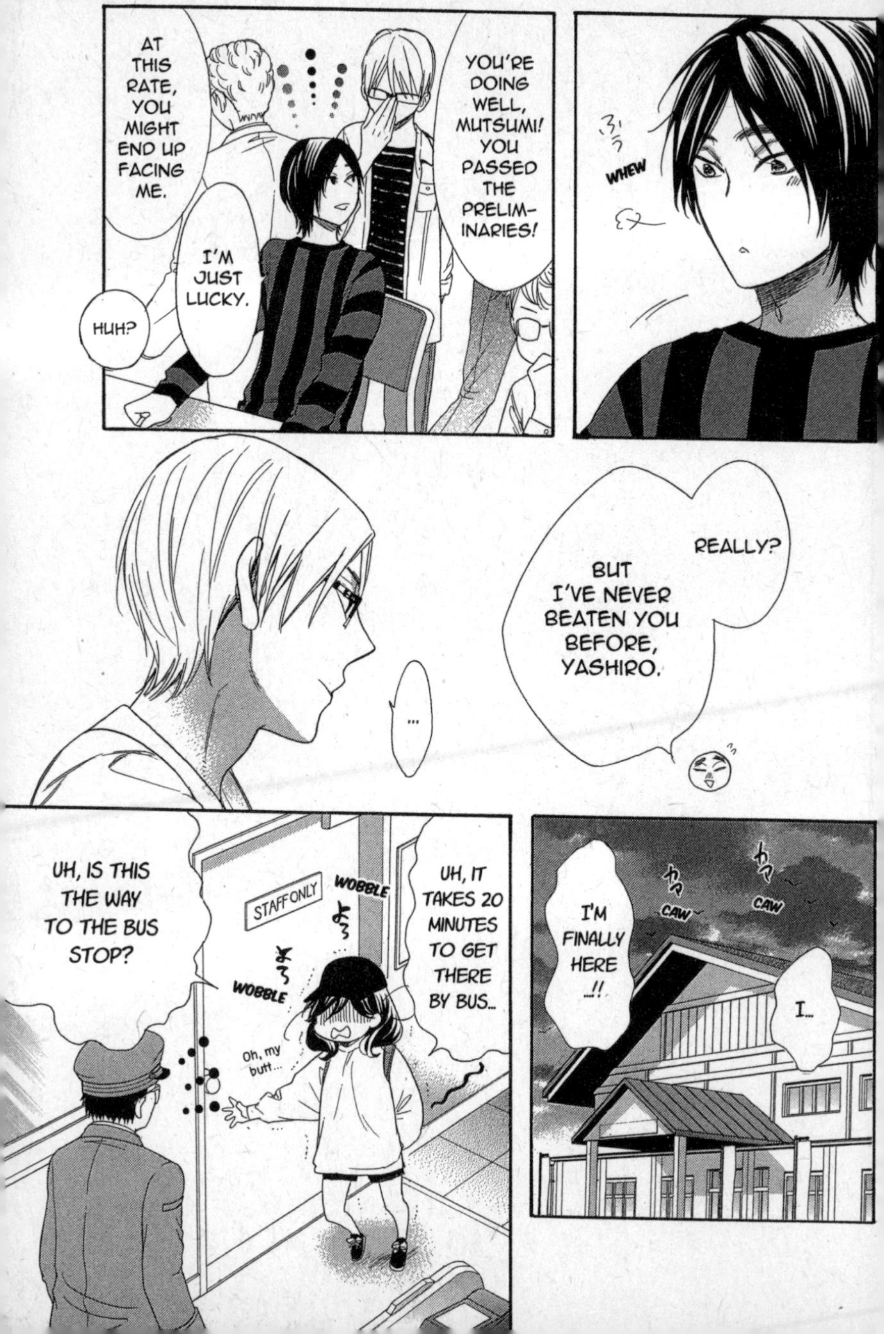
WHEW
YOU'RE DOING WELL, MUTSUMI! YOU PASSED THE PRELIM-INARIES!
AT THIS RATE, YOU MIGHT END UP FACING ME.
I'M JUST LUCKY.
HUH?
REALLY?
BUT I'VE NEVER BEATEN YOU BEFORE, YASHIRO.
...
CAW
CAW
I'M FINALLY HERE ...!!
I...
UH, IT TAKES 20 MINUTES TO GET THERE BY BUS...
WOBBLE
STAFF ONLY
WOBBLE
Oh, my butt...
UH, IS THIS THE WAY TO THE BUS STOP?

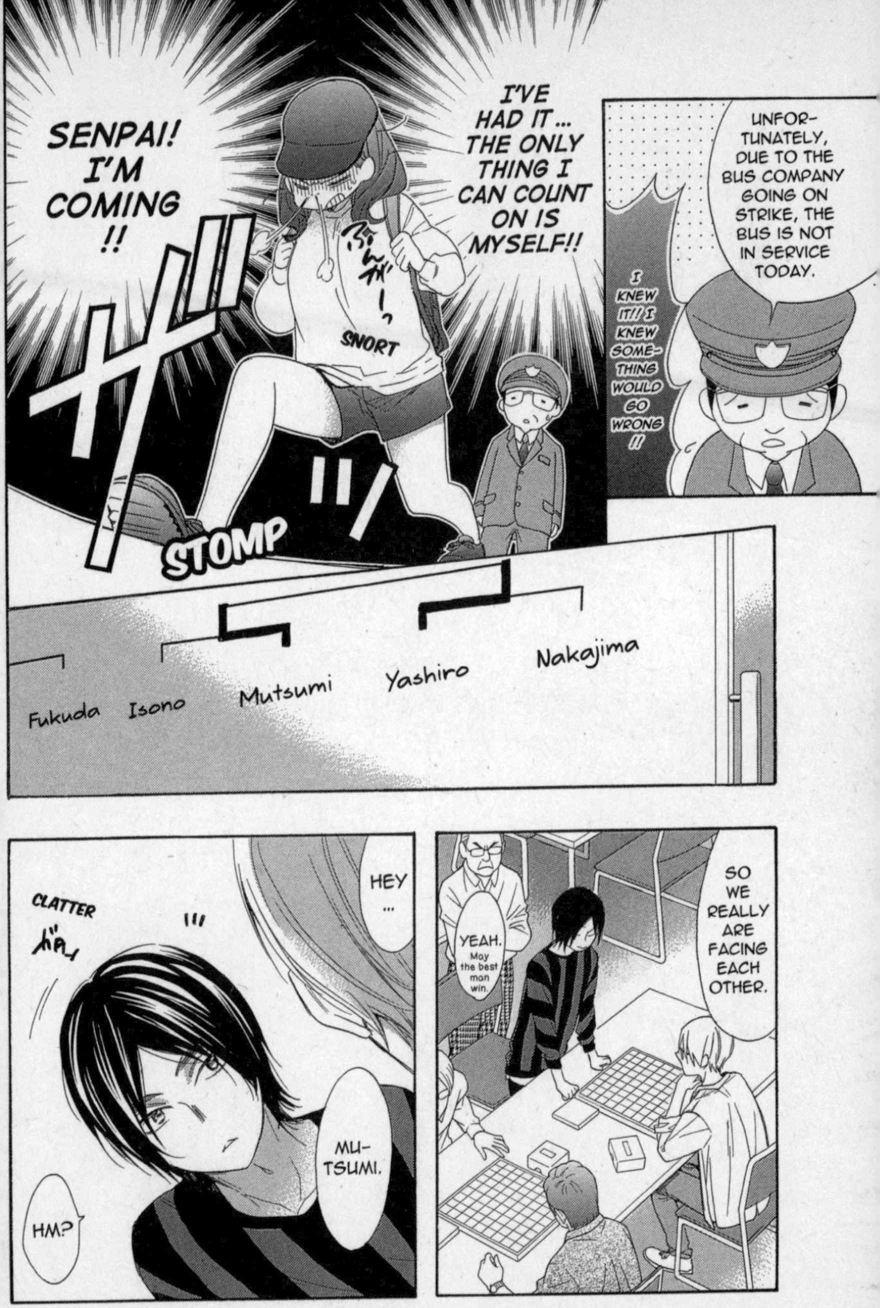
UNFORTUNATELY, DUE TO THE BUS COMPANY GOING ON STRIKE, THE BUS IS NOT IN SERVICE TODAY.
I KNEW IT!! I KNEW SOMETHING WOULD GO WRONG!!
I'VE HAD IT... THE ONLY THING I CAN COUNT ON IS MYSELF!!
SENPAI! I'M COMING!!
SNORT
STOMP
Nakajima
Yashiro
Mutsumi
Isono
Fukuda
SO WE REALLY ARE FACING EACH OTHER.
YEAH. May the best man win.
HEY ...
MU-TSUMI.
HM?
CLATTER

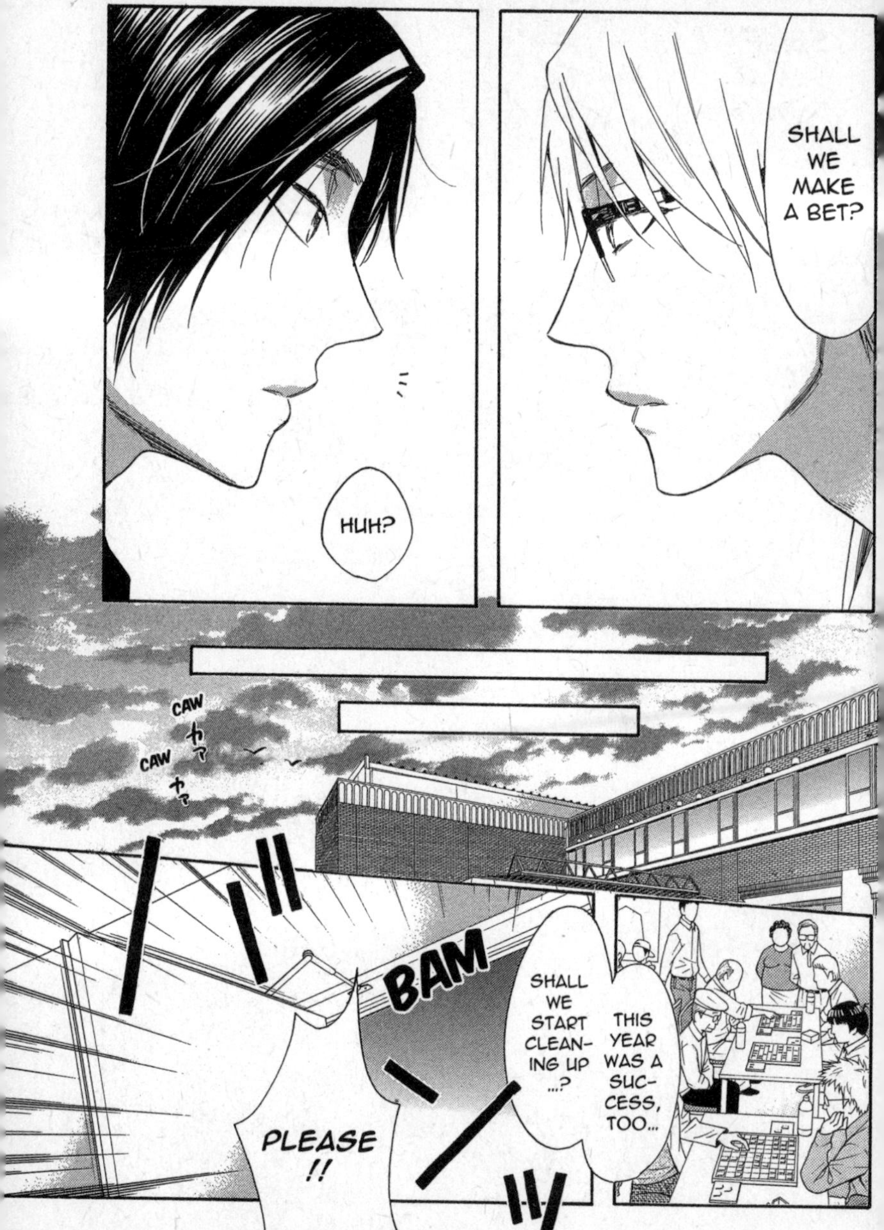
SHALL WE MAKE A BET?
HUH?
CAW
カァ
CAW
カァ
THIS YEAR WAS A SUCCESS, TOO...
SHALL WE START CLEANING UP ...?
BAM
PLEASE !!

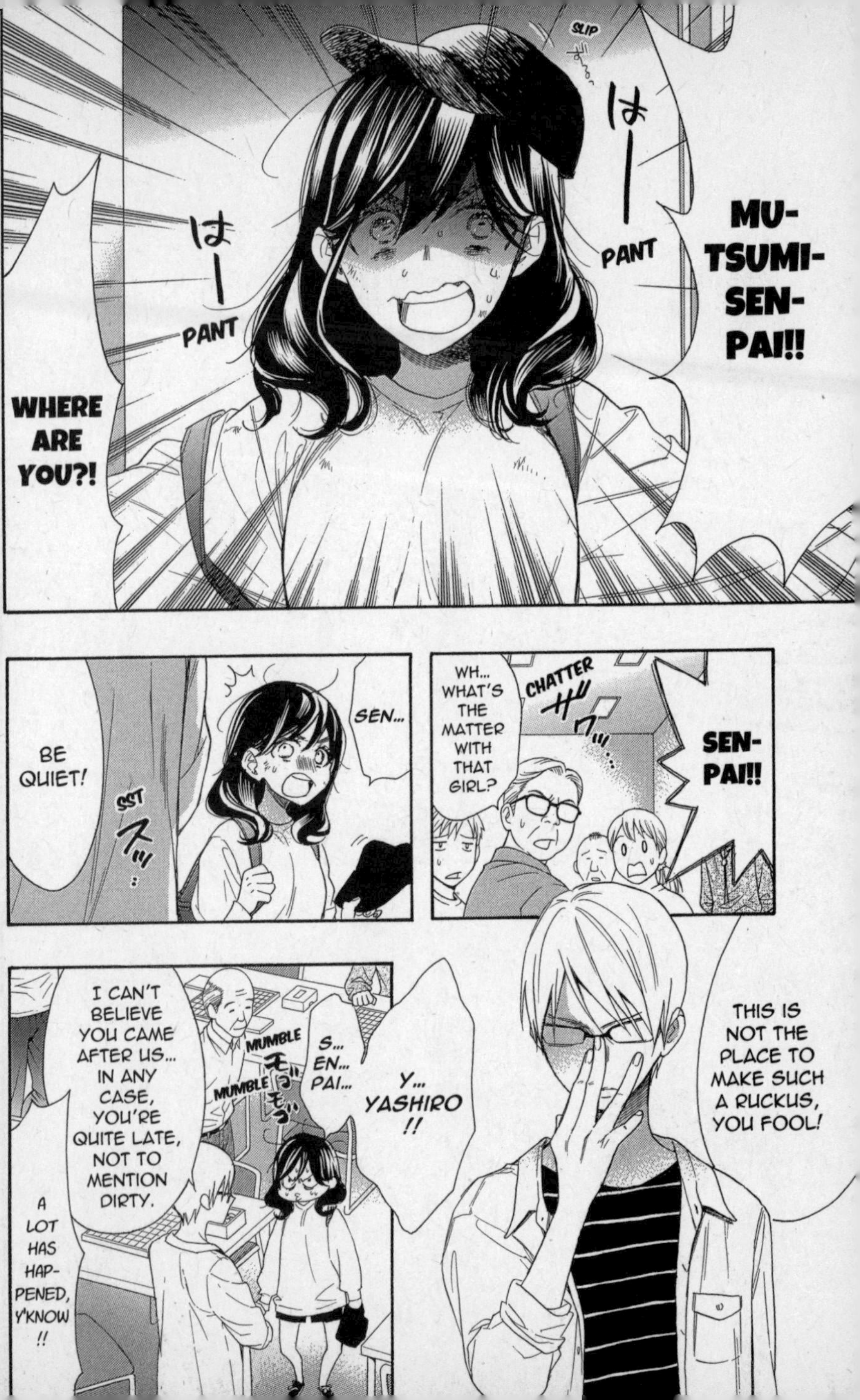

MU-TSUMI-SEN-PAI!!
SLIP
はー
PANT
はー
PANT
WHERE ARE YOU?!
SEN-PAI!!
WH... WHAT'S THE MATTER WITH THAT GIRL?
CHATTER
SEN...
SST
BE QUIET!
THIS IS NOT THE PLACE TO MAKE SUCH A RUCKUS, YOU FOOL!
Y... YASHIRO!!
S... EN... PAI...
MUMBLE
MUMBLE
I CAN'T BELIEVE YOU CAME AFTER US... IN ANY CASE, YOU'RE QUITE LATE, NOT TO MENTION DIRTY.
A LOT HAS HAP-PENED, Y'KNOW!!

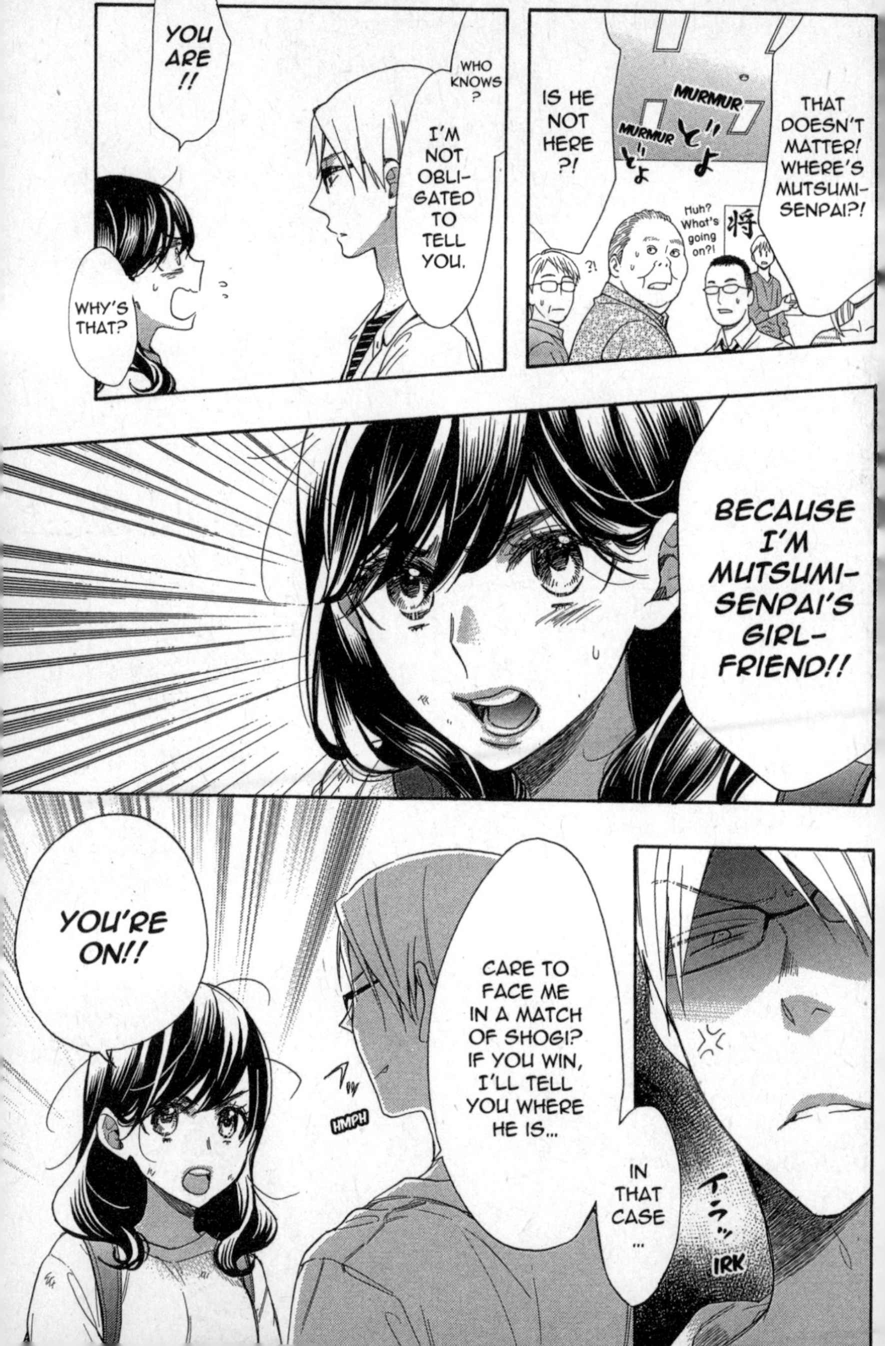
THAT DOESN'T MATTER! WHERE'S MUTSUMI-SENPAI?!
MURMUR
MURMUR
IS HE NOT HERE ?!
Huh? What's going on?!
?!
WHO KNOWS ?
I'M NOT OBLIGATED TO TELL YOU.
YOU ARE !!
WHY'S THAT?
BECAUSE I'M MUTSUMI-SENPAI'S GIRLFRIEND!!
IRK
IN THAT CASE ...
CARE TO FACE ME IN A MATCH OF SHOGI? IF YOU WIN, I'LL TELL YOU WHERE HE IS...
HMPH
YOU'RE ON!!

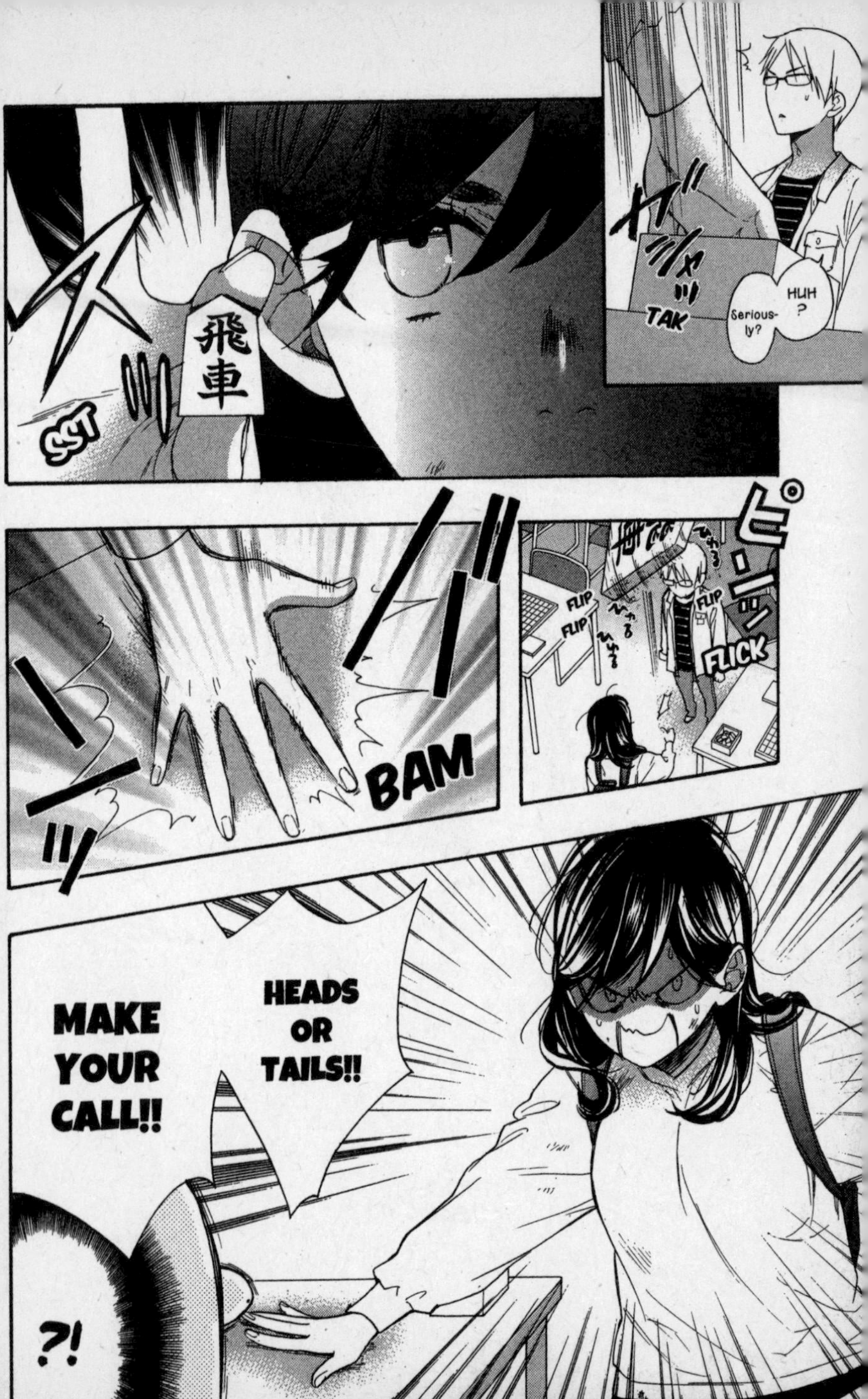
TAK
HUH?
Serious-ly?
SST
FLIP
FLIP
FLIP
FLICK
BAM
HEADS OR TAILS!!
MAKE YOUR CALL!!
?!

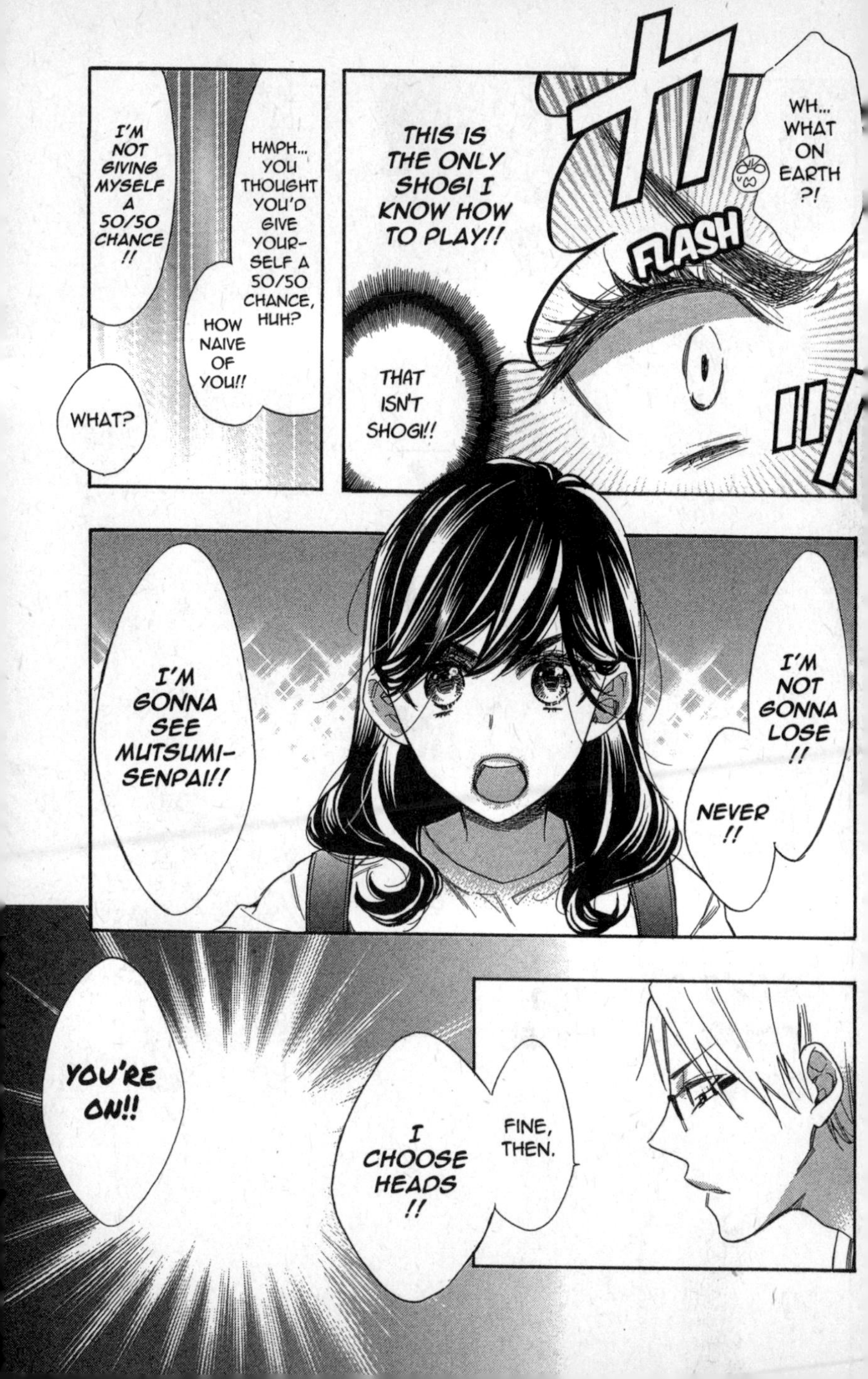
WH... WHAT ON EARTH?!
FLASH
THIS IS THE ONLY SHOGI I KNOW HOW TO PLAY!!
THAT ISN'T SHOGI!!
HMPH... YOU THOUGHT YOU'D GIVE YOUR-SELF A 50/50 CHANCE, HUH?
I'M NOT GIVING MYSELF A 50/50 CHANCE!!
HOW NAIVE OF YOU!!
WHAT?
I'M NOT GONNA LOSE!!
NEVER!!
I'M GONNA SEE MUTSUMI-SENPAI!!
FINE, THEN.
I CHOOSE HEADS!!
YOU'RE ON!!

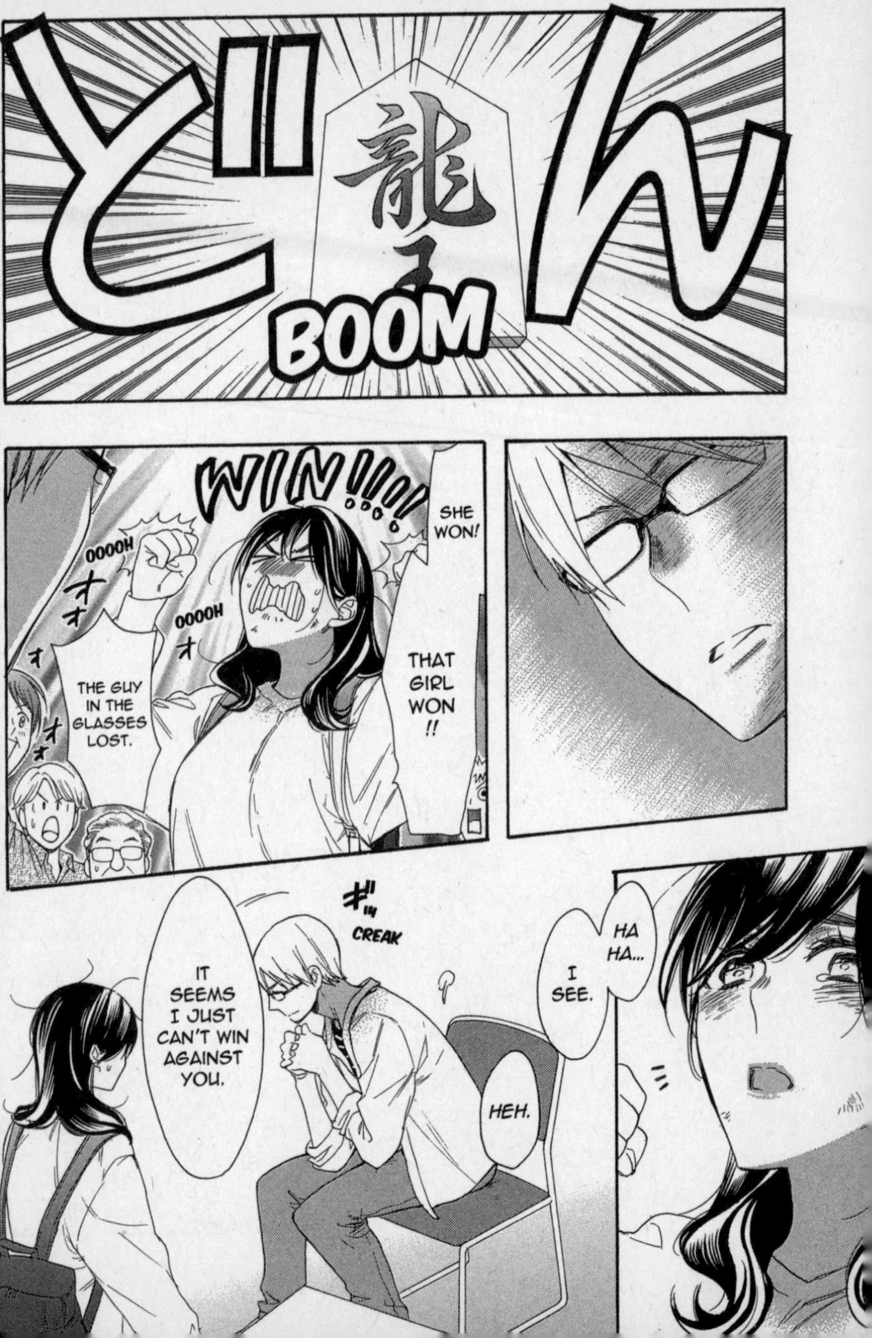
どん
龍王
BOOM
WIN!!!!!
SHE WON!
THAT GIRL WON !!
OOOOH
オ
OOOOH
オオ
オオオ
THE GUY IN THE GLASSES LOST.
HA HA...
I SEE.
HEH.
ギ
CREAK
IT SEEMS I JUST CAN'T WIN AGAINST YOU.

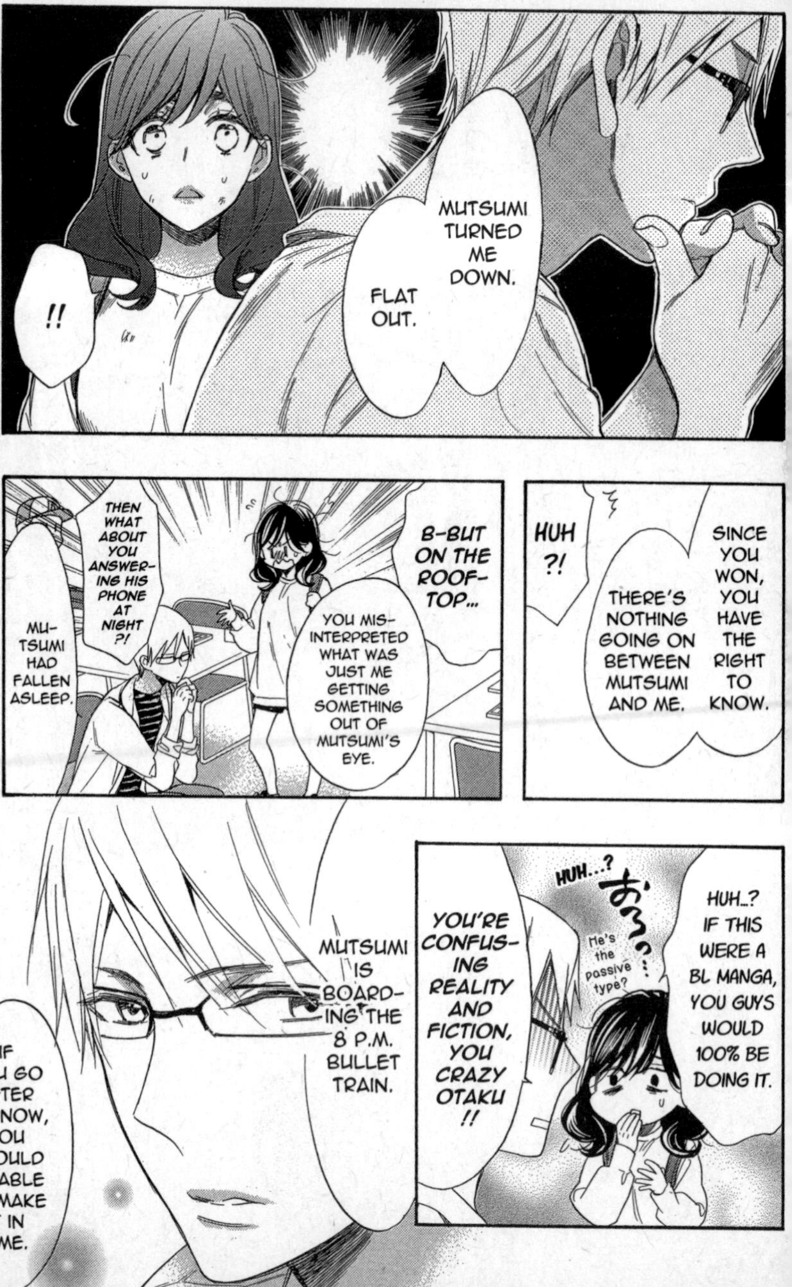
MUTSUMI TURNED ME DOWN.
FLAT OUT.
!!
SINCE YOU WON, YOU HAVE THE RIGHT TO KNOW.
THERE'S NOTHING GOING ON BETWEEN MUTSUMI AND ME.
HUH ?!
B-BUT ON THE ROOF-TOP...
YOU MIS-INTERPRETED WHAT WAS JUST ME GETTING SOMETHING OUT OF MUTSUMI'S EYE.
THEN WHAT ABOUT YOU ANSWER-ING HIS PHONE AT NIGHT ?!
MU-TSUMI HAD FALLEN ASLEEP.
HUH..? IF THIS WERE A BL MANGA, YOU GUYS WOULD 100% BE DOING IT.
HUH...?
He's the passive type?
YOU'RE CONFUS-ING REALITY AND FICTION, YOU CRAZY OTAKU !!
MUTSUMI IS BOARD-ING THE 8 P.M. BULLET TRAIN.
IF YOU GO AFTER HIM NOW, YOU SHOULD BE ABLE TO MAKE IT IN TIME.

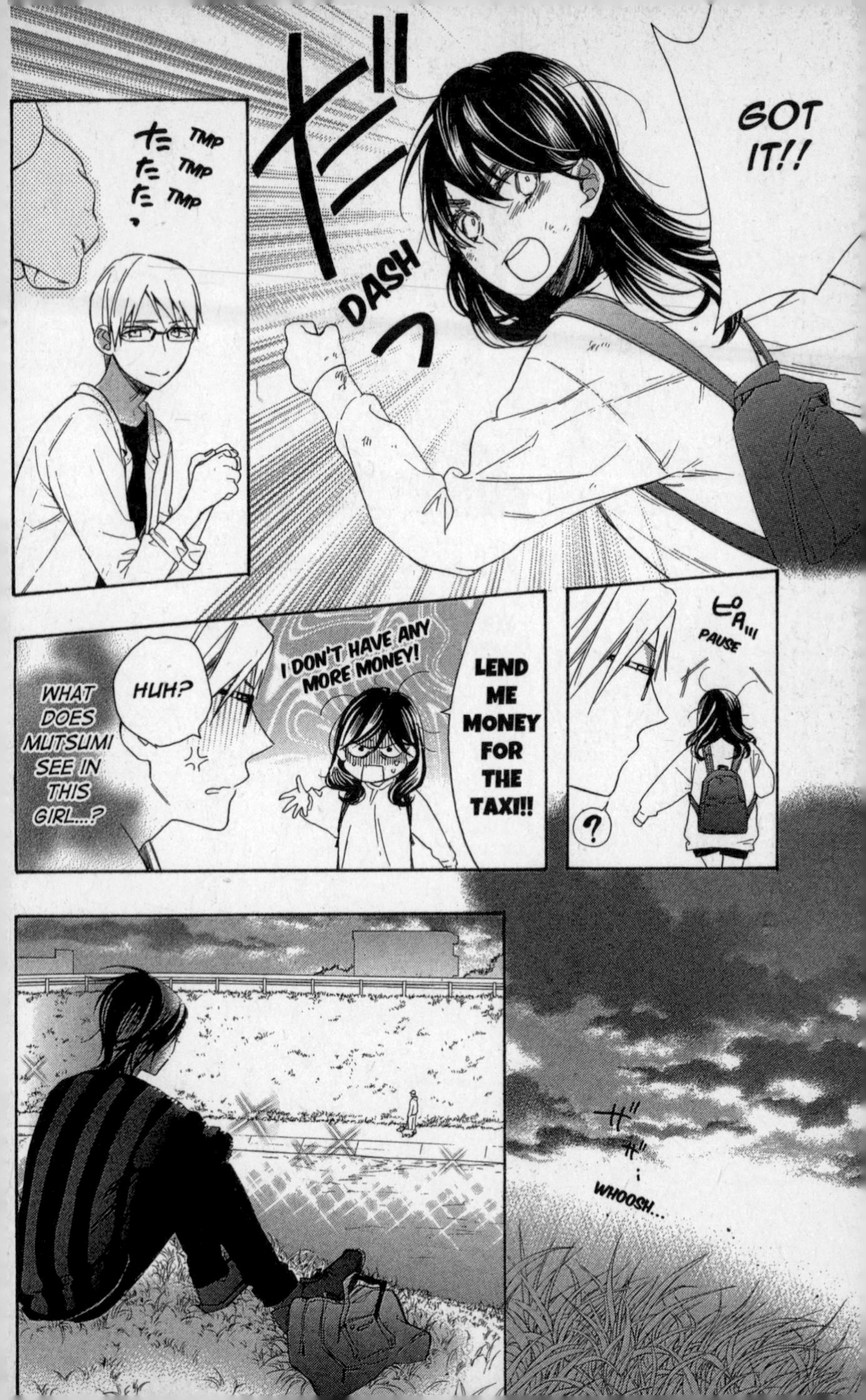
GOT IT!!
DASH
たたた、
TMP TMP TMP
ピタ…
PAUSE
?
LEND ME MONEY FOR THE TAXI!!
I DON'T HAVE ANY MORE MONEY!
HUH?
WHAT DOES MUTSUMI SEE IN THIS GIRL...?
ザ ザ
WHOOSH...

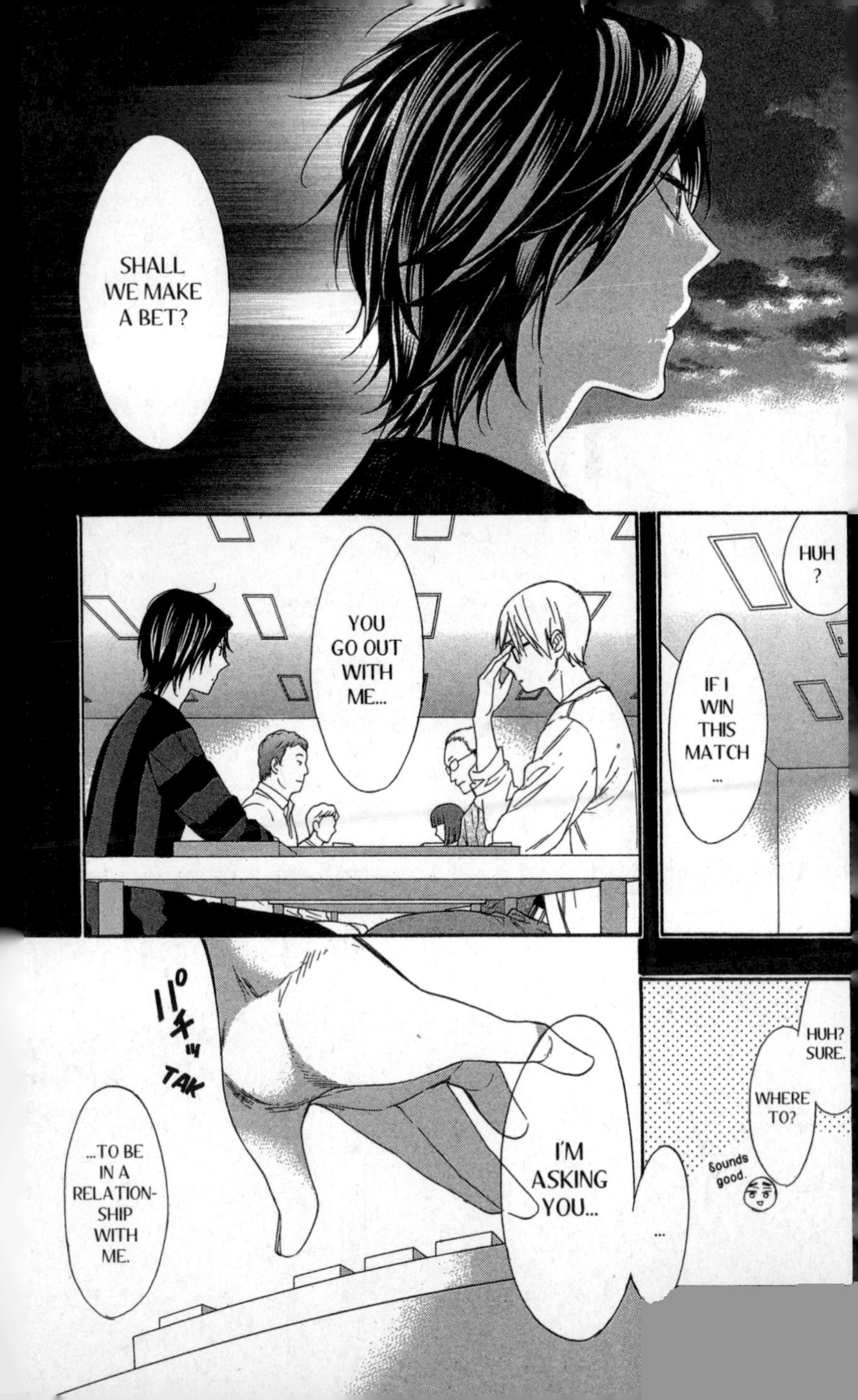
SHALL WE MAKE A BET?
HUH?
IF I WIN THIS MATCH...
YOU GO OUT WITH ME...
HUH? SURE.
WHERE TO?
Sounds good.
I'M ASKING YOU...
...
TAK
...TO BE IN A RELATIONSHIP WITH ME.

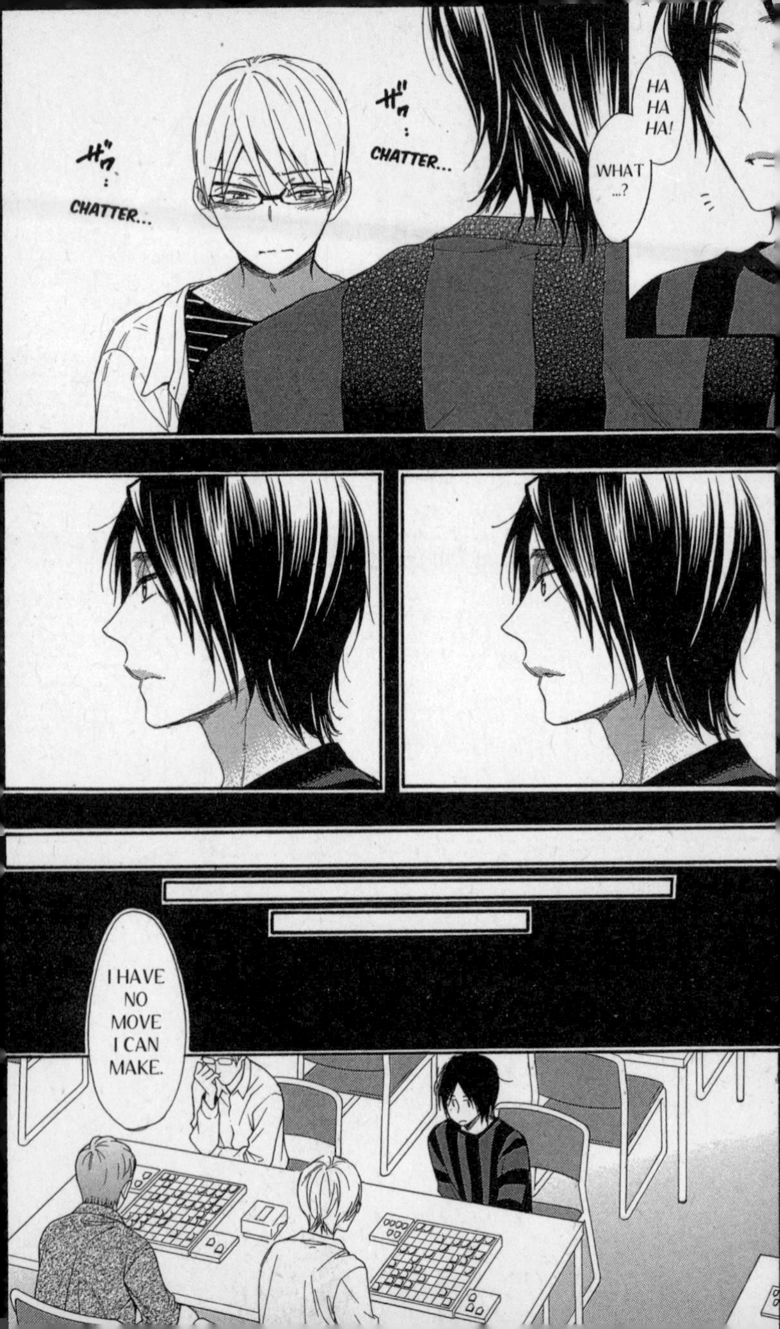
HA HA HA!
WHAT ...?
ザワ
CHATTER...
ザワ
CHATTER...
I HAVE NO MOVE I CAN MAKE.

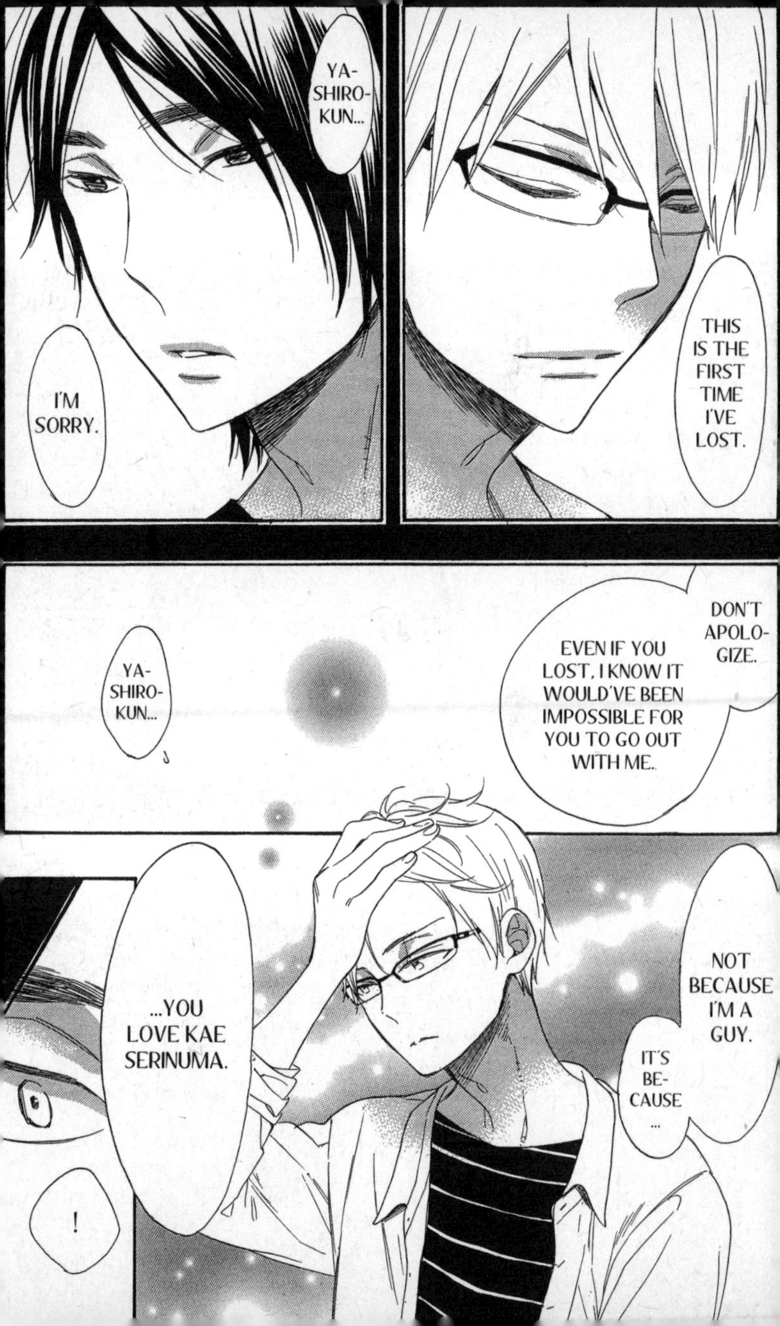
THIS IS THE FIRST TIME I'VE LOST.
YA-SHIRO-KUN...
I'M SORRY.
DON'T APOLO-GIZE.
EVEN IF YOU LOST, I KNOW IT WOULD'VE BEEN IMPOSSIBLE FOR YOU TO GO OUT WITH ME.
YA-SHIRO-KUN...
NOT BECAUSE I'M A GUY.
IT'S BE-CAUSE ...
...YOU LOVE KAE SERINUMA.
!

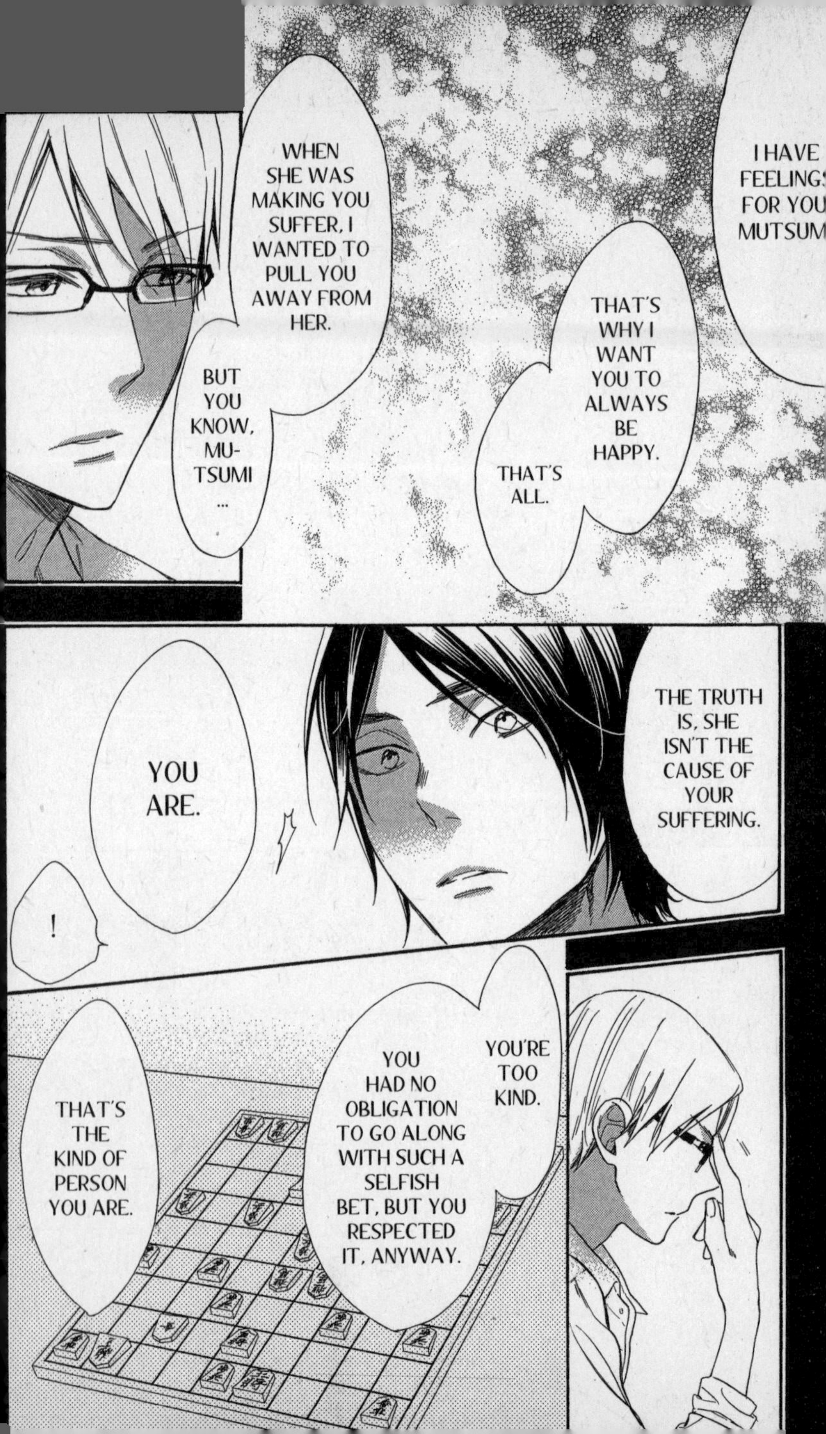
I HAVE FEELINGS FOR YOU MUTSUM
THAT'S WHY I WANT YOU TO ALWAYS BE HAPPY.
THAT'S ALL.
WHEN SHE WAS MAKING YOU SUFFER, I WANTED TO PULL YOU AWAY FROM HER.
BUT YOU KNOW, MU-TSUMI ...
THE TRUTH IS, SHE ISN'T THE CAUSE OF YOUR SUFFERING.
YOU ARE.
!
YOU'RE TOO KIND.
YOU HAD NO OBLIGATION TO GO ALONG WITH SUCH A SELFISH BET, BUT YOU RESPECTED IT, ANYWAY.
THAT'S THE KIND OF PERSON YOU ARE.

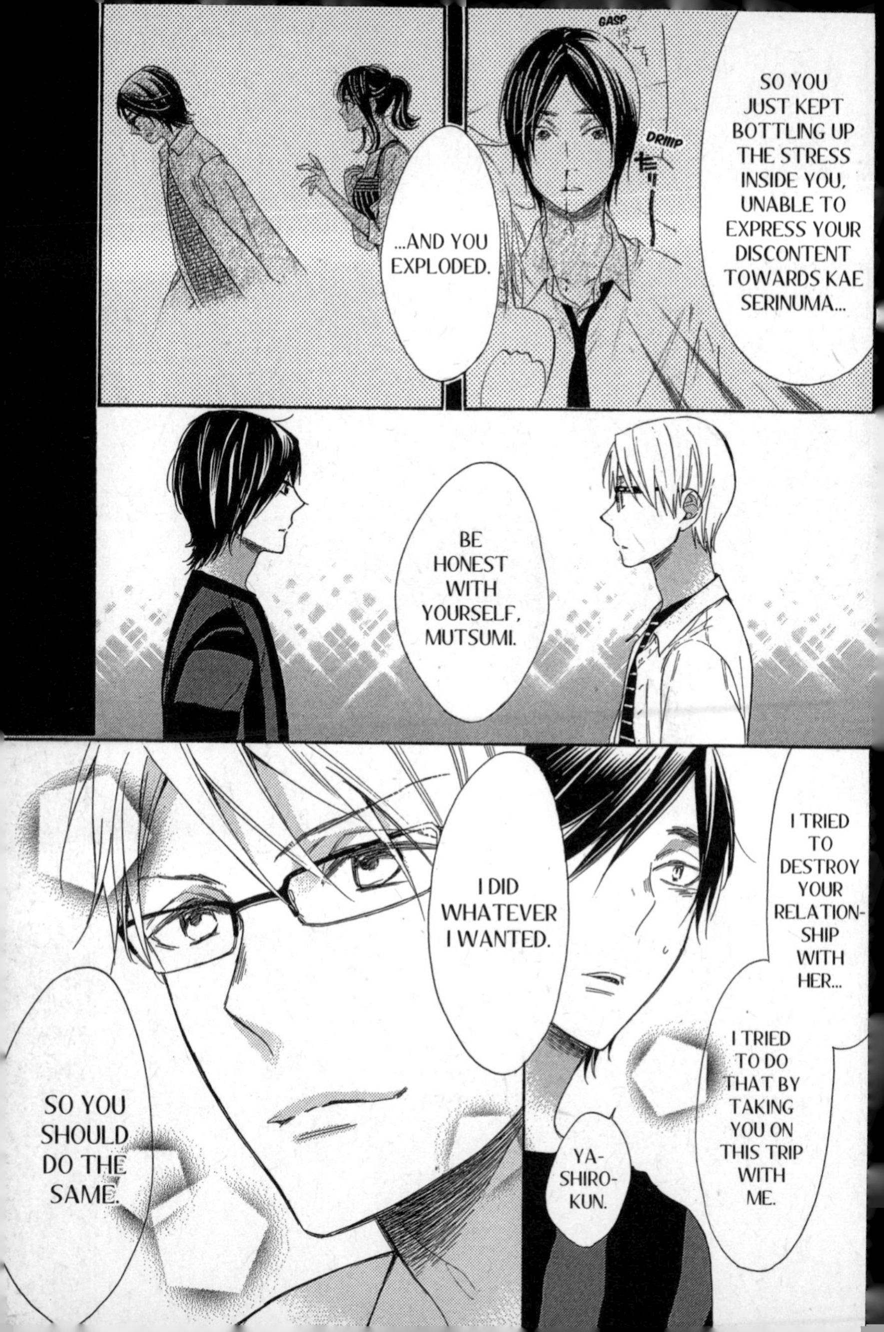
GASP
DRIIIP
SO YOU JUST KEPT BOTTLING UP THE STRESS INSIDE YOU, UNABLE TO EXPRESS YOUR DISCONTENT TOWARDS KAE SERINUMA...
...AND YOU EXPLODED.
BE HONEST WITH YOURSELF, MUTSUMI.
I TRIED TO DESTROY YOUR RELATION-SHIP WITH HER...
I TRIED TO DO THAT BY TAKING YOU ON THIS TRIP WITH ME.
YA-SHIRO-KUN.
I DID WHATEVER I WANTED.
SO YOU SHOULD DO THE SAME.

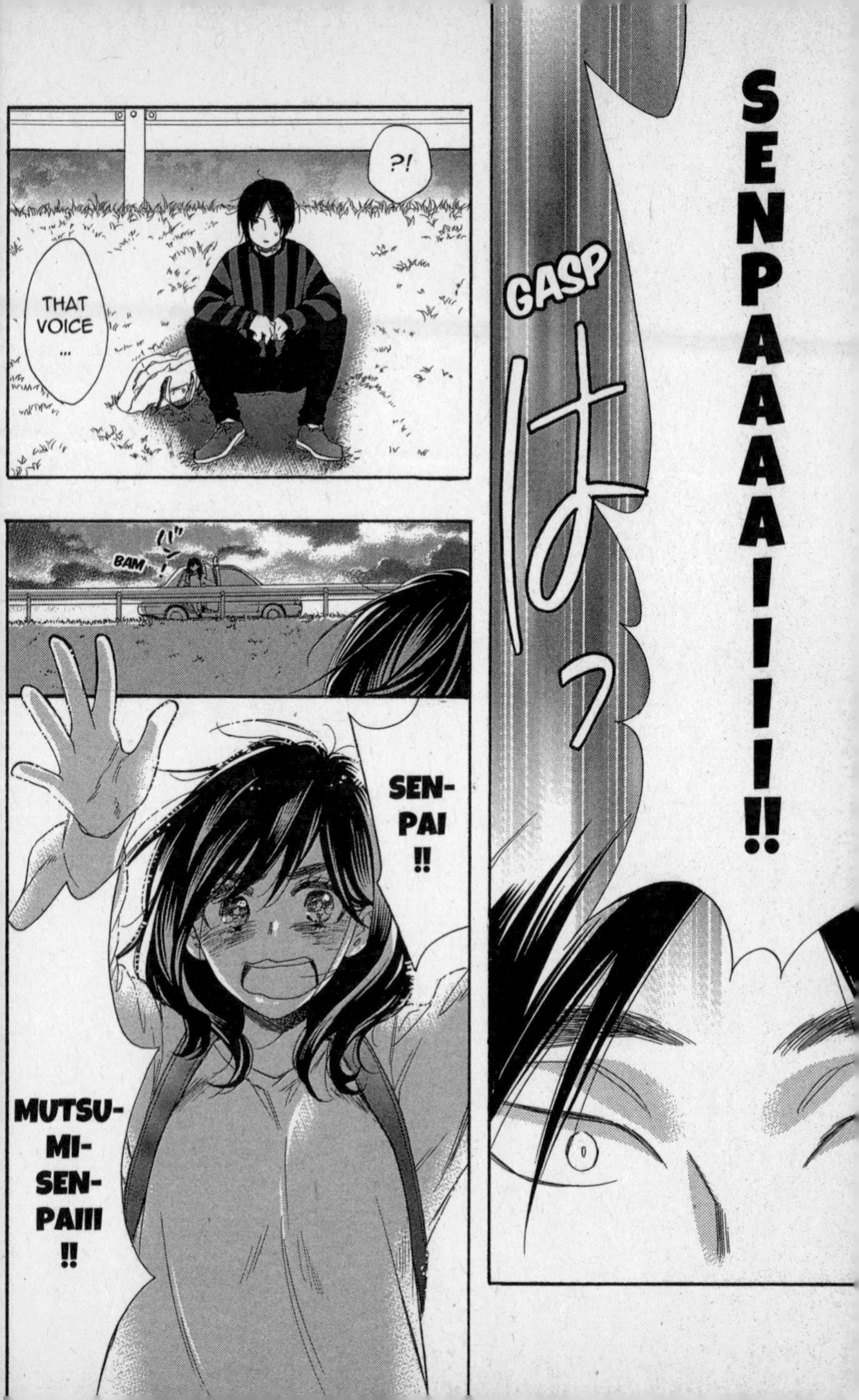
SENPAAAAIIII!!
GASP
はっ
?!
THAT VOICE ...
BAM
バ
SEN-PAI !!
MUTSU-MI-SEN-PAIII !!

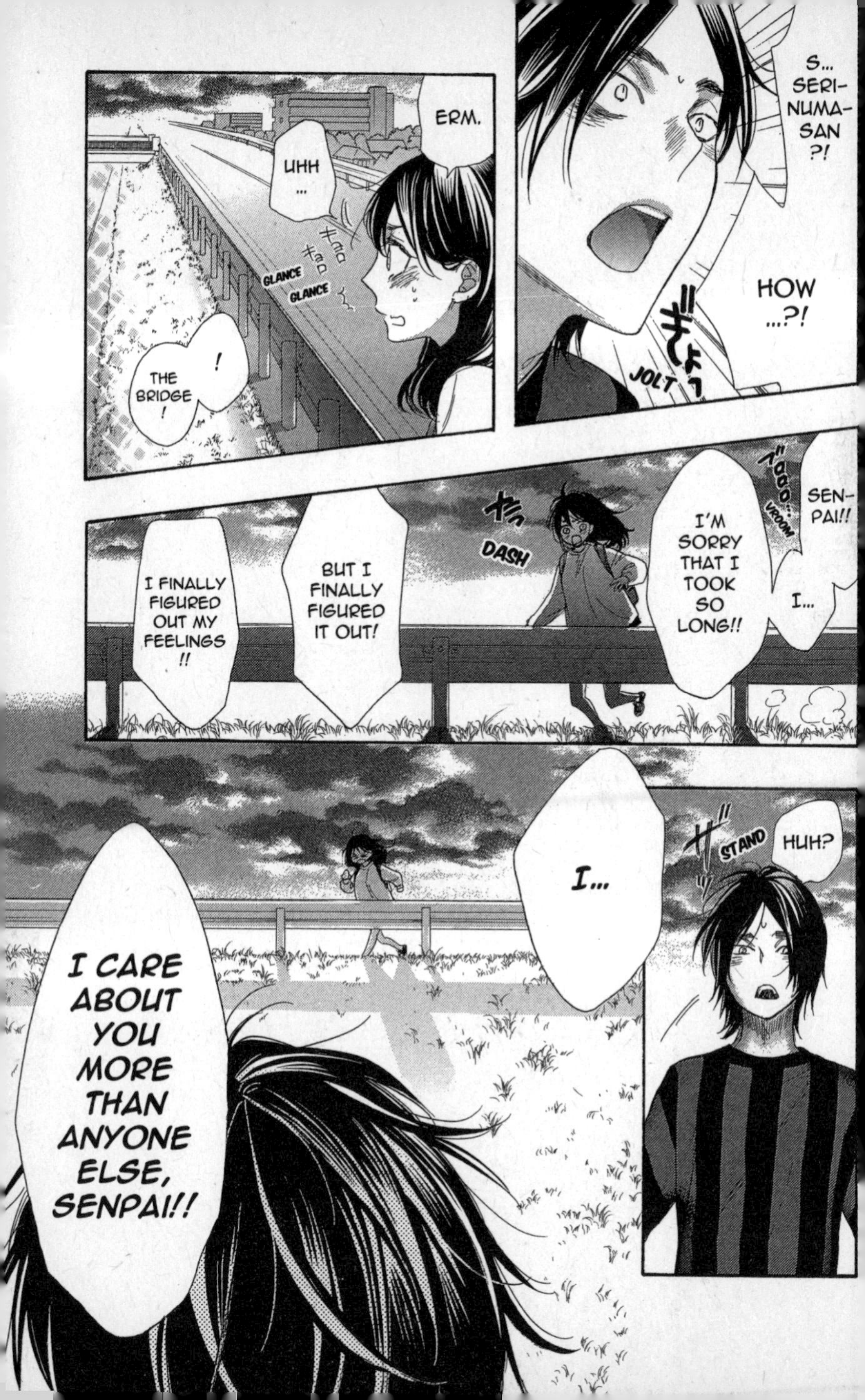
S... SERI-NUMA-SAN?!
HOW...?!
JOLT
ERM.
UHH...
GLANCE GLANCE
!
THE BRIDGE!
SEN-PAI!!
I...
VROOM
I'M SORRY THAT I TOOK SO LONG!!
DASH
BUT I FINALLY FIGURED IT OUT!
I FINALLY FIGURED OUT MY FEELINGS!!
HUH?
STAND
I...
I CARE ABOUT YOU MORE THAN ANYONE ELSE, SENPAI!!

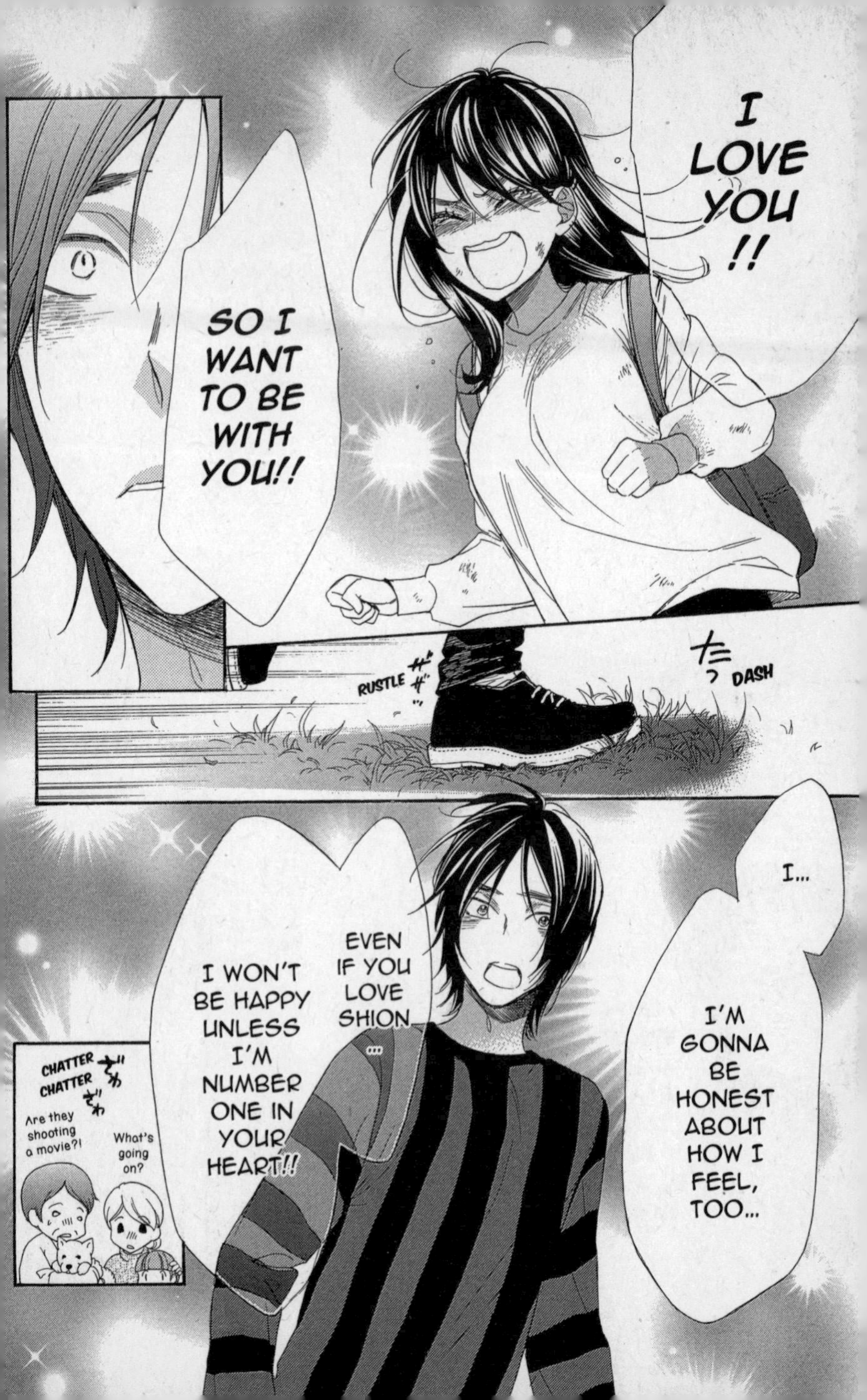
I LOVE YOU!!
SO I WANT TO BE WITH YOU!!
DASH
RUSTLE
I...
I'M GONNA BE HONEST ABOUT HOW I FEEL, TOO...
EVEN IF YOU LOVE SHION
I WON'T BE HAPPY UNLESS I'M NUMBER ONE IN YOUR HEART!!
...
CHATTER CHATTER
What's going on?
Are they shooting a movie?!

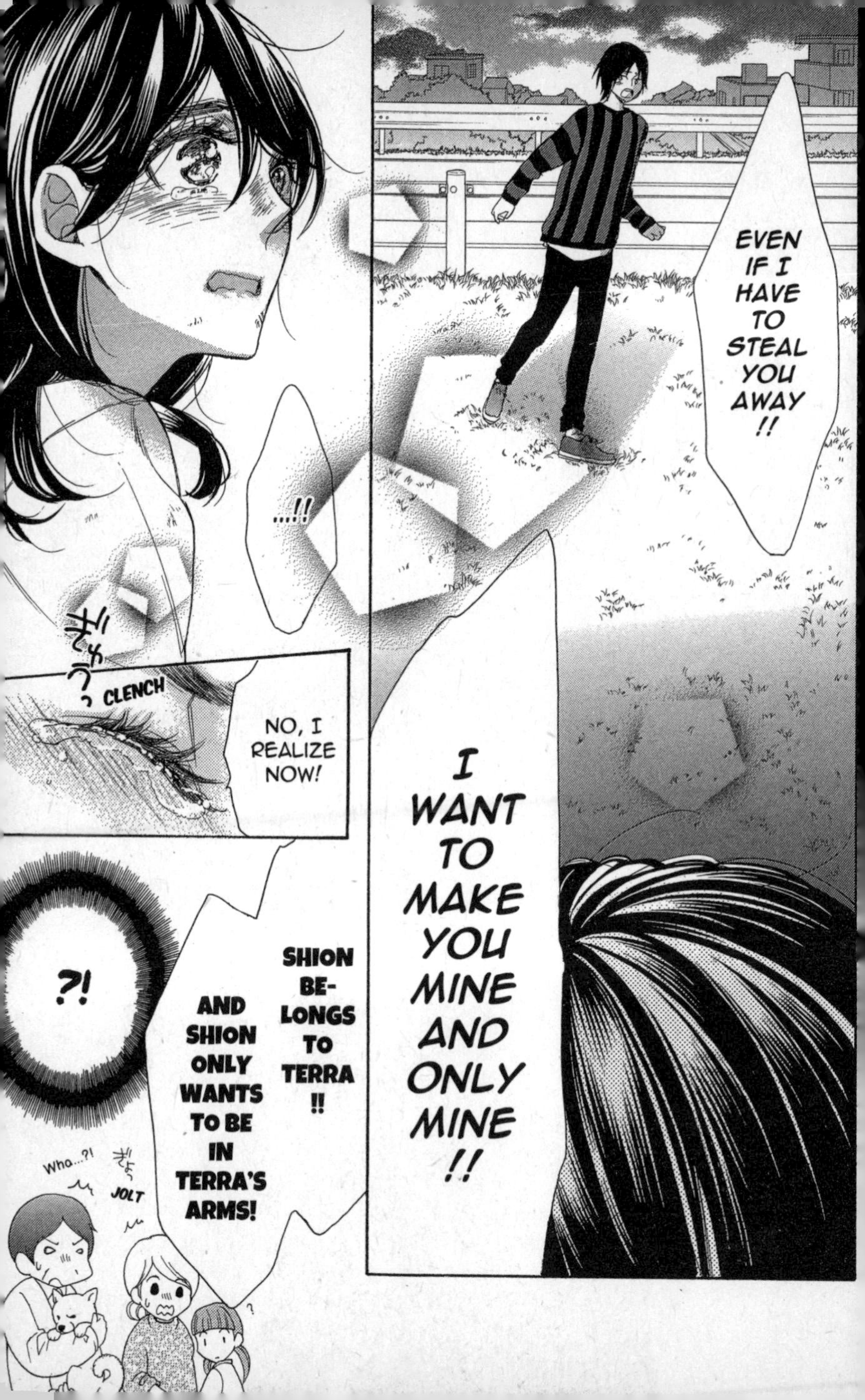
EVEN IF I HAVE TO STEAL YOU AWAY!!
I WANT TO MAKE YOU MINE AND ONLY MINE!!
...!!
CLENCH
NO, I REALIZE NOW!
SHION BE-LONGS TO TERRA!!
AND SHION ONLY WANTS TO BE IN TERRA'S ARMS!
?!
Who...?!
JOLT
?

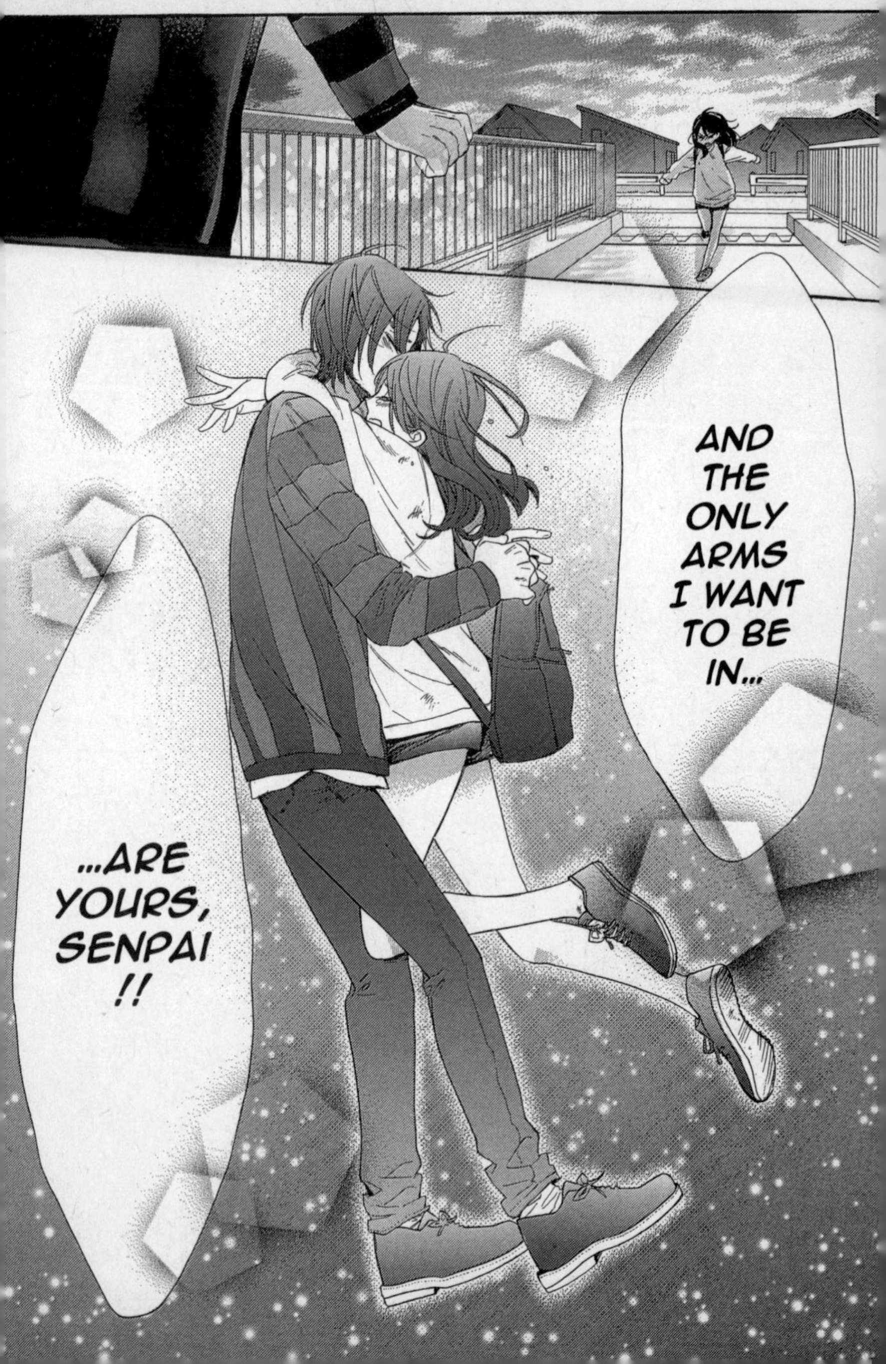
AND THE ONLY ARMS I WANT TO BE IN...
...ARE YOURS, SENPAI!!

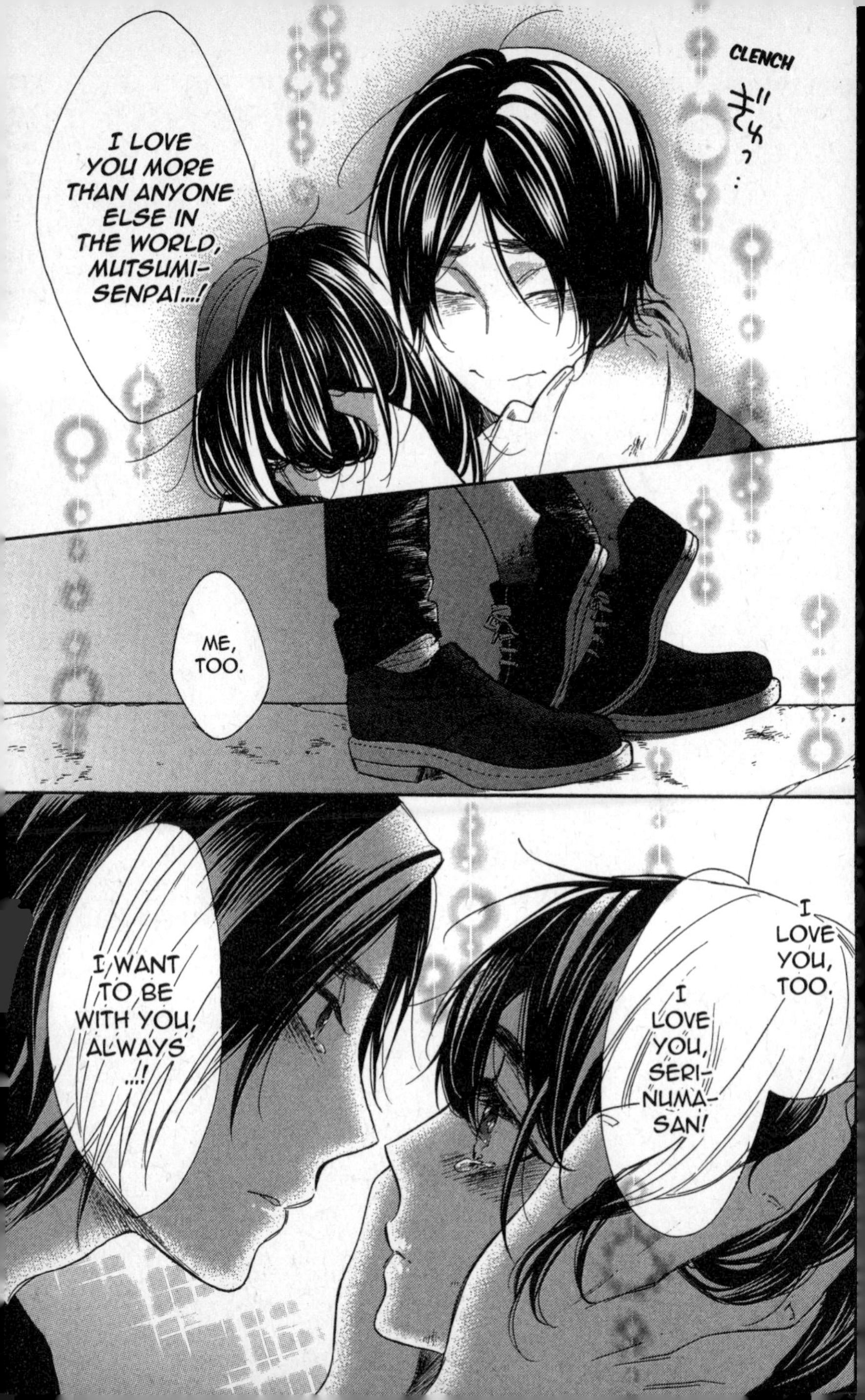
CLENCH
ぎゅっ
I LOVE YOU MORE THAN ANYONE ELSE IN THE WORLD, MUTSUMI-SENPAI...!
ME, TOO.
I LOVE YOU, TOO.
I LOVE YOU, SERI-NUMA-SAN!
I WANT TO BE WITH YOU, ALWAYS ...!!

RIP

FWIP...

SO...

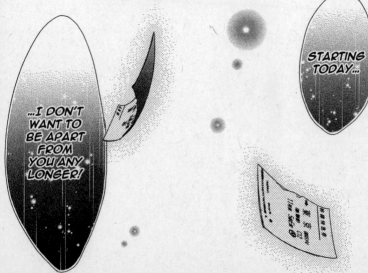

STARTING TODAY...

...I DON'T WANT TO BE APART FROM YOU ANY LONGER!

KISS HIM,
NOT ME!

THANK YOU!

It's the 13th volume!

I never thought that this series would get this far. I'm so thankful.

I hope you enjoyed this volume as well.

You'll get the most out of the body-switching story if you listen to the CD while reading the manga. ♡

You can find it in the 11th volume.

When I wrote the body-switching story, I thought the story would be interesting as a voice dramatization, so I'm glad I got to see it happen! It's a standout voice dramatization on CD, and holds its own next to the previous two.

This is the third time! What a surprise! We had the anime cast reprise their roles.

Also, we've released another special edition (in Japan) that includes a voice dramatization on CD.

Mitsuboshi also makes his first appearance!! I was so moved. ♡♡

Yashiro's role in the series is small, but he's become an interesting character. I think he was sent off in a cool way, too (if I do say so myself). I hope he'll find himself a nice boyfriend and be happy (Haha).

Anyway, this series, which has thankfully gone a long time, will come to an end next volume. I hope you keep up with Kae and the rest of the gang in *Kiss Him, Not Me!* until the very end! See you in the next volume...!

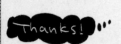

Thanks!...

SPECIAL ADVISOR / EIKI EIKI-SENSEI

STAFF / AKI-SAN, SHIROE-SAN, ROKKU-SAN, YUKI-SAN, UZUKI-SAN, O-SAN

EDITOR / A-SAN

AND EVERYONE ELSE INVOLVED IN THIS WORK!

AUTHOR'S NOTE

THE 13TH VOLUME!
WHEN I THINK ABOUT IT,
WE'VE COME A LONG WAY,
HAVEN'T WE?
PLEASE STAY WITH ME FOR
JUST A BIT LONGER!

-JUNKO

I ❤
BL

Translation Notes

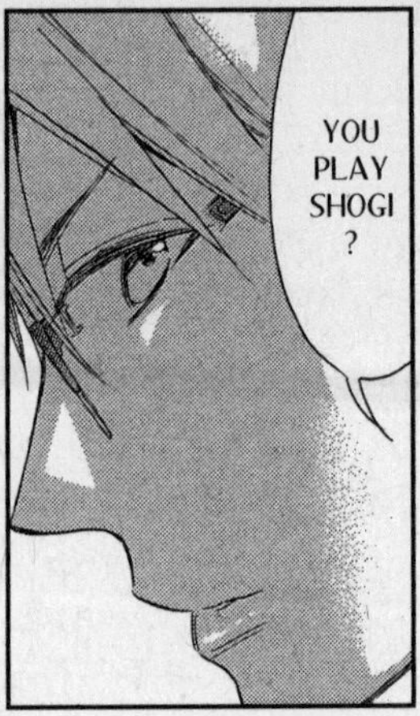
YOU PLAY SHOGI ?

Shogi, page 58

Shogi, also known as the general's game, is a two-player strategy board game in the same family as chess, and is the most popular of chess variants native to Japan (which is why it's sometimes called "Japanese chess"). Similar to Western chess, shogi consists of king, pawn, rook, bishop, and knight pieces, but also has pieces that are not found in Western chess, such as gold generals, silver generals, and the lance. Other differences include playing on a 9x9 board as opposed to an 8x8 board, and using 20 flat pieces per player instead of 16. Chinese characters are also written on both sides of each piece, and when a regular piece reaches a certain point in enemy territory, it can be flipped and promoted to a stronger rank. A major difference between shogi and chess is that when opposing pieces are captured in shogi, they become loyal to the player that captured them. .

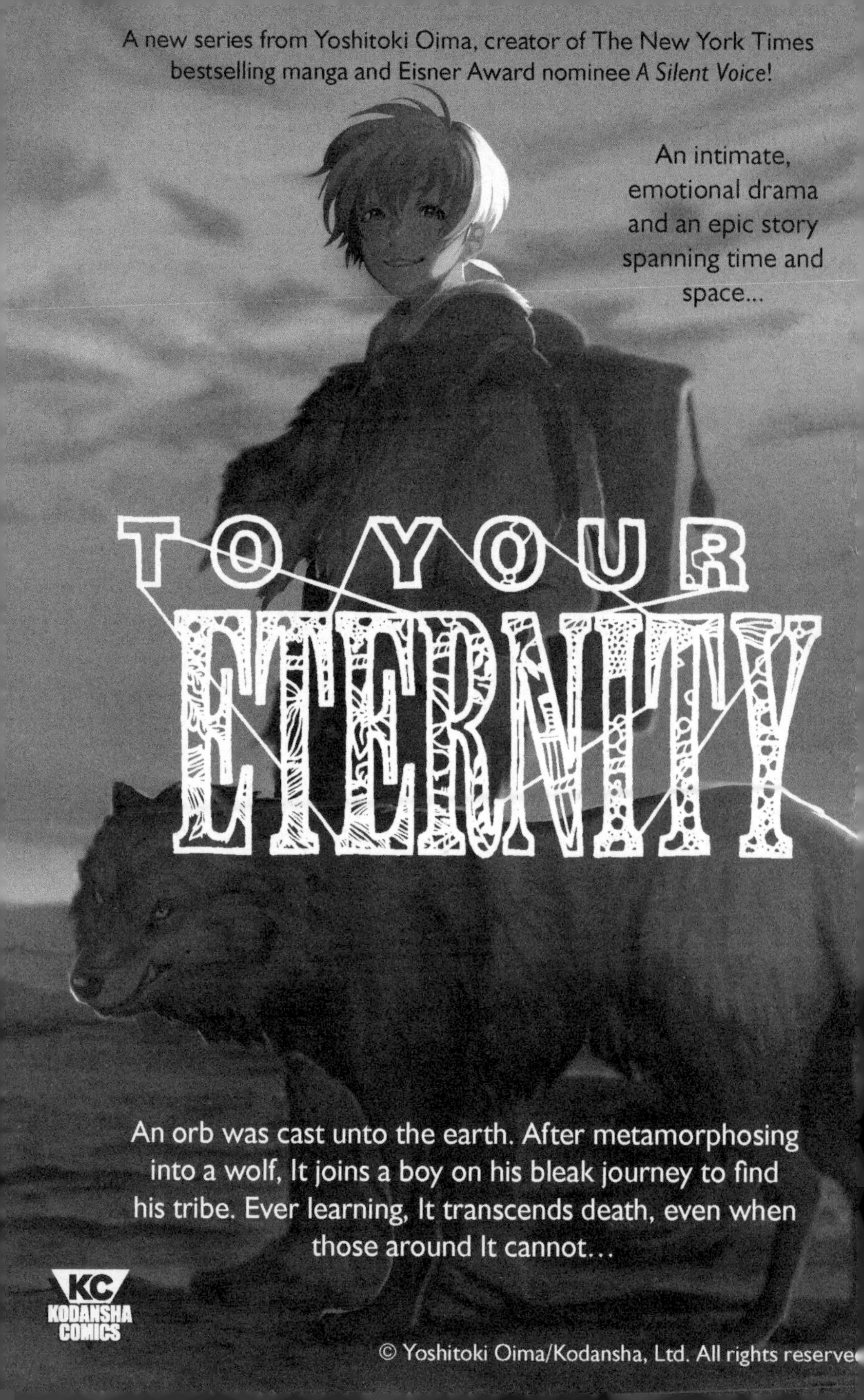
A new series from Yoshitoki Oima, creator of The New York Times bestselling manga and Eisner Award nominee *A Silent Voice*!
An intimate, emotional drama and an epic story spanning time and space...
TO YOUR ETERNITY
An orb was cast unto the earth. After metamorphosing into a wolf, It joins a boy on his bleak journey to find his tribe. Ever learning, It transcends death, even when those around It cannot...
KC KODANSHA COMICS
© Yoshitoki Oima/Kodansha, Ltd. All rights reserve

KC KODANSHA COMICS

"I'm pleasantly surprised to find modern shojo using cross-dressing as a dramatic device to deliver social commentary... Recommended."

-Otaku USA Magazine

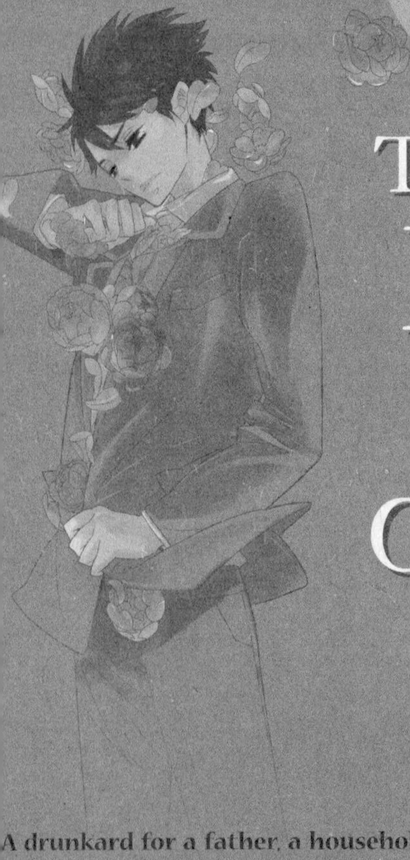

the prince in his dark days

By Hico Yamanaka

A drunkard for a father, a household of poverty... For 17-year-old Atsuko, misfortune is all she knows and believes in. Until one day, a chance encounter with Itaru–the wealthy heir of a huge corporation–changes everything. The two look identical, uncannily so. When Itaru curiously goes missing, Atsuko is roped into being his stand-in. There, in his shoes, Atsuko must parade like a prince in a palace. She encounters many new experiences, but at what cost...?

Having lost his wife, high school teacher Kōhei Inuzuka is doing his best to raise his young daughter Tsumugi as a single father. He's pretty bad at cooking and doesn't have a huge appetite to begin with, but chance brings his little family together with one of his students, the lonely Kotori. The three of them are anything but comfortable in the kitchen, but the healing power of home cooking might just work on their grieving hearts.

"This season's number-one feel-good anime!" —Anime News Network

"A beautifully-drawn story about comfort food and family and grief. Recommended." —Otaku USA Magazine

sweetness & lightning

By Gido Amagakure

Japan's most powerful spirit medium delves into the ghost world's greatest mysteries!

Story by Kyo Shirodaira, famed author of mystery fiction and creator of *Spiral*, *Blast of Tempest*, and *The Record of a Fallen Vampire*.

Both touched by spirits called yôkai, Kotoko and Kurô have gained unique superhuman powers. But to gain her powers Kotoko has given up an eye and a leg, and Kurô's personal life is in shambles. So when Kotoko suggests they team up to deal with renegades from the spirit world, Kurô doesn't have many other choices, but Kotoko might just have a few ulterior motives...

IN/SPECTRE

STORY BY **KYO SHIRODAIRA**
ART BY **CHASHIBA KATASE**

"An emotional and artistic tour de force! We see incredible triumph, and crushing defeat... each panel [is] a thrill!"
—Anitay

"A journey that's instantly compelling."
—Anime News Network

WELCOME TO THE BALLROOM

By Tomo Takeuchi

Feckless high school student Tatara Fujita wants to be good at something—anything. Unfortunately, he's about as average as a slouchy teen can be. The local bullies know this, and make it a habit to hit him up for cash, but all that changes when the debonair Kaname Sengoku sends them packing. Sengoku's not the neighborhood watch, though. He's a professional ballroom dancer. And once Tatara Fujita gets pulled into the world of ballroom, his life will never be the same.

KC KODANSHA COMICS

A Kodansha Comics Trade Paperback Original.

Kiss Him, Not Me volume 13 copyright © 2017 Junko
English translation copyright © 2018 Junko

All rights reserved.

Published in the United States by Kodansha Comics,
an imprint of Kodansha USA Publishing, LLC, New York.

Publication rights for this English edition arranged through Kodansha Ltd.,
Tokyo.

First published in Japan in 2017 by Kodansha Ltd., Tokyo, as *Watashi Ga
Motete Dousunda* volume 13.

ISBN 978-1-63236-556-9

Printed in the United States of America.

www.kodanshacomics.com

9 8 7 6 5 4 3 2 1

Translation: David Rhie
Lettering: Jacqueline Wee
Editing: Ajani Oloye
Kodansha Comics edition cover design: Phil Balsman